CAMBRIDGE LATIN AMERICAN STUDIES

EDITORS

DAVID JOSLIN JOHN STREET TIMOTHY KING

7

REGIONAL ECONOMIC
DEVELOPMENT

THE SERIES

REGIONAL ECONOMIC DEVELOPMENT

THE RIVER BASIN APPROACH IN MEXICO

BY

DAVID BARKIN

AND

TIMOTHY KING

CAMBRIDGE
AT THE UNIVERSITY PRESS
1970

Published by the Syndics of the Cambridge University Press
Bentley House, 200 Euston Road, London N.W.1
American Branch: 32 East 57th Street, New York, N.Y. 10022

Library of Congress Catalogue Card Number: 76–111122

ISBN: 0 521 07837 7

Printed in Great Britain
at the University Press
Aberdeen

CONTENTS

LIST OF FIGURES

vi

LIST OF TABLES

PREFACE

This book has its origins in our Ph.D. dissertations and is based on research in Mexico during the past six years. King's dissertation was written for the Department of Agricultural Economics at the University of California at Berkeley in 1963–4. It was concerned with problems of evaluating large scale development projects, carried out in pursuit of a multiplicity of objectives, whose success depended on the nature of private sector reaction to public sector action. This was discussed in the context of the Mexican attempt to promote regional development by integrated river basin investment projects and taking the Tepalcatepec project as a case study. Barkin's dissertation, written for the Department of Economics, Yale University, in 1965–6, studied the contribution that the Tepalcatepec Commission had made to Mexican national and regional development in considerably greater detail. After some correspondence, we had an opportunity to meet and discuss the possibility of a joint book while we were both in residence at El Colegio de México in the summer of 1967. We were later able to work together for short periods in Cambridge in July and August 1968 and in New York in December 1968 to January 1969.

The first two sections of this book are based primarily on King's dissertation and the third on Barkin's; but the revision of all sections involved so much joint work both in adding new ideas and data and in eliminating old material, that the whole book must be considered a joint effort, even if we have not been able to reconcile our writing styles. In its present form, the first part of the book is a survey of the way in which government policies may attempt to solve regional development problems in less developed countries and consequently how such policies should be evaluated. The second section describes Mexican regional development problems and policies in both economic and political aspects, paying, in Chapter 4, particular attention to the postwar history of river basin development in Mexico but discussing other regional development programmes as well. In the third part we analyse and assess in detail the work of the

Tepalcatepec Commission since its formation in 1947. Finally we use this assessment, together with the earlier analysis of other schemes, to evaluate the strategy of using river basin projects as the core of regional development policies, considered both from economic and political angles.

Although we are both economists we have tried to make this book intelligible to those without a training in economics who are interested in Mexican development as a whole, or in particular political or economic issues, but who have no interest in the economics of project evaluation. We have probably not succeeded entirely and the latter half of Chapter 1 in particular would be difficult for the non-economist to follow; this can be readily omitted.

Over the long gestation period of this book, we were helped with advice and finance from a host of individuals and institutions. It is impossible to mention by name everyone who gave one or both of us assistance. We should, however, mention our gratitude to our dissertation committees at Yale and at Berkeley, chaired by Professors Lloyd Reynolds and David Allee respectively. The advice of Clark Reynolds, based on his own long study of Mexico, was especially valuable to both of us; he was also a member of Barkin's dissertation committee. We are very grateful to a large number of people who helped us in Mexico, and particularly, to Sr. Victor Urquidi, to Lic. Gustavo Petriciolli, and to Ing. César Buenrostro, who as Executive Secretary of the Río Balsas Commission was extremely helpful in providing not only personal advice but also facilities and personnel to assist the studies. Other members of the Commission also gave unstintingly of their time and knowledge.

The original research was financed by grants from the Giannini Foundation of Agricultural Economics and the Center for Latin American Studies, both of the University of California at Berkeley; and by the Foreign Area Fellowship Program and the Yale University Councils on International Relations and Latin American Studies. Support for turning this research into this book came from the Agricultural Development Council, Washington and New York Universities and the Nuffield Foundation.

April 1969   D.B. and T.K.

REGIONAL DEVELOPMENT POLICY IN LESS DEVELOPED COUNTRIES

THE OBJECTIVES OF REGIONAL DEVELOPMENT POLICY

The process of economic development does not at any stage affect all the regions of an economy equally. Changing patterns of output may cause a changing locational pattern of economic activity. Industrial growth will be concentrated in a few densely populated urban areas. These will draw food and raw materials from certain agricultural regions, which may flourish, perhaps at the expense of previously growing agricultural regions. Other regions may remain sparsely populated from a lack of demand for their potential production or for want of investment in transport or power facilities. In later stages of industrialization, regions heavily dependent on older industries may lose ground relatively to regions where the industrial structure is newer. Since the mobility of factors is never perfect, the wages of labour and the profit on capital are likely to be higher in rapidly expanding areas than elsewhere. In areas which are economically declining or growing relatively slowly, there will be relatively greater unemployment, and productive resources will tend to leave these areas for the regions of faster economic growth.

This uneven pattern of regional growth is, to a greater or lesser extent, inevitable. Regional inequality is in this respect like all economic inequality. Social justice might be better served if it could be avoided but in a world in which natural resources and talents are unequally distributed, almost the only mechanism yet devised for allocating those resources and talents to their most productive uses is to allow their prices to be an indication of relative scarcities and for such price variations to be reflected in the incomes of their owners. This is not to argue that the unfettered play of the price mechanism will generally lead to the optimum allocation of resources, however defined, and that in consequence, governments are unwise to try to alter the regional pattern of growth. For several reasons, governments do not usually look on unmoved at the uneven nature of regional economic growth, but adopt a variety of policies to try to reduce the unevenness. This book is primarily concerned with the attempts of the government of Mexico in this respect, and, in particular, with its adoption of the particular strategy of investing heavily in river basin development to do this.

The anxiety that governments feel about regional development may either be mainly about the income per head of those who are already inhabitants of the region or chiefly about the total output of the region. In the first case, the prime motive will be a concern that the distribution of *per capita* income should be as equal as is compatible with other social objectives. This concern may simply be humanitarian, but in any case, since regional discontent may give rise to defeat at the polls or to internal revolution, self-preservation is likely to require it.

Opinions that are locally concentrated will, in this respect, be proportionately more influential than those that are evenly spread throughout the entire population—governments will probably therefore be more concerned with regional *per capita* income differentials than with equivalent differentials between different social groups. Sometimes the government may be less concerned about the individual welfare of the disadvantaged regional inhabitants than it is anxious to avoid the appearance of leaving some group totally outside the modern economic growth that the rest of the economy is enjoying, and upsetting the image of modernity that the rest of the economy conveys. This, as we shall explain, is an important cause of Mexican anxiety about regional problems. In such a case, the concern of the government may not be so much simply with regional *per capita* money income, but with the provision of certain services—education and health are obvious examples.

In other cases, governments are less anxious to raise *per capita* regional income than to increase the population of the region at the same time as increasing regional output. In these circumstances, regional development might take place but income per head in the region fall. Perhaps it is felt that to leave an area sparsely settled is to invite some neighbouring country to seize it openly by force or covertly to colonize it. Nowadays this seems perhaps a little improbable in most parts of the world, but it has certainly inspired Mexican regional development efforts in the past.

Modern governments are more likely to be anxious to reduce congestion in certain regions. There are undoubtedly gains to society from the close locational grouping of firms. These are often called 'economies of agglomeration'. Customers and suppliers established close together reduce the cost of communication between them; economies of scale can be obtained in the supply of specialist and public services, and specialist institutions can be established to train a labour force. From the point of view of households, the larger the city, the greater the variety of cultural and leisure activities it is likely to offer. For these reasons the natural tendency towards the locational concentration of industry has some beneficial social effects. But the beneficial effects must be set against disadvantages of congestion that arise from this concentration of economic activity. Normal market forces left to themselves will not ensure that, from any point of view, the best balance between social advantages and disadvantages is obtained. Newly established firms typically pay the same for services as all firms in an area, but since, where congestion exists, their establishment raises the costs for all the firms already in the area, what the new firm considers as costs underestimates the costs for society as a whole. Congestion also increases costs for households, but it is often difficult to translate these into financial terms.

If at some point a government feels that any benefits from economies of agglomeration or from increasing city size are outweighed by the social costs of congestion, this provides a further motive for trying to decentralize economic activity. A related objective which sometimes stimulates regional activity is the desire to reduce the flow of people to cities, in order to limit the growth of slums and reduce urban unemployment. Such a flow does indeed create social problems, but it is the very essence of the industrialization process. Urban unemployment is probably socially more costly than rural unemployment, since food needs to be transported to the towns, and housing and other facilities consumed may be greater. It might well have been desirable if the urban unemployed had remained living with, and supported by, their rural families. On the other hand, a certain amount of urban unemployment is probably needed to enable expanding industry to draw on a steady flow of labour. To try to stamp out unemployment may increase the cost of labour to industrializing firms, who will then be induced to invest in techniques which replace labour by machinery and thereby restrict the increase of employment.

The desire to reduce congestion is a possible reason for wishing to develop areas which are at present scarcely inhabited. Another is a belief that there exist in an area natural resources, whose exploitation would be profitable, but which require a minimum scale of investment much larger than can be provided by private investment. For several activities, including the supply of power and transport facilities, economies of scale are important. Investments here might not be justifiable economically, unless the regional economy reached a certain minimum size, but might then have a high return. In other words, there may be a case to be made out for public action to promote regional development parallel to the infant industry argument for protecting domestic industry. It is also sometimes argued that the settlement of a previously underdeveloped region could lead to the addition to the productive resources of an economy in unexpected ways— perhaps it may lead to the discovery of mineral resources, or attract pioneer settlers, whose enterprise and initiative was previously untapped, but who now find and seize opportunities to start new activities, which raise their own income, employ un-utilized resources and represent an addition to the scarce entrepreneurial talent of the nation.

The above are the various objectives of a policy concerned with inter-regional differences in the degree of development. They are not, of course, all the objectives of government activity in any particular region. All national economic objectives—the growth of national income, price stability, the diversification of the economy, the strengthening of the balance of payments, etc.— are as likely to be among the objectives of regional policies as the specifically regional ones.

THE PROCESS OF REGIONAL DEVELOPMENT

The particular objectives pursued by a government will, of course, affect its choice of policies, and these will be discussed in the next section. But all policies have the basic aim of promoting regional growth, and an understanding of the process of regional economic development is essential in analysing particular policies. In what follows, it will be generally assumed that the context of the analysis is that of a developing country—implying, for example, that more than 40 per cent of the labour force is engaged in agriculture, and that a considerable proportion of the rural labour force is underemployed, except possibly at peak seasons. Most of what is said, however, does not depend on these assumptions and would be equally relevant to all types of economy.

Much has been written about regional problems, and from the point of view of every discipline. National questions generally have regional counterparts, so that the studies of regions may have as broad a scope as that of nations. In addition, all economic action and its effects take place in one region or another, and usually with unequal regional impact. A discussion of the process of regional development might therefore include every aspect of national development. But what we are concerned with are the points on which the process of regional development will differ, in degree or kind, from the process of national development. There are three such points—in the role that inter-regional trade plays in the development process as against international trade, in the questions of how growth in one region affects growth elsewhere in the economy, and in the mechanisms by which inter-regional payments may be balanced. We shall discuss each of these in turn.

In the first place, external trade will account for a much larger part of the output and consumption of a region than of a nation. Except in a purely subsistence economy, the importance of exports for any area is likely to be a function of that area's size.[1] One man may depend entirely on his ability to export his services; for the world as a whole, there are no exports. It is obviously less realistic to develop a theory of growth for, say, an individual country on the assumption that neither goods nor factors could move across

[1] This is pointed out by Charles N. Tiebout in 'Exports and Regional Economic Growth', *Journal of Political Economy*, LXIV (April 1956), pp. 160–4.

boundaries than it would be for the whole of North America. Because of the clear importance of trade to regional growth, a number of writers have placed great weight on the role of exports. The 'export-base' theory of regional development, as put forward by Douglass C. North, is perhaps the clearest expression of this, although many writers have discussed similar ideas.[1] The theory is very simple. Growth within a region is initiated and continues to be led by a demand for products in which the region has a comparative advantage. Regional production, investment and incomes rise, and complementary industries are established. Local savings are invested locally and their multiplier effects are local. In particular, a number of 'residentiary activities' are likely to be developed within the region providing goods and services for the local market. In North's version of this theory, the export sector remains dominant for the region, playing a vital role in determining the level of income in the region and in transmitting national cyclical fluctuations to the region. The character of the export-base determines the character of the region, whether 'industrialized' or 'agricultural'; and it may change through time so that a region may start by exporting principally local primary products and later export commodities that could be termed locationally 'footloose'.

As a simple model of the way in which regions grow, the 'export-base' model has no rival. The exact role of the export-base will, of course, be affected by the definition of the region chosen, and it may be possible to conceive of geographical regions in whose growth exports have played only a small part. But if one is considering the development of regions in less developed countries, where even national domestic markets are on the small side for supporting modern industrial activities, then quite clearly the establishment of an export-base must be a major objective of regional economic policy. The particular policy adopted in the pursuit of regional development will determine the nature of the export-base and in consequence the sort of regional development that can be achieved. The ideal product for the export-base would clearly have very good long-term economic

[1] D. C. North, 'Location Theory and Regional Economic Growth', *Journal of Political Economy*, LXIII (June 1955), pp. 243–58.

prospects, and would offer many opportunities to invest in industries supplying it or using its products (i.e. potential 'linkage' effects are large) with the proviso that it could be satisfactorily established without these complementary industries so that the minimum amount of investment needed to start it would not be prohibitively large. Usually, where the region is less developed than the rest of the economy, one would expect the export-base to be of primary products. In a few historical instances, this may not have been the case—for example, recent growth in Puerto Rico, which for certain purposes, might be considered a region of the United States economy, has been based on exports of goods manufactured from imported raw materials. But where, as in this study, the region in question is a sparsely populated area of a less developed country, the only feasible exports will at first be of either agricultural or mineral products.

Building on a similar analysis to the export-base theory, other authors have gone on to discuss the extent to which, if left to themselves, normal market forces will tend to concentrate economic growth in a few regions, leaving the rest lagging behind. This leads us to another difference between the economic analysis of inter-regional and international trade—this time by making different assumptions about the degree of factor mobility, which affects the way in which growth in one region affects growth in other regions. International trade theory usually assumes that factors of production are immobile between countries, but completely mobile internally. Though not completely true, international migration of labour and investment are sufficiently small to make this an acceptable approximation for many analytical purposes. In the analysis of inter-regional trade, however, inter-regional immobility of factors would be too unrealistic an assumption to make the results interesting. To assume perfect mobility, so that factors move to eliminate any inter-regional differences in the rate of payment to factors would also be very unrealistic and this assumption would eliminate a major reason for interest in regional development. In consequence, some mobility of factors must be assumed but insufficient to assure equal factor rewards and levels of employment in all regions.

The question whether if left to itself growth will tend to

equalize regional income differences or cause these to diverge has attracted much discussion and opposing answers, but cannot be answered without reference to particular situations. The issues that will determine the answer, however, are fairly clear. In the first place, the rate of growth of exports will be of great importance. These exports are likely to be of primary products. It is widely accepted that the world market prospects for most primary products are not promising in the foreseeable future, though there are individual exceptions. Demand for such products usually rises relatively slowly in proportion to rising world incomes and a fall in price is not likely to lead to a compensatory increase in the quantity sold. This is certainly the case for most food products. Demand for raw materials usually rises less fast than demand for the products in which the materials are incorporated, since economies in raw material use are often made and synthetic substitutes developed. With raw material costs only a small proportion of the costs of the finished product, price elasticities of demand for raw materials are also likely to be low. On the supply side, increasing output of raw materials might be expected to run into diminishing returns to fixed natural resources. This may well cause a rise in price of some minerals, and, in the distant future, of foods produced in temperate zones. As things are at present, however, the scope for increasing the output of tropical agricultural products in Africa and Latin America is extremely wide, and there seems little prospect of the demand tending to outstrip supply. In consequence these products in particular face stagnant or falling world prices.

For this reason it may seem as though the growth of regions dependent on agricultural exports must inevitably lag behind more industrial ones. This is much too simple a view. Any single region is only a small supplier of the world output of a particular commodity—expansion here will have little effect on world prices. Of course, declining world and national prices will have some adverse effect on earnings and hence on the growth of the export-base, but this would be more than offset by the rapid expansion of output.

There are other reasons, however, why some writers have argued that growth will tend to be fastest in a few regions, in which industrial growth will be concentrated, and that other regions will tend to lag increasingly behind. In regional analysis by Myrdal, market forces left to themselves tend to this result.[1] As in North's theory, the increase in demand for consumption goods and for productive factors which results from the initial investment is felt principally within the region in which the investment takes place. Opportunities will be more profitable here. Banking, transport, trading facilities, and other elements of social overhead capital will be developed here rather than elsewhere. Mobility of factors tends to reinforce this cumulative process, slowing the rise of factor prices in the growing areas that might otherwise have halted expansion. Growth in one region will spread to other regions through a demand for imports from these regions but only to a limited extent. Myrdal calls these effects of regional development 'spread effects' and argues that they are normally more important in advanced countries—which he attributes to a fuller utilization of potential human resources in such countries—so that growth will tend less to be concentrated in a few areas. This is an important point: wage differentials and differences in the availability of labour between regions may be a potent force in attracting industry in developed countries—as the postwar experience of the US South and Puerto Rico have demonstrated. Less developed countries, however, are normally characterized by high levels of unemployment in all regions and from an economic point of view one would expect that wages would not be far above subsistence anywhere. Even though in many countries political factors keep urban wages much more above rural ones than would be justified by cost-of-living differences, these differentials are unlikely to offset the other attractions of industrial areas—skills, social overhead facilities and specialist firms—as a magnet for attracting industry.

Hirschman, who has a similar but rather more optimistic analysis than Myrdal, has pointed out that entrepreneurs are likely to overestimate external economies existing in a growing region from lack of knowledge of opportunities existing elsewhere, or lack of courage or imagination to try them.[2] This will encourage

[1] Gunnar Myrdal, *Rich Lands and Poor* (New York: Harper, 1957), pp. 23–38.
[2] A. O. Hirschman, *The Strategy of Economic Development* (New Haven: Yale University Press, 1958), pp. 183–201.

the polarization of economic growth, and so will the fact that the most mobile men are likely to be those with training, skill or entrepreneurial talent who would be just the people to start development in the backward regions.

The third principal difference between analysing regional and national problems is the way in which inter-regional balances of payments are adjusted. To some degree, this adjustment is eased by the fact that the region has the same currency as the rest of the economy, and that, in consequence, a wide variety of assets can be used to finance inter-regional transactions. There is therefore no regional problem comparable to the question of whether foreign exchange reserves are adequate to meet fluctuations in the balance of payments—the adequacy of 'regional liquidity' is never an issue.

On the other hand, long term disequilibrium in the balance of payments of a region may be a good deal harder to correct than that in the national balance of payments. If a nation finds that at present exchange rates equilibrium in the balance of payments is attainable only by enduring a high level of unemployment, it can always adjust the external value of its currency and so expand export earnings and lead to a substitution of domestic production for imports, to permit both full employment and balance of payments equilibrium to be reached. By a suitable choice of exchange rate, it will be possible to expand exports of the products in which the nation has a comparative advantage. This is true even if, following exchange rate changes, export expansion and import reduction take considerable time and effort so that, in the short run, it makes sense to talk in terms of balance of payments constraints on economic development—implying that there are unemployed domestic resources which cannot be used to earn foreign exchange (because of limited substitution possibilities).[1] We shall shortly say a little more about this when discussing project appraisal. The option to alter the national exchange rate has no equivalent in regional policy. Exports to other regions must be developed on the basis of the existing exchange rate. Possibly indirect tax exemptions, if given selectively by region,

---

[1] There is a large literature on this. A good discussion is that in R. I. McKinnon, 'Foreign Exchange Constraints in Economic Development and Efficient Aid Allocation', *Economic Journal*, LXXIV (June 1964), pp. 388–409.

may have some effect in this direction, but only if such taxes are an important component of production costs. Unfortunately, it is frequently hard to achieve much by this approach since in backward regions the tax base may already be very narrow, and revenue from indirect taxes cannot be sacrificed. The possibility that a higher level of unemployment will lead to the lowering of wages and prices is remote—the inflexibility of money prices downwards is widely accepted. This is particularly the case for prices in one region relatively to those elsewhere in the economy since many of the forces that determine prices operate equally in all regions, and production in one region has to use inputs imported from other regions.

Successful regional policy has therefore to find an export-base product in which the region has not merely a comparative advantage with respect to other regions, but which it can produce at competitive prices. The ability of any regional policy to do this must be a major criterion by which it should be judged. The extent and the nature of cumulative development which will follow the establishment of an export-base must also be appraised when selecting policies to promote regional development. The alternative approaches which governments may follow in promoting regional development will be answered in the next section.

REGIONAL DEVELOPMENT POLICIES

It is not the purpose of this section to consider in detail all the alternative policies that governments might pursue or have at times pursued. Instead we shall try to classify the different approaches to policy in terms of the differing roles they assign to public and private action and in terms of the sort of development envisaged. One can distinguish here three types of approach. The first are negative approaches, which merely restrict certain actions of the private sector; the second are approaches which try to induce private firms to act—these are sometimes described as 'permissive'; and the third those that involve more direct action. In discussing all these cases, we assume the sort of mixed economy that is general outside Communist countries. Here private enterprise is encouraged to a greater or lesser degree, but the government plays an active part in the planning and promoting of economic development. The choice of regional policy may of course reflect the extent to which there are fairly demarcated 'spheres of influence' for the private and public sector—and therefore the extent to which the government feels able to take the lead in carrying out activities in one region which the private sector is performing in another.

The negative approach involves the mere prevention of the free establishment of firms in regions which are considered relatively too developed or congested. Licenses might be required, taxes levied or an outright prohibition (such as the prohibition of new office building in Central London) adopted. The criticism generally levied against licensing or other direct controls is that they allow the gains from such a policy to be captured in the form of monopoly profits by those who obtain permission to become established or are already there. In a developed country, it may reasonably be hoped that firms unable to locate in their preferred region will go somewhere else—or at least that the productive resources that would have been invested in that region will be invested elsewhere—although, strictly speaking, one might expect that investment which was only marginally profitable in the preferred region might not now take place. But in any case, the loss of investment will be small. In a developing economy, where any manifestation of the spirit of enterprise needs to be carefully nurtured, and where the difference in the attractiveness of different regions as a location for industry is very wide, controls on where firms may locate may reduce total investment. Small firms, in particular, which find survival and growth difficult in any case, and which prefer the security of being established where it is clear that others in the same industry are surviving and where there are markets plainly available, are unlikely to move into non-industrial regions if unable to become established in those regions that are already industrialized. For this reason, regional policy in developing countries will probably not include controls on industrial location, but rather inducements to locate elsewhere.

These inducements aim to operate to reduce costs or increase returns for profit-seeking economic activity in order to offset the disadvantages of less developed regions. Because of its concern with regional problems, the government may be prepared to do this even if it makes national income smaller by its action, though, as noted, one of the motivations for its actions may be a belief that once established, regional development may in fact prove socially profitable. The reasons why firms locate in one place rather than another has never occupied a central place in economics but there is a great deal of literature on the subject. What has emerged has taken one of two paths—neither very useful to the government in selecting its regional development policy. Most of location theory has been concerned with isolating the effects of distance either on the overall pattern of economic activity within a region, as in the work of von Thunen or Losch, or, as in much of Weber's work, on the location decision of a firm.[1] Isard suggests that the von Thunen approach might be of more value to the work of regional or national planners than the more limited approach, but it is not easy to see why, since planners are not usually faced with the isolated plains of considerable extent, which the von Thunen approach assumes, and regional development is going to be largely concerned with production for a market outside the relevant region and perhaps with production that draws raw materials from outside the region. It is true, however, that the planner may be realistically assumed to face a less narrow choice of industry than the private entrepreneur.

Theories to explain the micro-economics of the decision where to locate have been developed for a wide variety of circumstances and to a high level of precision. These include programming models, which can take account of the fact that trade flows along networks rather than continuously in all directions, and that there are different limitations on transport facilities and resource availability.[2] Other models have incorporated spatial factors into a conventional analysis of production functions.[3] Not all the

[1] Johann Heinrich von Thunen, *The Isolated State*, ed. Peter Hall (London: Pergamon Press, 1965); August Losch, *The Economics of Location*, trans. from 2nd ed. by William H. Woglom (German ed. 1943. New Haven: Yale University Press, 1954); and Alfred Weber, *Alfred Weber's Theory of the Location of Industries*, English translation and notes by Carl J. Friendrich (German ed. 1909. Chicago: University of Chicago Press, 1929).

[2] Louis Lefeber, *Allocation in Space: Production, Transport and Industrial Location* (Amsterdam: North-Holland Publishing Co., 1958).

[3] Leon Moses, 'Location and the Theory of Production', *Quarterly Journal of Economics*, LXXIII (May 1958), pp. 259–72.

13

location theories stress merely distance. Some also mention agglomerative (and deglomerative) factors and a miscellaneous category comprising the several costs associated with labour, power, water, taxes, insurance, interest (as a payment for the services of capital), climate, topography, social and political milieu, and a number of other items.[1] Analysis based on such models might help governments to predict the results of actions to encourage private investment, or to estimate the necessary magnitude of cost reductions to induce a response from profit-seeking activity. Apart from this, the models themselves do not give a great deal of guidance to policy-makers in the selection of actual policies.

'Permissive' policies involve either tax policies, which operate in the main to make already profitable actions more profitable, or the provision of various sorts of social overhead capital (SOC) which lowers costs. The latter course may merely involve bringing a neglected region up to the average national standard in schools, power, transport facilities and so on. The type of private investment attracted will obviously depend then on the nature of the region and the facilities provided. Obviously, irrigation will foster agricultural development, while hydroelectric power may have its own particular effects on the location of industry.

Investment in SOC is a controversial strategy for a government to follow, and, as usual in development economics, the controversy can be resolved only by resorting to empirical study. It is obvious that some SOC is essential for economic development, and the thing that distinguishes it from other equally necessary capital goods is that it cannot be imported. (Although power may be transmitted inter-regionally, or even internationally, the facilities for transmitting it must be constructed within the receiving region.) Furthermore, it is generally accepted that the government must carry out such investment. Often there are considerable economies of scale—a pricing policy which charged consumers only the marginal costs of supplying them would mean the enterprise would make losses. Frequently because of the effects of such activities in reducing the costs of other enterprises the full benefits of the investment cannot be captured by the first

[1] See Walter Isard, *Location and Space Economy* (Boston and New York: The Technology Press of M.I.T. and Wiley, 1956), p. 138.

enterprise and it may even be impossible to have a practicable pricing policy at all—as in the case of road investment. Quite apart from this, it may be difficult in an underdeveloped country to find private investors prepared to undertake investment with such a long period of gestation and expected life. Since duplication of facilities in this area is wasteful but without duplication a private owner would have a monopolistic position, it is also accepted the field is a proper one which requires government control. Nobody will deny the need for at least a bare minimum of government activity in this area.

Those who stress the desirability of placing particular emphasis on this type of investment go further than this. They argue that since such capital is essential for economic development and its gestation period long, it must of necessity precede investment in more directly productive activities and will not be profitable at first in terms of private criteria. Paul Rosenstein-Rodan has also pointed out that the construction of SOC raises effective demand, and in that way, leads to further private investment and a cumulative growth of income.[1]

On the other hand, Hirschman argues that the importance of SOC has been exaggerated.[2] Much investment in it, he suggests, has been done as a matter of faith, since it often appears difficult to apply the usual sort of investment criteria that we consider later in the chapter. Where Hirschman differs most markedly from Rosenstein-Rodan is over the necessary sequence of SOC investment and investment in directly productive activities (DPA). Of course, a minimum of SOC is needed—one must be able to reach a region in order to develop it. But he suggests that the range of choice open on the matter is much wider than is usually supposed. Beyond a minimum point, SOC has diminishing returns with respect to lowering the cost of DPA. The difference, at this point of the argument, between the two views turns mainly on the point that SOC is necessarily 'lumpy'. Given that a minimum

[1] Paul N. Rosenstein-Rodan, 'How to Industrialize an Underdeveloped Area', *Regional Economic Planning: Techniques of Analysis for Less Developed Areas*, Papers and Proceedings of the First Study Conference on Problems of Economic Development Organized by the European Productivity Agency, Bellagio, Italy, 19 June–1 July 1960, ed. Walter Isard and John H. Cumberland (Paris: E.P.A., 1961), pp. 205–11.

[2] Hirschman, *Strategy of Economic Development*, pp. 83–97.

is necessary for development, and that it cannot be added in strictly marginal amounts, the difference so far is only in the minimum size of the lumps. It may well be true, as Hirschman argues, that because development planners are principally concerned with government investment, and SOC is an unquestioned field for government activity, they tend to overestimate the size of the lump.

But Hirschman goes further in contrasting SOC investment with investment in DPA and produces some hypotheses which, though not logically compelling, certainly merit empirical examination. Given that the relation between SOC and DPA is not, within wide limits, technologically determined, and given that the government has limited investment funds and so must choose between investment in each of them, he argues that preference should be given to the sequence of investment that maximizes 'induced' decision-making. This is in line with a belief that it is more the lack of entrepreneurship to exploit potential savings that holds back development than other bottlenecks, and that the government should above all try to establish mechanisms to induce the utilization of these resources. Without necessarily accepting that the first proposition is true for all underdeveloped countries, this offers an important and unique role for government in a developing economy. Hirschman argues that supplying SOC ahead of demand will induce far less private investment than letting SOC investment itself be induced by a shortage, making the initial step in the sequence investment in DPA. He argues that excess SOC is permissive. It invites people to use it. A shortage, on the other hand, creates a number of people who are directly affected by the shortage and who have a direct incentive to go out and try to get the situation remedied. It is argued that this is a particularly important consideration in regional development strategy, since a mere provision of SOC will not be enough to get entrepreneurs to go into a region they are accustomed to considering backward.

This is plausible, if not wholly convincing. For example, suppose an investment in a road will reduce the costs of a potential industry by 20 per cent, making its location in a particular region newly profitable. It is possible that costs might alternatively be reduced by the same amount by investment in a supplying industry. It is possible that the second investment may induce the establishment of the potential industry, while the road investment will fail to do so, because in their search for markets, the supplying industry is likely to be more active in attempting to stimulate complementary activity than are road builders. If both, however, are part of the government, this may not be the case. Furthermore, the development of a road is likely to reduce costs for a much wider range of industries than investment in a particular branch of DPA, and consequently, the aggregate effect of it may be much greater, even if, for particular lines of production, there are potential entrepreneurs who fail to take advantage of its effects on profits. In any case, the actual inducement effects can only be determined by extensive empirical study, eventually providing a large enough sample to isolate the inducement effects of different types of investment.

Investment in DPA may have two inducement effects—one on the suppliers of inputs (which Hirschman calls 'backward linkage effects'), and another, on the users of its outputs ('forward linkage effects'). Certain industries can be considered 'satellites' of a major industry. In this connection, Hirschman gives an example that is of interest to us. Processing mills, he states, generally have no backward linkage effects on the production of the agricultural product processed; he argues that it is unrealistic to think of rice production, for example, as being 'induced' by the existence of rice mills. Such mills are rather to be considered as satellite industries through a process of forward linkage. Quite often, however, as in the case of the sugar industry the world over, backward linkage does appear in agricultural industries.

Hirschman also suggests that the percentage of output represented by the purchase of inputs from other industries and the percentage sold as inputs to other industries provide an indication of the potential linkage effects that might result from the establishment of these industries. This is difficult to accept; an enthusiast for 'balanced growth' might use the same list as the industries to avoid, as likely to provoke the greatest bottlenecks. The question 'when is a bottleneck a bottleneck, and when a stimulus to further development' is answerable only by empirical research.

A regional development policy entailing a little more government involvement is a programme of setting up industrial estates.
Sometimes this merely involves making building land available,
and is almost indistinguishable from the general strategy of providing social overhead capital. Other programmes provide
factories for rent. If this is done principally to reduce the initial
costs of establishment for small firms, the rent might be the private market one. A more determined policy could charge low
rents in order to subsidize capital costs. An industrial estate policy
may at its best offer the promise of obtaining economies of agglomeration relatively quickly, and by concentrating industrial
growth into one area of a particular city, some of the urbanization
costs which might be incurred in haphazard sprawling development may be reduced.

Tax policies can be used to promote regional development in a
large number of ways. Exemption from income and profits tax,
or more generous depreciation allowances on new investment, can
make investments which earn lower pre-tax profits in backward
regions than elsewhere, earn a relatively higher after-tax rate. In
an economy where the disparity between profits to be earned in
different regions is not very great—i.e. in many industrial countries—this may be a useful inducement, but it is unlikely to tempt
pioneer industrial investment into the backward areas of less
developed countries.

Exemptions or reductions in local taxes are likely to be even
less effective than exemptions from central government taxes.
Local taxes are usually so small as to be insignificant in most locational decisions and in those cases where they may make a difference, the reductions granted by one local taxing authority are
likely to be quickly matched by other localities, also anxious to
attract the industry. From the point of view of a local authority it
will be better to have a non-tax-paying industry than no industry
at all, and if this seems to be the choice then generous concessions
will be given. With all local authorities giving similar concessions,
the effects on the location of industry cancel out, but the local
authorities are deprived of the tax revenue. Discriminating concessions by a central government are likely to be much more
effective. An example of a scheme that has apparently been very

successful in attracting investment funds is that now being tried in the Brazilian northeast.[1] Firms have been able to use part of the funds that would otherwise be paid in Federal income tax to invest in the region.

Selective reductions in indirect taxes may influence the location of firms, but the only concession here that is likely to be really important in developing countries is exemption from import duties on intermediate imports. As will be described in Chapter 4, Mexico has adopted this approach to encourage the establishment of industries along her border with the United States.

An alternative regional policy involves direct government investment in productive activities. We have just contrasted this as a strategy with a policy that invests heavily in social overhead facilities. There is not a great deal more that can be said in the abstract. The basic rationale for direct government investment is either that social returns from investment exceed private returns, for one or more of the reasons described, or, as Hirschman argued, because entrepreneurial talent is scarce and needs encouraging. It may, of course, be argued that if entrepreneurial talent is particularly scarce it is unlikely that the government has very much of it. Nevertheless, where providing incentives to increase private sector investment is an important government objective, directly productive investment may be the most efficient way to encourage it.

PROJECT SELECTION

The previous section discussed some of the considerations to be taken into account when the government is choosing broad policies to stimulate regional development. This section is more concerned with the making of choices between particular items of expenditure than with the overall strategy behind policy selection. Economists have usually treated these two things separately. But, at least in principle, they cannot be satisfactorily separated. A government cannot select a policy of, say, heavy investment in transport facilities, without some details of what the outcome of

[1] A. O. Hirschman, 'Industrial Development in the Brazilian Northeast and the Tax Credit Scheme of Article 34/18', *Journal of Development Studies* (October 1968), pp. 5–28.

such investment is likely to be compared with the investment of a comparable quantity of productive resources in something quite different—perhaps an educational programme. Policy selection must take account of the return on individual investments, to prevent the waste of resources that would result if the commitment of funds in one sector earned a much lower return than in other sectors. The measurement of the return on investments, however, can only be made in the light of the objectives behind the making of these investments, and these objectives are determined both by the aims and by the nature of the broad policies. For example, an investment project may be assessed in one light if the objective is to maximize the gross income of a particular region and in another if the aim is maximum *per capita* regional income. A project designed to stimulate private entrepreneurial activity will be assessed differently from one which simply aims to produce consumer goods.

Although some of what will be said in this section might apply to the choosing of tax policies or direct controls on private investment, we are concerned primarily with investment projects and especially with investments to fulfill regional development objectives. Every project involves the commitment of inputs in a stream through time and the generation of output through time. The project proposed may describe the inputs and outputs quite precisely as though the outcome of the expenditure was quite certain, or it may recognize the fact of uncertainty by trying to assign probabilities to different outcomes. In the case of regional development projects in developing countries the information needed to be able to assign such probabilities is almost certain not to be available. This does not mean that project planners will always use the expected outcome of uncertain events in their calculation —they might be anxious, for example, to avoid catastrophe and play safe, or uncertainty may make it worthwhile to keep as much flexibility as possible, even at some cost. We are not in this book going to be much concerned with the inevitable fact of uncertainty or its effects on decision-making. As with most writing on this subject we shall tend to assume that the outcome of any action is completely predictable. The fact that the consequences of an activity can only be imperfectly predicted has, however, recently been discussed in an interesting book by A. O. Hirschman, which suggests that failure to appreciate all the problems that may arise in the course of operation of a project may have its beneficial side.[1] Often a development project has encountered unexpected problems, which if anticipated would have prevented its approval, but which in the event turned out to be soluble. It is useful to be aware of this—if only because it may mean that it becomes easier in future to predict man's capacity to solve problems—and in our description of what happened to regional development policies in Mexico it will be important to ask to what extent the outcome was predictable and whether any unexpected results were beneficial or unbeneficial.

Even if ignorance of the difficulties which may be ahead is sometimes bliss, in general one must proceed on the assumption that rational decisions require information and the more accurate the information the better. But information is costly and sometimes difficult to obtain and process. It is clear that for a centralized decision-maker to obtain enough information on all potential courses of action to be able to compare the outcome of every possible use of resources would in practice be impossible because of the quantity of information to be obtained and processed. The use of prices might seem to avoid this problem. By providing an immediate indication of the relative degrees of scarcity of different factors of production and different outputs, and by allowing an immediate calculation of the increment to output that could result from the commitment of resources to investment rather than to current consumption they make it possible to establish rules for making decisions to give some assurance that the basis for relating public expenditure in one sector of the economy will not differ from that used in another sector. It is now widely accepted that there may be many circumstances in which the government of an underdeveloped country will be wiser to calculate its own system of accounting or shadow prices rather than use prevailing market prices, and economists have written a good deal on what would be the most appropriate prices to use and how to use them.

[1] A. O. Hirschman, *Development Projects Observed* (Washington, D.C.: The Brookings Institution, 1967).

Indeed it has sometimes appeared as though almost the sole problem in project selection was the choice of appropriate prices —after this the prices could be used in well established formulae and sufficient information on which to make decisions about any project would be automatically forthcoming. We shall suggest, however, that this is a rather over-simplified view of the process of project appraisal, at least in the present state of the art. Although it may be conceptually possible to envisage the determination of some set of prices to measure ideally the costs and benefits of all projects, we are a long way from being able to do this. We shall come to the question of the actual prices to be used at the end of this chapter.

The key part of project appraisal is the measurement of the benefits of the project. In the last resort, the costs of any project are the benefits from the use of the resources in the best project that has to be foregone if the project in question is undertaken. Consequently, we must ask how we should measure the benefits of an investment project designed to promote regional development.

Handling the multiple objectives of public investment

The first thing to note is the probable multiplicity of objectives of public investment projects—as illustrated by our discussion of regional policies. Expenditures here will aim to increase national income. They will, however, be especially concerned to increase regional income—but this may either be primarily *per capita* income or total regional income. Where the concern is *per capita* income, the government may be interested in the regional average *per capita* income or in the *per capita* income of certain groups living in the region. The provision of employment may be a separate goal—and this again may either aim at the reduction of unemployment locally or the attraction of labour from other regions. The project may also lead to the discovery and utilization of other sorts of resources—whether natural resources, entrepreneurial ability or potential sources of saving—which would otherwise be untapped.

The outcome of any project can be expressed in terms of the

degree of fulfillment of these objectives.[1] The real measure of objective fulfillment would go much further than this, since it would allow for a particularly high level of fulfillment of one objective to compensate for a particularly low level of achievement of another and arrive at a single measure of the benefits of a project. Since not all the ways in which objectives are expressed make the outcomes directly commensurable, money equivalents must be assigned to those not expressed in money terms. This may not itself be inherently possible. Most, but emphatically not all, of the benefits which do not increase total national income can theoretically be expressed in terms of the distribution of that income. Thus, fuller employment may be desired primarily to increase the share of income available to the unemployed and inflation may be regarded as harmful because of its adverse effects on income distribution. Unfortunately the ideal measure of benefits would not involve the mere definition of weights to all outcomes expressed in money terms in advance and maximizing the weighted sum—the weight assigned to one objective must itself vary with the level of achievement of other objectives. A given reduction of unemployment may be a very important objective when *per capita* incomes are $1,000 and unimportant when they are $100.

To state what an ideal measure of objective fulfillment would involve is simultaneously to demonstrate how impossible it is to achieve. The alternatives sometimes suggested are to maximize the fulfillment of one objective or weighted combination of objectives, subject to constraints in terms of other desirable goals.[2] Though conceptually not ideal, it does offer some hope that it can be applied. It is not really too implausible to imagine a government being prepared to state explicitly the constraints on, say, maximizing the rate of growth in terms of other goals, such as price stability. Governments probably do have some idea of what is a tolerable level of inflation or unemployment. It may be

[1] Several of the points made in the following paragraph are dealt with more fully in Timothy King, 'Development Strategy and Investment Criteria: Complementary or Competitive?' *Quarterly Journal of Economics*, LXXX (February 1966), pp. 108–20.

[2] See Otto Eckstein, 'A Survey of the Theory of Public Expenditure Criteria', in *The Public Finances: Needs, Sources and Utilization*, A conference of the Universities-National Bureau Committee for Economic Research (Princeton: Princeton University Press, 1961), pp. 439–94.

impossible, if only for political reasons, for a government to spell out what level of unemployment or inflation it would tolerate, but it probably will have revealed its preferences sufficiently in the past for an economist to attempt to express them explicitly.[1] Furthermore, economists know a lot about the technical manipulation of an objective function subject to constraints.

The objective function is easiest to handle when we maximize one objective and put in all other desirable goals as constraints. Where we want to put several objectives into the function to maximize the weighted sum, we encounter the problem that such weighting is bound to be arbitrary and that we run the risk of producing, as Eckstein says, 'either a meaningless hodgepodge, or a slighting of all objectives other than tangible output'.[2]

Attempts by the US Bureau of Reclamation to establish a set of uniform measures of indirect benefits other than the contribution made by the project to gross national income led to the making of so many arbitrary assumptions that the whole concept of benefits other than economic efficiency fell into disrepute.[3] Spurious precision may be worse than no precision at all, since it may hide the places where a real choice has to be made.

Given the difficulties that are involved here, it would be nice to be persuaded that an elaborate attempt to consider a multiplicity of objectives carefully is unnecessary. Lindblom has argued this—not merely because it is difficult to formulate objectives, but because he attacks the whole idea of a division between ends (objectives) and means, and also because he sees real merit in an

---

[1] In a very interesting discussion of this, Arthur Maass shows that what amounts to a trade-off between economic efficiency and the single most non-economic objective can and does emerge from the US legislative process. This has occurred both in Federal roads and housing programmes, though not in water resource development. During the legislative process, after extensive discussion, and consideration of alternatives, a trade-off point was reached. As Maass points out, the explicit recognition of trading-off the fulfillment of one objective for the fulfillment of another is a considerable step forward from the view that projects should be designed solely to achieve an economic efficiency objective and doctored later, since the multiplicity of objectives will affect the design of the projects. See Arthur Maass, 'Benefit-cost Analysis: Its Relevance to Public Investment Decisions', *Quarterly Journal of Economics*, LXXX (May 1966), pp. 208–26.

[2] Eckstein, 'Survey of the Theory of Public Expenditure Criteria', p. 448.

[3] There is a very good discussion of this in Hirschman, *Development Projects Observed*, pp. 175–80. The final chapter of his book, 'Project Appraisal', pp. 160–88, overlaps with the analysis in this section of this chapter at many points.

alternative approach which would involve making policy-decisions in small steps, with each step aiming to fulfill only a limited range of objectives and considering only a small number of alternative possibilities.[1] This is an important argument, since such a procedure would get round some of the difficulties mentioned earlier about the high cost of information in centralized decision-making, and with the undeniable fact that all decisions rest on predictions about an uncertain future. It does, however, go against the assumption that is usually made in discussing government choice and indeed the assumption made so far in this chapter—the assumption that policies be selected after a careful and comprehensive consideration of alternatives, evaluated in the light of carefully formulated objectives—an approach that Lindblom classifies as 'synoptic'.

Society, Lindblom argues, is not able to separate the ends it seeks from the means employed to achieve them, since society is a collection of individuals and what some members of it regard as an end in itself others will regard as a means to quite some other end. For some in society, increasing defence expenditure is desirable in order to increase national strength, and reducing unemployment merely the means to this end. For others, the end is full employment, and increasing defence expenditure the means chosen. In these circumstances it is easier to obtain agreement on the policy to be followed than on social ends. However it should be noted that the idea of social objectives is not one that seems foreign to most governments. The latter appear ready to talk about 'progress' or 'development' or to be prepared to say that one social situation is preferred to another, which implies some notion of social objectives.

Lindblom contrasts the problems of a synoptic approach with the virtues of allowing policies to emerge from numbers of small un-co-ordinated steps taken after policy analysis, evaluation, and decision have taken place independently at a large number of points throughout society. This procedure permits the representation of a much wider range of values in policy decisions than would be

[1] Lindblom has expressed these views in several articles and book reviews, but for the most complete expression of his ideas, see David Braybrooke and Charles E. Lindblom, *A Strategy of Decision: Policy Evaluation as a Social Process* (New York: Free Press of Glencoe, 1963), pp. 6–143.

considered by a single decision-maker. Where unanticipated adverse consequences result from a policy, later steps can be taken to correct them. If one group presses for, and obtains, a policy that neglects important aspects of the problem, another group will stress the neglected factors, and government decision-makers and others will act as watch-dogs to see that certain values are not neglected.

There are, however, grave difficulties with this approach, especially when it comes to correcting mistakes.[1] Reversing an investment decision may often be extremely wasteful of resources, or even physically out of the question. The more often any course of policy has become an accepted part of the general context in

[1] It is interesting in this context to contrast Lindblom's views of a traffic engineer, with those of Peter Hall, writing on the future growth of London.

'A city traffic engineer, for example, might propose the allocation of certain streets to one-way traffic. He may be quite unable to predict how many serious bottlenecks in traffic will arise and where. Nevertheless, he may confidently make his recommendations, assuming that, as bottlenecks arise, appropriate steps to solve the new problem will be taken at the time—new traffic lights, assignment of traffic patrolmen, or further revision of the one-way plan itself. He may also correctly anticipate certain other consequences, such as business losses in certain locations from rerouting customer traffic. Some of these consequences he will nevertheless ignore in drawing up his traffic plan. Instead, he will, in separate consideration of each of various anticipated problems, decide to alter parking regulations, ease pedestrian traffic in certain areas, or turn to some other policy to reduce the business losses ruled irrelevant to his first policy problem.' (Lindblom and Braybrooke, p. 125.)

'The traffic engineer is paid to make traffic flow; he does just this; other considerations are irrelevant to him. In a city as ill-planned for the motor vehicle as London, the result may be a disaster in terms of true planning. The two most spectacular cases of this so far are the routing of a main West End traffic stream through London's handsomest surviving Georgian square; and the plan to bring heavy lorries, northbound from the docks and central markets, throught the old village centre of Highgate. [A footnote points out that the latter plan was modified by the Ministry of Transport in January 1963, after considerable protest, and thus perhaps partially vindicates Lindblom, in this particular instance.] But there are many other cases which are no less disturbing, but which get less spectacular publicity because they do not involve aesthetics or because the people affected are less vocal than in Highgate. Any and every residential backwater is now likely to have its peace and quiet ended by the diversion of a main traffic flow.

'Based on considerations of traffic flow alone, traffic engineering techniques bid to erode the Londoner's standard of decent living more quickly than any other development. But based on a careful weighing of costs and benefits to everyone involved—motorists, residents, pedestrian school children and shoppers—they could point the way to a cheap and quick method of making London a better place to live *and* drive in, until we can spare the resources for more radical reconstruction.' Peter Hall, *London 2000* (London: Faber and Faber, 1963), pp. 120–1.

which other decisions are taken, the harder it is to reverse such a policy, from both political and economic standpoints. In addition, the fact that government policies are not subject to abrupt changes and reversals may, in a mixed economy, be turned to good advantage, since it may be presumed that a reduction of uncertainty will improve private decisions and lead to a better allocation of resources.

Where policies are virtually irreversible then something of a synoptic approach must be adopted, even if the difficulties involved are fully appreciated, and even if the results are only partially successful. This is true where there is considerable interdependence between government decisions, as is very frequently the case with investment in developing countries.

Finally, unless we are sure that each section of the community is served by a strong interest group, and that such groups are reasonably balanced in the political process, there is little guarantee that what would emerge from a Lindblom process of bargaining over policy decisions together with frequent amendments to existing policies would be an improvement over a reasonable attempt to be synoptic.

Nevertheless, remember that this is a matter of emphasis. The synoptic approach is not operational in any full and complete sense. It is possible to conceive of a situation in which an enormous computer, fed with a completely specified social welfare function and a complete list of all resources, could grind out a simultaneous solution to all policy decisions, but it is impossible to believe that any society will ever attempt that. Some decentralization of decision-making is inevitable. It is useful to be reminded that what is often 'sub-optimization' by decentralized units, which may involve decisions taken with respect to criteria that are inconsistent with 'higher level' criteria, and which fail to take into account their effects on the activities of other decentralized units, is not always harmful.[1] But, in any case, administrative practice often tries to minimize the negative consequence of ignoring side effects by establishing agencies with power to co-ordinate

[1] On the problem of suboptimization see Ronald N. McKean, *Efficiency in Government Through Systems Analysis, with Emphasis on Water Resources Development*, A RAND Corporation Research Study (New York: John Wiley & Sons, 1958), pp. 29–34.

the activities of other decision-makers just where the side effects of their policies are most harmful. Rather than see a traffic engineer as an example of the virtues of the incrementalist approach, it was implied that city planning on a reasonably synoptic basis was needed. It is quite likely, however, that the city planning authority will not be greatly concerned about the raw sewage that the city is dumping into the river. It is the inhabitants of the next city downstream who worry about that. In such a case, a central government might create an agency to co-ordinate sewage disposal throughout the basin.

In our later example of Mexico, the River Basin Commissions can be envisaged as using a synoptic approach to making decisions for river basins as a whole but ignoring side effects outside each basin. But in making budget proposals, officials of the other agencies involved—the Ministry of Water Resources, the Treasury, and the Presidential Ministry in this example—may also use something of a synoptic approach, but one that is based on different considerations. The net result is far from a neat synoptic investment decision with all alternatives weighed in the light of all objectives. It is indeed possible that some of the decision criteria used by a Commission will contradict the higher level criteria of the Presidential Ministry. The procedures certainly offer no guarantee that the marginal productivity of the last 100,000 pesos spent by a River Basin Commission in terms of fulfillment of the set of national objectives will be the same as that of the last 100,000 spent by the Ministry of Communications. They can perhaps do something, however, to prevent these marginal productivities from getting too much out of line with each other.

We return here then to the simple but not obvious point of view that at present it may be better to state the objectives as clearly as possible, and to indicate beforehand trade-offs between them as far as can be known as a guide in designing investment projects. When alternatives are presented for decision perhaps the most that can at present be hoped for is that the degree of fulfillment of each objective is shown and that where it is possible to show trade-offs between alternatives these are shown as precisely as possible. In the long run perhaps one may hope that more satisfactory indices of objective fulfillment can be constructed.

Linkage effects

How, in this sort of framework of selecting projects, do the seemingly qualitative considerations of the sort mentioned in the section on regional development policies—for example, the difference between social overhead capital and directly productive investment—enter questions of investment appraisal? The difference is not in the reasons why the government is pursuing regional development policy. At least some of the ways in which projects fulfill objectives are the same for all types of investment projects. All produce outputs, which may be sold directly to the consumer, sold to producers or which, where this output cannot be conveniently captured by the producer and therefore priced, such as with a road, can at least be clearly identified and a value placed upon them for the purposes of appraising the project. The appropriate prices to use will be discussed shortly.

The output of public projects will usually be sold to the private sector (including households) and inputs will be bought from the private sector. There will, however, be a difference between types of project in the degree to which they make purchases from or sales to the private sector, and hence in the number of profitable opportunities they offer to utilize their products or sell imports to them. There will be a difference in the extent to which such opportunities are likely to be noticed by existing or potential entrepreneurs and in the sort of entrepreneur who will be able to take advantage of the opportunities. There will also be a difference in the extent to which employment is offered in other industries and in the degree to which profit opportunities are stronger locally than elsewhere.

These opportunities for profit are, of course, the 'linkage' effects introduced in the discussion of regional policy.[1] How should they be handled in project appraisal? In benefit-cost

[1] They may also be described as an important class of 'pecuniary' external effects that one producer may have on the prices facing other producers. 'Pecuniary' external effects imply no direct technological relationship between one producer's action and the productivity of action by other producers—such external effect is often known as a 'technological' external effect. It is generally agreed that if a technological relationship exists between two projects, they should be planned and appraised as though they were a single project. There is more disagreement about the way in which 'pecuniary' effects should be treated.

analyses in advanced countries they are usually ignored for the good reason that full employment can be assumed, and seizing the profit opportunities means diverting resources from some other uses almost equally profitable. The gain to the economy from linkage effects is therefore negligible. But even in advanced countries the fact that different projects have different regional impacts may be a reason for selecting one rather than the other where an important objective is regional development. This was the motive behind the proposed use of secondary benefits by the US Bureau of Reclamation.

Where linkage effects concern regional income or employment objectives, project appraisal involves trying to measure what would or would not happen without the project. The regional employment and income generated in complementary activities will presumably be given a greater implicit weight than an equal amount of income and employment which might have been generated in other regions. This does not give rise to any special difficulties of valuation. Much more difficult to handle is the possibility that offering profitable opportunities will release untapped entrepreneurial talent and lead to a switch of resources from consumption to investment. In the case of the increase of savings, the difficulty arises from predicting what will happen. The question of the extent to which a greater valuation should be placed on savings than on consumption is a matter to be discussed shortly, since it forms an essential part of the choice of shadow prices.

Entrepreneurship is even more difficult to handle. A decade after Hirschman expressed very strongly the belief that a major task of government in developing countries was to find ways to utilize the potential stock of entrepreneurs, there is still very little empirical evidence to substantiate or to reject this view, and very little knowledge about what sort of projects do this best. In starting off a process of cumulative regional growth, obviously the initial steps are critical and encouraging local entrepreneurs is clearly desirable. How should one value entrepreneurship? Normal factors can be valued in terms of the stream of services offered, but with entrepreneurs it is not at all clear what their contribution has been. It is not at all clear to what extent and in what societies, within the limits of the supply of investable resources, the most profitable opportunities are seized. It is easy to observe that there are differences between societies and between social groups in the apparent search for profit-making activity and in the extent to which industrial rather than commercial activities are carried out. An obvious example is the difference in economic behaviour between immigrants and others both in the society from which they have come and in the society to which they have migrated. But how far opportunities have made the men, or men the opportunities could be endlessly debated, and how far the 'obviousness' of the opportunities affect this is also uncertain. Nevertheless it is clear that the more a regional development project can tap entrepreneurial talent from inside the region rather than divert it from elsewhere, the better it is.

A related issue concerns foreign investment. In most circumstances direct investment by foreign firms will be welcome, since it offers to the recipient country an increase in total investment, often backed by the provision of know-how and the training of the domestic labour force. Foreign investment may itself offer linkages which stimulate domestic activity. Where there is unemployment of labour, and where capital and trained management is imported, foreign investment need not imply much of a diversion of resources from other activities and so the whole output of the project may seem a net gain. Against this, however, have to be weighed possible political disadvantages—the fact that foreigners control significant amounts of the capital assets of the country is widely disliked by governments, perhaps because they feel some loss of political control is involved. Foreign investment also has effects on the balance of payments—providing foreign exchange while the initial investment is taking place, but setting up potential future liabilities in terms of the profits remitted. In many countries a shortage of foreign exchange appears to be the major bottleneck on the rate of growth—there appears to be domestic capacity underutilized for want of the needed foreign exchange to import intermediate goods and raw materials. The effect of this on the price of foreign exchange in terms of the domestic currency—which is an important element in any calculation of costs and benefits of a project—will be discussed shortly. In circumstances where balance of payments difficulties are expected to continue, the acceptability of foreign investment needs rather careful inspection—but an analysis of this is outside the scope of this present discussion.

In summary, the analysis of linkages must try to assess what would have happened in the absence of the project—not only in the region concerned but in the nation generally. The net contribution of the project to the various objectives can then be measured.

Prices

The prices for inputs and outputs to be used in calculating objective fulfillment will be discussed only rather briefly here—not because they are unimportant but because they are rather extensively discussed elsewhere.[1] The selection of prices to make decentralized decisions possible is bound to be approximate. We noted earlier that for various reasons (which we shall come to) the government may wish to depart from the use of market prices and calculate its own 'shadow' prices. The ideal set of prices would only emerge after all the alternative uses of resources had been compared in terms of their achievement of all social objectives and the best investment and production programme had been chosen. But if it were feasible and sensible to carry out such a thing there would be no need for decentralized decisions and hence for prices. The actual prices utilized, therefore, will be calculated on a much less ambitious basis and will usually try to represent the relative scarcities of products and factors in relation to one objective only—that of obtaining the best available temporal pattern of consumption.

One difficulty with the use of market prices is that the relative prices of goods may not reflect costs of production—because some are sold monopolistically, or because the impact of indirect taxes of all sorts is far from even. Where taxes (including import tariffs) are clearly imposed to discourage the use or production of a commodity, then these would be included in the prices of inputs

[1] A very clear introduction to this subject is I. M. D. Little and J. M. Mirrlees, *Manual of Cost Benefit Analysis* (Paris: OECD Development Centre, 1969). Seeing a preliminary draft of certain chapters of the *Manual* has greatly clarified the present section.

and outputs. But where the levels of these are very haphazard, resulting primarily from a series of historical accidents, the use of the set of prices that would prevail under free international trade with an exchange rate in equilibrium is theoretically very attractive.

The rationale for this use of prices is that in theory all tradable output is available to be exported or replaces a potential import and that the use of the price at which it would be exported or would replace an import is its value to the economy. It is not in practice easy to calculate what the appropriate exchange rate should be. If tariff levels are high, it is probable that the existing exchange rate is undervalued and is incorrect for the purpose of calculating shadow prices. One way to get round this problem is to work in dollar terms, using international prices. This is not to argue that the commercial policy of less developed countries ought necessarily to be a free trade one, but merely that the protection afforded to one industry ought to be considered in the light of that industry's needs and that the social profitability of other industries should not be affected by their having to purchase inputs at above world prices from a protected industry. A possible objection might arise here from the frequent argument that the growth of an economy is peculiarly constrained by a shortage of foreign exchange, while domestic resources are not fully utilized. How valid is this as an objection?

It is certainly possible to conceive of a situation in which the production possibilities within an economy and the pattern of demand for the economy's products is such that there are unemployed resources which cannot be employed without additional foreign exchange. The most probable reason for this is that investment requires imports which cannot be produced domestically, but it is also possible that a high marginal propensity to import consumer goods combined with a tax system unable to prevent personal incomes from rising, might have the same effect. Production and market possibilities might prevent the use of unemployed domestic resources to earn foreign exchange—perhaps because, on the supply side, needed complementary natural resources to expand primary product exports are not available, and the present level of quality of manufactured goods makes these unacceptable abroad, or because on the demand side the country is already maximizing foreign exchange earnings from other exports. It is at least theoretically possible that, no matter what the exchange rate or pattern of multiple exchange rates, a limited range of potential exports and an unfavourable pattern of demand, perhaps with foreign markets controlled by commodity agreements or import quotas, could combine to set an upper limit on potential foreign earnings. Dependence on a single exchange rate without export taxes may make this earning limit still lower, since the rate of exchange cannot then be adjusted for each export commodity separately to maximize foreign exchange earnings.

One may reasonably object here that this situation may be improbable except in the very long run. Altering exchange rates or adopting multiple rates is often politically very difficult. It may of course take a long time for domestic producers and foreign importers to respond to price changes, and there are all sorts of reasons why expansion of certain types of exports may be difficult. A switch in production from the home market to exports may be hard enough to obtain in developed countries where the changes in the structure of production and trade required are smaller, where factors of production are more mobile, and whose response to price incentives is likely to be faster. In short-run planning in less developed countries it may well make sense to distinguish between foreign resources and domestic resources, since the latter cannot be quickly substituted for the former. It is, however, much more dubious to do this when trying to determine long run development strategy and to assume *a priori* that specialization in goods in which a country has a comparative advantage will not provide sufficient earnings of foreign exchange. If foreign exchange availability were identified to be the single bottleneck on output, with surplus capacity elsewhere in the economy quite general, then project selection would be narrowed down to maximizing the attainment of objectives with the foreign exchange available. This would not, however, end the problem of choosing prices. It would still be necessary to select an interest rate for discounting purposes and to determine the correct wage rate, but this time only the intertemporal earning and allocation of foreign exchange would be considered instead of the more usual time pattern of aggregate investment and consumption. We shall discuss wage and interest rates shortly.

Using free trade prices might seem to be difficult in the case of certain goods, such as the output of social overhead capital projects which are not tradable internationally. But their production does use imports that are tradable or can be incorporated into tradable goods. By going back down the chain of production it is possible to reduce the cost of production of non-tradable goods into tradable goods and labour. There are some further problems in pricing the output of such projects, however. The use of actual prices charged (where these can be charged) may reflect deliberate elements of subsidy (common in irrigation projects for example). In addition projects are frequently economical only if undertaken on a large scale, which involves a change in the prices of outputs, and perhaps of inputs as well. This is a likely consequence of regional development projects—linkage effects, for example, are likely to manifest themselves as changes in prices which make other productive opportunities profitable.

Where an expansion of output leads to a fall in the prices that would prevail in a competitive market, multiplying the output by the price at which it can all be sold underestimates its social value since the benefit of the price reduction to former consumers is not measured. In these circumstances it is generally accepted that the best measure of the social value of providing a good or service is what the consumers of the good or service would be willing to pay for it. Where the amounts involved are large in relation to the total expenditure of consumers, and the good involved is a consumer good, it is difficult to estimate what consumers would be willing to pay since actually paying this amount would affect the income available for other commodities and lead to a reallocation of expenditure. A measure of willingness to pay cannot be obtained by looking at the demand for one commodity alone. There is no comparable effect where the good is bought as an input into production. The value then assigned to the provision of, for example, irrigation water is usually calculated on the assumption that after paying the market price for all other inputs the producer would, if necessary, be prepared to pay up to the whole of his profit for water, rather than go without it.[1] If we are considering the case for going or not going ahead with an investment project this is the measure to use, however incongruous the results may sometimes appear. If, without investment in water supplies costing less than one million dollars, the whole industrial development of a river basin yielding hundreds of millions of dollars above the alternative uses of the other resources involved cannot go ahead, then the benefits to a small expenditure can be very large indeed. If without the proverbial horse-shoe nail the kingdom will be lost then the return to providing such a nail is very high indeed. The fact that other inputs are equally indispensable and that the surplus over alternative uses could equally be assigned to them if their production was at issue does not alter the analysis.

The pricing of outputs and inputs, at least where traded internationally, is a theoretically much simpler affair than the pricing of unskilled labour and the determination of a satisfactory procedure for discounting future project benefits. In discussing briefly the questions at issue here we must warn the reader that we are skimming over the surface of very deep water indeed. It is not the purpose of this discussion to derive formulae to guide the making of actual decisions or to discuss the very complex differences in views about social welfare that is implied in the choice of one investment criterion rather than another.[2] Society saves and invests because by postponing consumption, more consumption can be obtained in later years, as long as the return on investment is positive. The more saving takes place, the lower the marginal return on it becomes. Society—or at least the government's interpretation of social wants—will not normally wish to see income saved until the point at which the marginal return on it becomes zero. This is partly because as more consumption becomes available the marginal valuation of a unit of it will probably become smaller—nobody would argue that the average

---

[1] This is well explained in Stephen A. Marglin, *Public Investment Criteria* (London: George Allen and Unwin, 1967), pp. 41–4.

[2] For further discussion see Little and Mirrlees, *Manual of Cost Benefit Analysis;* Marglin, *Public Investment Criteria*, pp. 47–71 and Stephen A. Marglin, 'The Rate of Interest and the Value of Capital with Unlimited Supplies of Labor', in Karl Shell (ed.) *Essays on the Theory of Optimal Growth* (Cambridge, Mass.: M.I.T. Press, 1967), pp. 141–63.

Indian alive today should forego 10 rupees of consumption in order that his descendants a century later (living perhaps at current European levels) could enjoy 11 rupees of consumption—partly also because the present generation is mortal and it is the present generation that elects the government, and the willingness of the present generation to forego consumption so that its children can consume more is probably limited.

Nevertheless the government may well feel that the proportion of income currently saved is inadequate in view of the high return in terms of future consumption that can be earned on investment, but be unable in view of its limited ability to tax, to raise the rate of investment to the level it regards as adequate. There are two important consequences of this, one concerning the choice of the shadow wage of labour, and the other, the choice of the rates at which future benefits are discounted. In the first place, a pattern of investment that leads to a lower level of current consumption and higher savings would be preferable, other things being equal, to one with higher current consumption and lower savings. This will affect the choice of investment projects and the techniques associated with them, since the shadow wage to be employed in appraising projects and selecting techniques must reflect not only the opportunity cost of labour in alternative uses, but the effect that the current consumption of that labour will have on the future stream of consumption available to the economy.

The opportunity cost of labour in most developing countries is likely to depend directly or indirectly on the marginal productivity of labour in agriculture and this is usually estimated to be very low—much lower than the wage that the labourer is likely to receive working in industry or on the public investment project. But more employment will usually involve more total consumption and therefore less saving. The increase in consumption associated with the employment of a worker on some project results both from additional consumption from those in agriculture now enjoying a higher income after the worker has left, and from the worker's own added consumption, and is likely to be considerable. This additional consumption is not entirely a cost to the economy, of course, but it will be regarded by the government as of less social value than if the entire additional income had been saved. The 'shadow wage' will then be between the marginal productivity of labour and the actual wage rate paid—and Little and Mirrlees show that with plausible assumptions about the magnitudes involved the shadow wage is likely to be much nearer to a worker's consumption out of wages (likely to be a very high proportion) than to zero, however low the marginal productivity of labour in agriculture may be. The results will be reinforced if there is any tendency for an increase in the employment of labour to bid up the wages of all employed labour—which may seem improbable in labour surplus economies but can happen with regional development projects in sparsely populated areas, and indeed occurred in the Mexican case.

The choice and use of a discount rate involves equally difficult issues. In the circumstances described above, the rate of return on the marginal project will be higher than the rate at which the government believes that future consumption should be discounted. Now it is desirable that, other things being equal, investment should receive as high a return as possible and if we are choosing between projects of equal life, with the same proportion of outputs being reinvested, making equal contributions to regional development and other development, we should not want to see investment taking place in a project which yielded 3 per cent if there was another yielding 15 per cent. If the government could control all investment and reinvestment and was able to predict accurately what return would be obtained for several decades as a consequence of any particular investment made now, irrespective of the length of life of the particular investment project concerned, it would then choose a discount rate which, when used to discount returns from all projects and selecting all those whose present value were greater than zero, made the total investments carried out just equal to the supply of investible resources. It would do this even if this interest rate were substantially in excess of what is regarded as the social discount rate. In these circumstances, it is assumed that the total amount of investment is unaltered by the allocation between public and private sectors. The marginal rate of return in both sectors ought therefore to be equal.

In practice, all the assumptions here are unrealistic. Public investment may be financed out of taxation and only partially displace private investment. There may be political reasons why the money thus raised could not be available to the private sector and this could be one justification for the government's investing in projects with a lower rate of return than is obtainable in the private sector. The economic life of all projects may not be the same and reinvestment out of revenue may differ. The government may then prefer a long-lived project with a comparatively low rate of return (though equal or in excess of the social discount rate) to a higher yielding project with a shorter life and for which the revenue is likely to be largely consumed or invested at a very low return. One way to deal with this is for the government to use the social discount rate in discounting projects, making an estimate of expected reinvestment and then (assuming the degree of fulfillment of other objectives is equal) choosing those that have the highest ratio of benefits to costs. Marglin has derived formulae for calculating the minimum benefit-cost ratio that a project need satisfy, taking into account the extent to which private investment is displaced by the project, the rate of return in the private sector and the proportion of revenue reinvested.[1]

We have used the expression 'marginal rate of return' rather loosely. For a project this may be associated with the 'internal rate of return' on the marginal investment project—that rate of interest which will make the present value of the benefits minus costs from the project equal to zero. Unfortunately this measure can sometimes be ambiguous—there may be several internal rates of return so defined. And for the reasons just explained a project with a higher internal rate of return may not always be preferred by investment to one with a lower internal rate of return. Nevertheless, the internal rate of return carefully calculated may be useful to the analyst in certain circumstances. In Chapter 7 we calculate such rates for a Mexican project under a variety of assumptions. We are not then trying to rank projects and have no information on what the social discount rate in Mexico should be. In these circumstances, the use of an internal rate of return

---

[1] The details are not important to this book. See Marglin, *Public Investment Criteria*, pp. 53–71 and Marglin, 'The Opportunity Costs of Public Investment', *Quarterly Journal of Economics*, LXXVII (May 1963), pp. 274–89.

means that there is no need to select a social discount rate. This procedure provides an easily understandable basis for comparing the rate of return with the profitability of private projects.

In practice, we can at present calculate the rate of return only with respect to the objectives that are easily expressed in income terms. This is no reason for ignoring other objectives. Indeed, as we shall see in the last chapters of this book, the project selected for close examination would fail to meet our test of profitability unless some of the objectives which cannot be measured in monetary terms are included in the calculations. Before proceeding to this evaluation, however, we shall discuss the way in which the considerations discussed in both parts of this chapter can be brought to bear on the history of regional development efforts in Mexico.

REGIONAL DEVELOPMENT IN MEXICO

In a country as large and as geographically varied as Mexico, uneven levels of regional economic development and rates of progress are almost inevitable. Mexico is very mountainous—only about one-third of its area could be described as level and more than half of the country is over 3,000 feet. The bulk of the population has always lived in upland areas and especially on the Mesa Central, the middle portion of a belt of mountains and high plateau that forms the backbone of the country. Separated from the coastal strips to east and west by steep escarpments, with deep valleys and wild mountains lying to the south and desert areas to the north, it has not historically been easy for the inhabitants of the Mesa Central to move away from it and there has usually been little temptation to do so. Even these inhabitants have never shared one culture, while elsewhere the population has been scattered in small groups in the relatively few areas where the soil has been rich enough, the water supply adequate, and the slope sufficiently level to support the growing of maize. In other parts of the country, internal mobility has also been restricted by geographical features. Only within the last twenty years have the limestone plains of Yucatán in the south-east been connected to the rest of the country by railway and only within the last ten, by road. Before that the difficulties of traversing the flood plains of the southern Gulf coast or the mountains lying behind them prevented land communication. The cultural, linguistic and economic isolation of different peoples has consequently been very considerable. Within the present boundaries of Mexico there are some fifty distinct Indian language groups.[1]

To describe in detail the variety of geographical features and local economies dominated by different products and their

[1] Leslie Byrd Simpson, *Many Mexicos* (Berkeley and Los Angeles: University of California Press, 1960), p. 10.

historical development would be an immense task. The following paragraphs merely attempt to sketch the main features of the pattern of regional development.

The dominant features of the Mesa Central resulted from volcanic activity that has taken place across a broad seam, some 100 miles wide and 800 miles long, stretching from the Pacific Coast almost all the way to the Gulf of Mexico. An older pattern of rounded hills, gentle slopes, and wide valleys was made more mountainous by the advent of the volcanoes, and the rivers draining the valleys were blocked by volcanic material, forming closed basins. Later, streams were able to cut deep, narrow valleys through the hills, and all the basins except the Valley of Mexico are now drained by rivers that reach the sea. The height of the floors of these basins varies between 5,000 feet above sea level in the Jalisco Basin and 8,000 feet in the Toluca Basin. The thousands of volcanic cones are of greatly varying heights; Orizaba, the highest, is over 18,000 feet.

Since pre-conquest times, the Mesa Central has been the most important region of Mexico from every standpoint: political, economic, and cultural. North of the volcanic seam, with its general level of between 5,000 and 8,000 feet, the plateau slopes gently downwards until at the Mexico–United States border the level is between 3,000 and 4,000 feet. The surface of the plateau is nowhere flat; its northern part resembles much of the country in the south-west of the United States, with gently sloping bolsons separated by ranges of block mountains that rise some 3,000 feet above them. This northern part is extremely dry, with some areas having less than 10 inches of rain a year and the remainder less than 20 inches. Further south, annual rainfall increases, and in part of the volcanic seam it exceeds 40 inches. It therefore became possible for Indian tribes migrating from the more arid north to settle and to become agricultural peoples, reaching much higher levels of culture than were ever obtained in the north where a settled agriculture was not possible.

On the Mesa Central the tribes found a temperate, thickly forested area, with many lakes and streams fed by the permanent snowcaps of the higher volcanoes. Generally, the floors of the seven basins (the three we have mentioned, and the basins of

Guanajuato and of Puebla, and the valleys of Aguascalientes and of Morelos) were swampy, and the borders of the basins and the lower slopes of the hills were settled earlier and more thickly than the lower areas. The Aztecs were the last of the Nahua tribes to settle in the Valley of Mexico and were forced to establish their capital city of Tenochtitlán on an island in the middle of a lake because it was the only place still open to settlement. A nation of warriors, they had achieved domination over much of the land to the south and levied tribute there by the time the Spaniard Cortés entered Tenochtitlán on 8 November 1519. In those two centuries, Tenochtitlán had grown until at the time of the conquest the Spaniards estimated its population at over 300,000 and marvelled at its beauty. Later one of them wrote:

When we saw so many cities and villages built in the water and other great towns on dry land and that straight and level causeway going towards Mexico, we were amazed and said it was like the enchantments they tell of in the legend of Amadis, on account of the great towers and cues (temples) and buildings rising from the water, and all built of masonry. And some of our soldiers even asked whether the things that we saw were not a dream. It is not to be wondered at that I here write it down in this manner, for there is so much to think over that I do not know how to describe it, seeing things as we did that had never been heard of or seen before, not even dreamed about.[1]

Following the siege and the destruction of Tenochtitlán in 1521, Cortés founded the City of Mexico on the same site and took over the Aztec empire in the name of the Crown of Spain. As a site for a capital city, it then left much, and now leaves more, to be desired. In the summer months, the rainy season in most of Mexico, the lakes on which the city was built often rose and flooded it. After several centuries of trying, the successful draining of the lake was achieved at the beginning of this century, and since then the problems of the city have changed but have not disappeared. Now the city is confronted with a serious shortage of water rather than a superfluity, and it is sinking into the spongy lake bed. We shall have more to say about these troubles when we consider current problems of regional development.

[1] Bernal Díaz del Castillo, *The Discovery and Conquest of Mexico*, trans. with an Introduction and Notes by A. P. Maudslay (New York: Grove Press, 1958), pp. 190–91.

43

The chief economic concern of the Spaniard was minerals and particularly silver and gold. Since most of the sources of these were found on the Mesa Central or elsewhere on the plateau to the north, there was no reason for any marked change in the distribution of population during the colonial period. At the time of independence, the haciendas (large estates) were mostly concentrated in this region, though there were also some in Yucatán.

There is no generally accepted figure for the total population of Mexico at the time of the conquest. A common estimate is 9 million, although it has sometimes been put as high as 25 million. Most lived on the Mesa Central; when the Spaniards arrived it was already quite densely populated. But once it became subject to the various epidemics that followed their arrival, the population fell rapidly and had not fully recovered by the time independence was achieved in 1821. The basis for existence of the Indian population was, and still is, maize, although beans, chile, squashes, sweet potatoes, maguey, and other crops were also grown. In the wooded mountain areas methods of cultivation were of the slash-and-burn variety, and this has contributed to the present acute problems of erosion. In the lake areas they required the frequent abandonment of land to recover its fertility, necessitating repeated migration of tribes within the area. Techniques were most primitive; ploughs were first introduced by the Spaniards. Often called 'the basic cereal zone', the Mesa Central was for centuries the chief agricultural region. But with the coming of the railways and large-scale irrigation, areas away from the cereal zone began to develop much more rapidly. The area retains its prominence in maize production, but this is because it is less suited to produce other cash crops, such as cotton, coffee, sugar, wheat and winter vegetables, which are commercially far more important than maize production in other areas, and whose growth, over the past half-century, has been the most important feature of Mexican agriculture. The total value of agricultural output on the Mesa Central has now been surpassed by the value of output of the irrigated agricultural region of the north-west. The Mesa Central still predominates in animal products because the most important market is located there.

44

North of the Mesa Central lies a sparsely populated area, often called the Mesa del Norte. The region's mining industry has stagnated for years, but important areas have thrived through the development of irrigation (although in some recent years, drought has taken a heavy toll). Irrigation has, however, been less important on this northern plateau than in the coastal areas to the west and to the east of it. Separating the plateau from the coasts are the rugged escarpments known as the Sierra Madre Occidental to the west and the Sierra Madre Oriental to the east. Both form major barriers to movement from the coasts up on to the plateau. One hundred miles wide in places, the Sierra Madre Occidental, in particular, has been hard to penetrate, although in recent years it has been crossed by two paved roads and by a railway. Its peaks rise up to more than 10,000 feet, while mountain streams, running southwards, have cut deep, steep-sided valleys in the escarpment and gorges through the narrow ridges separating them.

The northern coastal areas are very important agriculturally. The north-west coast is now the chief agricultural region of Mexico. The Fuerte River Basin Commission, whose work will be described in Chapter 4, is situated here, but its irrigation works are only a small part of the total irrigation of this region. Irrigation is essential for agriculture here—what is not irrigated is normally desert—and it has a long tradition. In what are now the states of Nayarit and Sinaloa, the first Spanish explorers found Indian tribes irrigating their agriculture along river flood plains. The area was never densely populated and within a few decades most of these people were wiped out by disease or carried off into slavery. It has been estimated that it took until 1920 for the population of Sonora, Sinaloa, and Nayarit to reach the population of 540,000 that had existed when the Spaniards first arrived.[1] In a few remote valleys, of which the most important is the Yaqui Valley, Indian communities still exist, but the bulk of the valley bottoms became the property of haciendas. In the 1930s these were replaced by *ejidos* (the farming communities established under the agrarian reform) or smaller private holdings.

The area combines hot, wet summers with mild, dry winters and is proving itself a formidable competitor of California in

[1] Preston E. James, *Latin America* (3rd ed. New York; Odyssey Press, 1959), p. 606,

certain United States and international markets. Included in the region are two agricultural zones, separated by a large stretch of desert. The more southerly zone, in the states of Sonora, Sinaloa, and Nayarit, has a fairly diversified agriculture, with cotton usually the chief crop. (The section of Chapter 4 that deals with the Fuerte River Basin Commission contains more information on the agriculture of the area.) The Río Colorado area of Baja California, the Mexican section of the Imperial Valley, usually produces almost entirely cotton and is the most important cotton area of Mexico.

Cotton is also the chief crop of the north-eastern coastal area. Of particular importance are the irrigated areas along the Rio Grande (the Río Bravo del Norte) which forms the border with the United States. The border has affected the economy of the north throughout its length. There is considerable opportunity to move across it, and this attracts a great number of people seeking this opportunity. For this reason, the border towns are, paradoxically, areas of relatively high *per capita* incomes and high unemployment. As we shall describe, these towns are now the object of a programme to absorb this unemployed labour into industrial employment. The most striking effect of the proximity to the United States has been in the west. Tijuana is in practice an appendage to the economy of southern California, and Baja California, the state in which Tijuana is located, has the highest *per capita* income of any state in Mexico.

The most important urban centre of the north, however, lies not on the border but about eighty miles from it, at the lower end of a pass leading from the north-eastern coastal strip on to the plateau. This is Monterrey, now the second most important industrial city in Mexico. It has grown from a population of 30,000 in 1880 to more than twenty times that size today, as the result of an industrial boom spurred by the growth of its steel industry. Although Monterrey is not the site of either iron ore or coal, it lies on the railway linking the capital to the United States, and in the early years of the century appears to have possessed a political climate favourable to the establishment of industry, and these seem to have been the major reasons why, in 1903, the Mexican steel industry had its beginnings here.

All along the eastern coastline of Mexico from just south of Monterrey, is the petroleum producing area which is productive enough to have made Mexico the second largest producer in the world for a short time after the First World War. The traditional centre of the petroleum industry has been in the north around Tampico although this focus has now shifted to the Poza Rica fields near Tuxpan. Production of petroleum in the south of the region, on the Isthmus of Tehuantepec and in the state of Tabasco, has been growing in importance.

This southern zone, beginning on the River Tamesi which forms the boundary between the states of Tamaulipas and Veracruz on the Gulf Coast, is also important because of the tropical agricultural products cultivated there. These coastal plains are hot and humid. Rainfall is abundant, increasing from between 40 and 50 inches a year in the north near Tampico, to between 80 and 100 inches along the southern part of the Gulf Coast. In part of the Oaxacan and Chiapas mountains which back this latter area and catch the saturated air masses moving in from the Caribbean, the rainfall is even higher. The rivers of this coast carry about half the total run-off of all the rivers of Mexico. The work of the Papaloapan and Grijalva Commissions in this area will be described in Chapter 4. Much of the land along this coast is flooded annually, but is considered to have high agricultural potential; there is extensive scope for expanding the cultivated area; the rivers here offer excellent opportunities for the production of hydroelectricity; from this we can see how river basin development is, in a sense, a natural strategy for the development of the region. The swampy forests and grasslands of southern Veracruz and the state of Tabasco have been little inhabited. There have been a few plantations that produce rubber, bananas, cocoa, chicle, and so on. The chief crop is coffee and this is grown not in the tropical Tierra Caliente (hot country) but in the Tierra Templada, the cooler zone between 3,000 and 5,000 feet. Apart from the port cities, the main towns of the region are situated in the Tierra Templada. Jalapa, Cordoba and Orizaba, on the road between Mexico City and Veracruz, are manufacturing centres.

It is only in the last ten years that it has been possible to cross the southern part of the Gulf region by road in summer to reach the Yucatán Peninsula, and the railway is not much older. The result has been the isolation of the flat, limestone peninsula. This does not mean that Yucatán has been economically unimportant. After 1880, the area around Mérida became the world's source of henequen fibre. Yucatán remains very largely a one-crop economy, and this has occasioned economic difficulties in the past and offers a gloomy outlook for the future. After agrarian reform in the 1930s and the expropriation of the plantations, the ejidos did not function efficiently to keep costs down and new planting was neglected, which meant that production fell rapidly in the early 1950s. But getting production up to its normal level (though only to about half the peak year of 1916) does not ensure prosperity in the fiercely competitive world fibre market.

The other regions of Mexico can be quickly described. To the south of the western half of the volcanic seam, the land drops into the valley of the Río Balsas, bounded on the other side by the forbidding mountains of the Sierra Madre del Sur, which in turn are separated from the Pacific Ocean by a narrow, inaccessible, and, except for Acapulco, underdeveloped coastal strip. The Balsas basin itself is the home of the most recent River Basin Commission which has absorbed the older Tepalcatepec Commission that had been developing the basin of one of its tributaries since 1947. It is this Tepalcatepec project that will provide us with our case study, so we shall have occasion to study this area further. The Balsas drains a highland region to the east that connects the central part of the state of Oaxaca with the Mesa Central. The Sierra Madre del Sur in Oaxaca and Guerrero is itself a dissected plateau, but streamcutting has produced a pattern of deep valleys and left very little flat land. There are a few isolated basins, such as that in which the city of Oaxaca lies.

The Sierra Madre del Sur drops steeply to the Isthmus of Tehuantepec. On the other side is another block of mountains, the Sierra Madre de Chiapas, running parallel to the coast. To the north-east of these mountains lies the Valley of Chiapas drained by the Río Grijalva in which the bulk of the population of this area is concentrated. On the other side of the Valley, mountains rise again to over 12,000 feet before dropping again to the plains of Yucatán. The main crops of the Valley are maize and coffee, and livestock production is also important.

In the mountains all over Mexico, but particularly in the mountains of Oaxaca and Chiapas, there are still many Indian villages scarcely touched by European influences. Official Mexico, mestizo (i.e. of mixed European and Indian blood) and proud of its Indian heritage, is very conscious of the problem they pose. Robert Scott characterizes the integration of the Indian and the village-dwelling peasant into the broader Mexican nation and its political life as one of the strongest goals and major achievements of the Mexican Revolution.[1] He argues that by comparison with the situation before 1910 this process has been very nearly completed. If awareness of the Mexican nation be taken as the critical element, then this may be true. There remain, however, isolated pockets lacking even this national awareness, and for mountain Indians generally, political integration has not necessarily implied economic advance. Although such advance is an important objective of the regional development policies of the Mexican government, it is uncertain how these Indians can be helped. They do not live for the most part in areas that are amenable to the adoption of modern agricultural techniques. Their handicrafts, though often remarkable, are not a sufficient basis for twentieth-century prosperity. But the government is obviously reluctant to leave them in abysmal poverty until they find their own way into the slums of the cities, there to make an extremely painful, if relatively rapid transition to modern life. Part of the work of the River Basin Commissions has been concerned with the existence of such people, and we shall have more to say on the matter later on.

REGIONAL DEVELOPMENT PROBLEMS
AND POLICY FROM 1821 TO 1947

At various times since independence, regional problems have played an important part in the thoughts and actions of the makers of economic policy and their advisers. Discussion of regional

[1] Robert E. Scott, *Mexican Government in Transition* (Urbana: University of Illinois Press, 1959), p. 12.

development has generally emphasized the settlement of the sparsely populated areas away from the Mesa Central. This section describes the different approaches taken by successive Governments, up to the start of the River Basin Commission programme in 1947. We shall not dwell on the economic and political rationale for the various policies—we shall discuss recent policies in the next chapter. But this short historical survey is intended to provide a background for our description of the contemporary state of regional development in the last section of this chapter and to the policies adopted to tackle regional problems that will be discussed in the following two chapters.

In the first two decades after independence, the dominant figure both in economic policies themselves and in writing about such policies was Lucas Alamán, who was a principal Minister in most of the governments of the period. Educated in Europe, and deeply impressed by what he had seen of the English Industrial Revolution and its effects on national power and political order, Alamán thought that Mexico, too, should industrialize. He thought that the smallness of population (about 6 million) was a barrier to this through a shortage of manpower for industry and his later writings also argued that population increases were necessary to provide a market for industrial production. The 6 million inhabitants nominally occupied over $1\frac{1}{2}$ million square miles. Alamán saw the danger inherent in the combination of empty Mexican lands and a growing United States. The Isthmus of Tehuantepec was almost uninhabited and a potential temptation to a United States seeking a route to the Pacific. To forestall this threat, Alamán attempted to colonize the Isthmus by creating a new province with its capital at Tehuantepec. European immigrants were avidly sought, with offers of passages and loans to get them established, and other inducements were also provided.

The only successful colonization, however, was that of Texas; initially encouraged in 1823, by 1826 the probable result was foreseen by the Mexican government which tried in vain to stop the colonizing. In 1830, Alamán imposed various restrictions such as forbidding colonists to bring in slaves. But these measures failed, and Mexican rejections of the Texans' demand for statehood merely irritated the settlers. In the ensuing war, the Mexican army was defeated in 1836 and the admission of Republic of Texas into the United States in 1845 led to further wars, this time with the United States. Again beaten, Mexico was forced to cede half her territory in 1848.

These wars were only part of a series of civil and foreign wars that kept Mexico in political chaos from 1830 to the later 1860s. In consequence, the economy stagnated and possibly income dropped. Government attempts to stimulate industrialization in the early 1820s by supplying finance to highly protected industries fizzled out in the early 1830s. The first railway, aiming to connect Mexico City and Veracruz, begun under Alamán in 1837, was still unfinished thirty years later. The only event to have a significant effect on the pattern of regional development was a law (the 'Ley Lerdo', embodied into the 1857 Constitution) which forbade corporations (i.e. religious foundations and civic communities) to hold real property. Passed by the Liberal political faction, it was aimed primarily at the economic power of the Church, but it was also hoped that the break-up of the communal Indian lands would create a new class of small proprietors, in accord with the Jeffersonian principles of the government. In the following years, the need of the Liberal governments for funds to finance civil war with the Conservatives and to defeat French intervention led to a number of colonization contracts.

Church property was to some extent reduced by the new laws, but nevertheless, it managed to retain a great deal of property and, under Porfirio Díaz, who seized power in 1876, this part of the reform became a dead letter. The institution that was most affected was the landholding village. Díaz and his *científicos* (the group of lawyers and economists who surrounded him) took the view that immigration could not play the same part in Mexico's development that it had played in Argentina and in the United States because the only healthy, fertile, and well-watered area, the Mesa Central, was already densely populated. To settle the other areas, large quantities of capital were needed, and this prompted generous concessions to foreigners. An 1883 law permitted land companies that surveyed public lands to claim one-third as payment and to buy the other two-thirds at reduced rates. This law specified that resale must be made to colonists in tracts of not more than 2,500 hectares.[1] In addition, the Díaz government set up some model colonies on the plateau, which were presented, together with working capital, to some Italian immigrants. Very few colonies were established, and by 1894, when the 1883 law was liberalized, the idea of colonization had been virtually discarded as a deliberate policy of regional development. Land concessions, however, continued as a way of rewarding political favourites and of strengthening the hold of the dictatorship throughout the country. The effect of land policy was less to settle the outlying areas than to change the pattern of land ownership which became increasingly concentrated. Whereas the hacienda system at the end of the colonial period had been concentrated mostly on the Mesa Central, by 1910 it was general throughout the country.

Indian villages lost communal lands, since they were unable to prove legal possession or registered title when confronted by the land companies, or had to abandon them after losing their water rights. Occasionally, there would be a rebellion; after it was crushed, the land of the villages involved would be confiscated, and those who took part would lose what little they possessed. Dispossessed Indians would find themselves living on haciendas and, before long, tied there in debt peonage. In 1910 about 800 haciendas contained 90 per cent of the land.[2] Over 80 per cent of rural families were landless.

These unhappy social consequences were not mitigated by favourable economic results. With the exception of certain commercial plantations producing for export, the hacienda was not a productive form of agricultural enterprise. It seems likely that the production of basic food crops—maize, wheat and beans—actually fell between 1880 and 1890, and after that date, the increase in these crops barely exceeded the rise in population.[3] In a poor year, maize would have to be imported, and wheat, flour, sugar, and salted meat were imported every year. Although by other indicators—miles of railway, growth of mineral production,

[1] A hectare is 2.47 acres.
[2] Daniel James, *Mexico and the Americans* (New York: Frederick A. Praeger, 1963), p. 79.
[3] Raymond Vernon, *The Dilemma of Mexico's Development: The Roles of the Private and Public Sectors* (Cambridge, Mass.: Harvard University Press, 1963), p. 53.

export performance, the beginnings of modern industry—the performance of the economy under Díaz was very successful, the social and economic costs of the land policy were high.

In 1910 came Revolution. Beginning as a middle-class political call for 'free suffrage and no re-election', it acquired momentum as a popular social movement, though its objectives were not always clear to those taking part, let alone generally agreed upon. The effect of the events in prerevolutionary Mexico on land ownership and agricultural output gave rise to extensive rural discontent and among the major revolutionary forces were a cry for land and an attack on large estates. The first product of the Revolution in the direction of social reform was a 1915 land reform law, which was later incorporated into the land reform provisions of the 1917 Constitution. This Constitution declared land and its subsoil to be the property of the Mexican nation and the right to exploit them to be revocable. Nationalism was another driving force behind the Revolution, although the early revolutionary governments did not feel secure enough to expropriate foreign property or to restrict the activities of the foreign investor on any large scale. The land reform laws, however, do limit the ability of a foreigner to own land.

Agrarian reform created the *ejido*, the land-holding village that is sometimes farmed collectively but more usually, and increasingly, farmed individually by *ejidatarios* who may farm land and pass it to their heirs, but who do not own it. Ejidos have usually been formed from land expropriated (almost always without compensation) from the haciendas. The redistribution aspects of land reform have been emphasized much more than colonization. Nevertheless the aim of settling lands away from the Mesa Central re-asserted itself as a policy after the Revolution. The remote regions offered the promise of providing land for those who could not be given it on the central plateau. In 1926, a colonization law was promulgated, laying down the conditions under which Mexicans, and those under which foreigners, might settle public lands. These were amended several times and eventually were superseded by a 1946 law which created a National Colonization Commission to promote, administer, and supervise settlement, with powers to make the necessary studies, to determine the necessary investments, and to select the colonists and the most appropriate crops. Somewhat incomplete figures suggest that about $1\frac{1}{4}$ million hectares, divided into nearly 14,000 lots, were colonized between 1919 and 1944.[1] In the early years of the Presidency of Miguel Alemán (1946–52), the rate of colonization was speeded up. It was under Alemán that the integrated river basin programme, linked in part to this colonization programme, was started.

All the way through the period since the Revolution, in legislative amendments to colonization laws, in the various Party programmes, in presidential speeches and elsewhere, the idea that the agricultural regions away from the Mesa Central must be settled and developed has received continual reiteration. One of the most famous pronouncements of this nature is the speech made by the President Avila Camacho in 1941:

The future of agriculture lies in the fertile lands of the coast. A march to the sea will relieve congestion in our central plateau, where worn-out lands must be devoted to crops which colonial policy denied them with the result that the traditional maize culture of the indigenous population has continued to be dominant. The fertility of the coastal plains will make it uneconomical to raise many products in the central plateau. But the march to the sea requires, as prerequisites, sanitary and health measures, the opening of communications, the reclamation and drainage of swamps, and, to make such projects possible, the expenditure of large sums of money. It will be necessary to organize a new kind of tropical agriculture, which, because of the very nature of its production, cannot be the small-scale type.[2]

This provides a clear statement of some of the important objectives of the schemes that we shall describe, and whose effects we shall analyse. It was not, however, Avila Camacho but his successor Alemán who took the most important steps to implement the policy.

THE PATTERN OF RECENT REGIONAL DEVELOPMENT

Since 1940 the growth of the Mexican economy has been extremely impressive. Tables 1 and 2 give the growth of domestic

[1] Moisés T. de la Peña, 'Problemas Demograficos y Agrarios', *Problemas Agrícolas e Industriales de México*, II, Nos. 3–4 (México, 1950), p. 10.

[2] Quoted by Sanford Mosk, *Industrial Revolution in Mexico* (Berkeley and Los Angeles: University of California Press, 1954), p. 220.

Table 1. *Gross domestic product, 1960 prices, selected years 1940–1964*

	('000 million pesos)					
	1940	1945	1950	1955	1960	1964
Agriculture, livestock, forestry, fishing	10·2	11·4	17·1	22·3	25·9	30·4
Manufacturing	7·6	12·3	16·4	22·6	33·3	45·7
Mining	2·0	2·1	2·0	2·3	2·7	2·7
Petroleum	1·1	1·3	1·9	2·6	3·9	5·2
Electricity	0·3	0·4	0·5	0·9	1·3	1·9
Construction	2·3	4·3	3·8	5·2	7·7	10·6
Transport	1·7	2·4	3·4	4·9	6·2	6·9
Commerce	10·0	15·2	20·7	27·4	36·9	47·2
Government	2·1	3·1	4·0	5·0	6·2	8·1
Other	8·2	12·1	15·5	21·7	31·7	40·0
Total	45·4	64·5	85·4	114·9	155·9	198·8

Source: Manual de Estadísticas Básicas, Banco de México.

Table 2. *Average annual rates of growth of gross domestic product, by sectors*

	1940/5	1945/50	1950/5	1955/60	1960/4	1940/64
Agriculture, livestock, forestry, fishing	2·2	8·6	5·5	3·0	4·1	4·6
Manufacturing	10·2	5·9	6·6	8·1	8·3	7·8
Mining	1·1	—0·6	2·9	2·8	0·3	1·4
Petroleum	3·3	8·6	6·4	8·7	7·0	6·8
Electricity	3·9	7·6	9·6	8·9	10·1	7·9
Construction	12·9	—2·2	6·4	8·1	8·3	6·5
Transport	7·4	7·4	7·5	5·0	2·8	6·1
Commerce	8·7	6·4	5·8	6·1	6·3	6·7
Government	8·3	5·2	4·3	4·4	7·2	5·9
Other	8·1	5·0	7·1	7·8	6·0	6·8
Total	7·3	5·8	6·1	6·3	6·3	6·3

Source: Table 1.

product by sectors and the growth rates of the principal sectors. The growth of output has averaged over 6 per cent per year in real terms, so that in spite of extremely rapid population growth, which has been rising throughout the period and has now reached a rate of about 3.5 per cent per year, average *per capita* income has risen substantially. The present population (1968) is about 47 million. Gross national product per head was an estimated $530 (US) in 1968.

The fastest-growing sectors were electric power, manufacturing industry, and petroleum, with manufacturing making by far the largest absolute contribution to the increase in output. The pattern of development of this sector has been one of import substitution under a system of protection which relies primarily on quantitative controls over imports, and only secondarily on import duties. Import substitution on a significant scale was first spurred by the shortages of the Second World War and, after a rapid rise in imports in the initial post-war period, by balance of payments difficulties. Government concern about unemployment in the face of such a rapid rate of growth of population also prompted industrial protection and promotion. Import substitution in non-durable consumer goods has never been important since the war, if measured in terms of the proportion of final demand supplied by imports, as is usually done.[1] Particularly since 1950, import substitution has been primarily in intermediate and investment goods. It has not been confined to manufacturing industry; it has also been important in basic food crops, most dramatically in wheat in the 1950s. The long-sought goal of self-sufficiency in foodstuffs has now been virtually achieved. Agriculture has grown fast by international standards and has also contributed substantially to the increase in export earnings that have made possible Mexico's growth. Agricultural products are by far the largest group of Mexican commodity exports. Resources for Mexico's development have come, of course, primarily from domestic sources, although nearly 10 per cent of gross fixed domestic

[1] This is not a very satisfactory measure since one effect of rising income will be to increase demand more than proportionately for complex and higher quality consumer goods, i. e., for those normally imported. So import substitution could be going on while the proportion of demand supplied by imports was unchanged.

capital formation between 1950 and 1965 was financed by foreign loans and direct investments.[1]

The regional impact of economic growth and industrialization has been, as would be expected, uneven, and the unevenness of existing levels of regional development is a principal cause for contemporary concern—a concern expressed in several books, as well as in political speeches, newspaper articles, conferences and other places.[2]

To describe the present pattern of regional development it is convenient to group state data into regions. Inevitably state boundaries do not follow physical divisions very closely, but the following breakdown will serve our need in describing regional variaitons[3]:

North Pacific

Baja California Norte, Baja California Sur, Sonora, Sinaloa, and Nayarit

North

Coahuila and Chihuahua

North Gulf

Nuevo León and Tamaulipas

[1] The Mexican investment statistics are undergoing a series of very substantial revisions and it is impossible therefore to make any precise statement about the magnitudes involved at present.

[2] See especially Ernesto López Malo, *Ensayo sobre Localización de la Industria en México* (México D.F.: UNAM, 1960); P. Lamartine Yates, *El Desarrollo Regional de México* (México D.F.: Banco de México, 1961); México, Sec. de Economía e Instituto Mexicano de Investigaciones Económicas, *Diagnóstico Económico Regional, 1958.* Under the direction of Fernando Zamora (México D.F., 1959).

[3] Regional scientists have spent a good deal of the time discussing problems of selecting regional boundaries for analytical and planning purposes. There has even been some debate as to whether such a thing as a 'true' region exists. See Walter Isard, 'Regional Science, The Concept of Region, and Regional Structure', *Papers and Proceedings of the Regional Science Association*, II (1956), pp. 13–26, and Morris E. Garnsey, 'The Dimensions of Regional Science', *ibid.* pp. 27–39. The concept certainly seems implausible. Natural geographic barriers might normally seem to be better boundaries for economic purposes than administrative divisions, although even if the country were a homogenous plain, we might still wish to talk about regions. In Mexico, officials of the Secretaría de la Presidencia have recently been working on a regional breakdown to use for the purpose of regional economic planning.

North Central

    Aguascalientes, Durango, San Luis Potosí and Zacatecas

West

    Colima, Jalisco and Michoacán

Central

    Federal District, Guanajuato, Hidalgo, México, Morelos, Puebla, Querétaro and Tlaxcala

Gulf

    Tabasco and Veracruz

Pacific

    Chiapas, Guerrero, and Oaxaca

Yucatán Peninsula

    Campeche, Quintana Roo, and Yucatán

Table 3 shows the density of population by region according to the Census of 1960. It can be seen that in the Central area the population is at its densest. This does not merely reflect the fact that the capital is much the largest centre of population and happens to be located in this zone—the states surrounding the Federal District all have densities of population greater than states in any other regions. Moving away from the Central regions, the density of population drops.

Table 3. *Density of population, by regions, 1960*

	Population ('000)	Area ('000 sq. miles)	Population density (persons per sq. mile)
North Pacific	2,613	160·0	16·3
North	2,135	153·9	14·0
North Gulf	2,103	55·7	37·8
North Central	2,870	101·8	28·2
West	4,459	56·2	79·3
Central	12,561	49·8	252·2
Gulf	3,224	37·6	85·7
South Pacific	4,125	90·0	45·8
Yucatán Peninsula	832	55·0	23·5

Source: Population Census, 1960.

FIG. I   Mexico: states and administrative regions.

Table 4 shows the distribution of industrial value-added by region. These figures are taken from the 1961 Industrial Census. While they are the best data available, they may exaggerate regional disparities in the levels of industrialization because of the way in which data is reported. The total value-added in the Census is very far below that given by national income figures (compare Table 1) and it seems likely that Census coverage and accuracy would be higher in areas with a relatively high proportion of large-scale industry—in other words, in the more industrial regions. Nevertheless, even making allowance for exaggerated diversity, it can be seen that the regional difference in the degree of industrialization are very substantial indeed. Output per man employed also suggests that in the least industrialized regions existing industries are of a very low labour productivity—presumably implying smallness of scale and little capital per man.

Table 4. *Industrial value-added per head of population,*
and per man employed in industry, 1960

	Industrial value-added (m. pesos)	Industrial value-added per head of population (pesos)	Index (national average= 100)	Industrial value-added per man employed in industry ('000 pesos)	Index (national average= 100)
Total Mexico	14,172	418	100·0	16·6	100·0
North Pacific	876	335	80·2	18·3	110·1
North	1,333	624	149·4	24·0	144·1
North Gulf	1,250	594	142·2	15·4	92·3
North Central	461	161	38·5	11·0	66·0
West	887	200	47·8	16·0	96·3
Central	8,160	650	155·4	16·8	101·3
Gulf	791	245	58·7	17·8	106·9
Pacific	174	56	13·3	11·1	66·6
Yucatán Peninsula	241	289	69·3	9·6	57·6

Source: Industrial Census, 1961.

Regional differences in agriculture are also striking, although here too, regional differences may be systematically distorted. Table 5 brings out statistically the agricultural differences described earlier. The northern coastal zones, particularly in the north-west, are the highly productive areas, with a very high share of irrigated land and relatively low production of subsistence crops (as represented by the low share of maize). The share of irrigation given by these figures is perhaps a little exaggerated in some respects. These are the figures for the areas irrigated in the large publicly-run projects, and they show very well where the government has exerted most of its irrigation efforts. If we had used total Census figures for irrigation of all types they would show a relatively smaller share in the northern coastal regions since in the central, western and southern areas of the country a relatively high proportion of irrigation is carried out using privately constructed works and pumps, and is not controlled by a local irrigation district. Figures for this other irrigation are much less reliable but show that the Water Resource Ministry's statistics given here cover only about half of all irrigation.

As can be seen, livestock output is a comparatively more important part of the production of the North region than of the other regions, and the central, western and southern regions are those in which maize production accounts for the highest share of total agricultural output. By implication, these last regions are the poorest areas agriculturally. They are also the areas of lowest total *per capita* income—as can be seen from the presence of their component states in the calculation of *per capita* income and welfare levels made by P. L. Yates (Table 6). This indicates very startling disparities between average *per capita* incomes in the richest and poorest states. As was mentioned earlier, the economic problems of the mountain Indians trouble many consciences, and the low levels of money incomes of these Indians account for a little of the disparities evident in Table 6. It is, however, unlikely that real income per head in the richest state is really 10.5 times that in the poorest. For example, in the poorer, more agricultural states a much larger proportion of output will never be marketed at all, and it is not clear how far, if at all, Yates's figures take this into account. Yates's Index of Welfare shows a narrower spread,

Table 5. *Value of agricultural and livestock production, maize output and area of large-scale irrigation, 1960, by region*

	Agricultural production (m. pesos)	Regional output as % of national	Maize production (m. pesos)	Regional maize output as % of national	Maize output as % of total regional agriculture output	Large-scale irrigation[a] ('000 hectares)	Regional irrigation as % of national	Value of livestock output (m. pesos)	Regional livestock output as % of national
Total Mexico	14,396	100.0	4,049	100.0	28.1	1,617	100.0	6,002	100.0
North Pacific	2,581	17.9	329	8.1	12.8	693	42.9	751	12.5
North	1,210	8.4	177	4.4	14.7	254	15.7	859	14.3
North Gulf	862	6.0	203	5.0	23.5	300	18.6	473	7.9
North Central	1,347	9.3	481	11.9	35.7	19	1.2	695	11.6
West	1,385	9.6	609	15.0	44.0	95	5.9	659	11.0
Central	2,550	17.7	1,038	25.6	40.8	237	14.5	1,067	17.8
Gulf	1,804	12.5	397	9.8	22.0	7	0.4	672	11.2
South Pacific	2,019	14.0	718	17.7	35.6	10	0.6	620	10.3
Yucatán Peninsula	638	4.4	96	2.4	15.0	2	0.1	206	3.4

[a] Large-scale irrigation under the auspicies of the Ministry of Water Resources Irrigation Districts, 1959–60.

Source: Agricultural Census, 1960.

but the upper figure is still approximately 475 per cent of the lower figure.

Table 6. *Income and welfare levels in the
richest and poorest states*

	GNP per capita 1960	Yates's welfare index[a]
(expressed as % of the national average = 100)		
B. California Norte	313	204
Distrito Federal	261	188
Nuevo León	186	144
Sonora	167	157
Tamaulipas	154	136
Coahuila	134	136
B. California Sur	124	148
Chihuahua	110	147
Guanajuato	49	65
Zacatecas	46	56
Querétaro	43	70
Tabasco	40	70
Chiapas	38	52
Guerrero	37	58
Michoacán	36	72
Tlaxcala	36	60
Hidalgo	33	65
Oaxaca	27	43

[a] Yates's Index of Welfare is the average score of a state for a number of indices—
the reciprocal of the death rate, the rate of literacy, the teacher-pupil ratio, the
percentage of dwellings with running water, the legal minimum wage, the
percentage of population covered by social security, the *per capita* consumption
of sugar, of electricity, of petrol and the *per capita* registration of motor vehicles.
For each index a state's score was its percentage of the national average. Most of
the indicators were for 1958, but some were for earlier years.
    Of course, no precise meaning is attached to such an index, but it provides an
interesting supplement to the GNP statistics.

Source: Paul Lamartine Yates, *El Desarrollo Regional de México*, p. 135.

The states with the lowest welfare and income levels are comparatively little industrialized, and industry in such states is of
very low productivity. Agricultural productivity is also extremely

low. It is not surprising to find low productivity and low incomes going hand in hand, and low incomes restrict the local market for other industries. Contrariwise, incomes are likely to be high where there is much manufacturing industry, not only because the money wages paid to unskilled labour may be higher, but also because of the large amount of skilled, white collar and managerial personnel employed. This will in turn tend to provide a market that can attract other industries, so that quite apart from other agglomerating forces such as the provision of specialized services, the availability of a skilled labour force, and so on, we might expect a cumulative process of industrial concentration to be taking place.

Are there forces that might substantially slow this process down? A shortage of labour in those areas which are experiencing the greatest industrial growth might, in some countries, lead to a greater rise in wages relative to an increase in productivity there than elsewhere. But in Mexico this is unlikely, in view of the unemployment, both open and disguised, found almost everywhere. Evidence for this is the plentiful supply of able-bodied lottery ticket sellers, shoeshine boys, and so on, available in all towns. At first sight, this might appear to be contradicted by differential levels in minimum wages in different zones which might be taken to indicate differential tightness in the market for unskilled labour in different states. In 1966–7, the minimum daily wage varied between 35.7 pesos ($2.86 US) in Baja California Norte and 10.00 pesos ($0.80 US) for agricultural workers in parts of Guerrero and Chiapas. In Mexico City, the minimum wage was 25 pesos ($2.00 US). Minimum wages are supposed mainly to reflect cost of living differences, but also to take account of the economic progress of each zone and its productivity. Unfortunately, one cannot take minimum wage data as evidence that there are market forces pushing wages higher in some places than in others (which would have implied that unemployment is not as general as we have suggested), because it is well known that in most areas the declared minimum wage is not paid. This is particularly true in rural zones. Of course, it is not only the local price of labour that might rise with industrial concentration, but also the price of other resources. An obvious candidate is the price of land, but this is usually a relatively unimportant influence on the location of manufacturing industry.

As we shall explain, in the Valley of Mexico (the Federal District and surrounding areas) there are now obvious signs of the increasing costs of congestion. It appears that this is now leading to the dispersion of industry to towns still in the Central Region but located outside the Valley, but this is a very recent phenomenon.

In the period 1940–60, at least, forces making for industrial dispersion were outweighed by those making for agglomeration. In the first chapter we described how economies of agglomeration could lead activities to locate close together. An additional incentive for locating in the Federal District compared with several other regions in the country may have been the relatively easy availability of electric power in the years after the Second World War when electric power shortages seriously impeded industrial growth in other places. The Valley of Mexico is not now especially favoured, since rates are the same all over the country, but the tariff structure provides no incentive to firms to locate close to the source of hydroelectric supplies.

Since it is almost essential to consult the central office of any government bureau to obtain necessary permits and licences as well as to obtain exemptions from existing regulations, firms must establish regular contracts with high officials in Mexico City. The absence of a highly developed and efficient communications network among government offices makes the process of obtaining even routine documents more tedious in outlying areas. Firms located elsewhere often find it necessary to establish small offices in the Federal District to transact their business with the government.

To support industrialization, large investments have been made in education, especially for technical training. One important feature of the growth of the educational system in large cities is its flexibility in developing programmes and schedules which permit the students to have full-time jobs in addition to pursuing their studies. Furthermore, a special programme of education for adults who did not go through the regular primary and secondary educational system is growing. This of course attracts people to

Mexico City; firms are also attracted by the relatively plentiful supply of skilled and educated labour.

So it is not surprising that in his book Yates showed that the degree of concentration of industry in the Valley of Mexico was increasing—the Valley's percentage of industrial value-added, as given by the 1940 and 1955 Industrial Censuses, rose from 40.1 per cent to 52.5 per cent between those two dates. In 1960, he estimated the percentage to have been between 55 per cent and 60 per cent. It is true that López Malo gives figures based on gross output and adapted from earlier industrial censuses that suggest that industrial concentration did not increase at all between 1930 and 1950.[1] But it is likely that for our purposes, these figures place too much weight on the processing of agricultural output in the areas of thriving commercial agriculture, with industry adding only a small amount of value to high agricultural output.

Data on the internal migration of population can be calculated from the Censuses of Population.[2] The figures for the periods 1940–50 and 1950–60 show a very marked movement into the Valley of Mexico, but out-migration from other states in the Central region. The rate of growth of the Federal District actually slowed down a little between 1950 and 1960, but the figures for internal migration suggest that the movement into the other parts of the Valley of Mexico fully compensated for this. Baja California Norte, with its much higher standard of living than elsewhere, experienced the fastest rate of growth, and all the border states except Coahuila—which does not have a large border town—experienced net in-migration. In all the northern regions, the opening up of irrigated zones was probably a factor in in-migration although Sinaloa was a net loser of population.

The major forces making for the push and pull of population are obvious. The border regions are growing fast not only agriculturally, but also industrially; there is here a thriving tourist industry, and there is the possibility of crossing, permanently or

[1] López Malo, *Ensayo sobre Localización de la Industria*, p. 87.
[2] This was first done for 1940–50 migration, using the 1950 Census, by Nathaniel Whetten and Robert Burnight, 'Internal Migration in Mexico', *Rural Sociology*, XXI (June 1956), pp. 140–51. Further data on the 1950–60 period may be found in Timothy King, *River Basin Projects and Regional Development*, unpublished Ph.D. Dissertation, University of California, 1965.

temporarily, legally or illegally, into the United States. The Valley of Mexico offers expanding industrial employment, though by no means at a sufficient rate to absorb all the new immigrants. The large number of people engaged in relatively unproductive service occupations is testimony to the lack of positions for unskilled people. Even for these people, however, the social services available in the city are much more abundant than in the rural areas; in addition to subsidized food, medical facilities, and education for all ages, recreational facilities are available for all and are heavily patronized by the poor.

Factors pushing migrants away from many states also contribute to migration flows. The slow rate of growth of productivity in subsistence agriculture, the lack of other employment opportunities, and the stagnation of the mining industry have forced many to leave their native states to seek industrial employment.

In summary, inter-regional disparities in levels of income and rates of progress are very marked in Mexico, and have caused a good deal of concern. The reasons for this can be divided into the purely economic and those with a strong political and ideological ingredient. The first category includes questions about the overall size of the national income. Whether the high concentration of industry tends to diminish or to increase national income depends on whether costs of congestion outweigh economies of agglomeration. We discussed the nature of economies of agglomeration in Chapter 1; unfortunately, it is not possible to give even a rough idea of the order of magnitude involved in the Mexican case for there is no known way of measuring them. There is, however, considerable evidence that the costs of concentration of industry in the Valley of Mexico, at least, if not in the whole Central Region, are very high, and in the remainder of this chapter we shall discuss this evidence. The political and ideological factors creating anxiety about the state of regional development are more appropriately discussed in Chapter 3.

Congestion implies that both the migration to the cities and the growth of new industry impose costs on the people and firms already established in the area as well as increasing the demands on public services. Neither group is required to pay these costs and as a result they do not think about the burden they impose on others. There are two types of costs which are incurred with the growth of the city; costs that result from the need for more social overhead capital and costs due to the increased congestion and air pollution as population and industry grows.

The influx of people and industry to the city requires an expansion of the whole range of public services offered to the population. Although the quantitative research on economies of scale in public services is far from adequate, it does suggest that a city the size of Mexico City is incurring substantial diseconomies in the provision of these public services as a result of urban growth. The most telling example of this is the problem of water supply in the Federal District. Mexico City is built on a lake bed, into whose subsoil it is now sinking. The most serious consequence of this is that the main area of the City is now in the lower part of the basin and drainage involves pumping sewage up to a height of 40 feet. The sinking will continue while the use of ground water continues to be above the level of recharge. The rate of sinking is uneven, with the result that seepage continually threatens the purity of the drinking water supply. The instability and plasticity of the subsoil creates building problems and increases the vulnerability of the city to earthquakes.[1] The successful drainage of the lakes has reduced the mildness of the climate and has increased dust storms in the spring.

The chief problem is the shortage of water in the Valley of Mexico, because this gives rise directly to the sinking of the City. The expansion of industry in the Valley clearly contributes to it. There are, it is true, severe restrictions on the sinking of new wells, but it is not always easy to enforce them. Water is now brought from the Lerma basin by aqueduct at a rate of 5 cubic metres a second. This was about one-sixth of the total amount used in 1960. One study discusses various plans for importing water under various assumptions about the size of the population and its geographic distribution within the Valley.[2] The details need not bother us, but two of the conclusions are interesting. Assuming a

[1] Federico Mooser, 'La Cuenca Lacustre del Valle de México', *Problemas del Valle de México* (México D.F.: Instituto Mexicano de Recursos Naturales Renovables, 1963), pp. 19–22.
[2] José Vicente Orozco, 'Plan Hidráulico para el Valle de México', *Problemas del Valle de México*, pp. 51–113.

diminution of the rate of growth of population in the Valley so that the 1990 population would be only a little more than double its present level, it would be necessary to import about five times the water imported in the early 1960s, tapping other river basins adjoining the Valley as well as the Lerma. If the rate of growth of population does not slow down, a population of 16 million in 1990 will have to import nearly eleven times the water imported in the early 1960s. The average cost of supplying water rises rapidly with the amount of water needed—from 20 centavos per cubic metre in 1960 to 60 centavos under the assumption of 12 million people in the Valley, and 90 centavos if the population is 16 million.[1] With average cost rising in this way one can see how high the marginal cost must be.

This marginal cost is not paid by new firms which cannot legally be charged more for their water than existing firms. Moreover, the Federal District residents are not likely to bear most of the costs of supplying this water, since, like the present Lerma aqueduct, the system will probably be built by the Ministry of Water Resources and financed by Federal taxation. If it were possible to discriminate in pricing and to charge new entrants to the Valley something like the marginal cost of supplying them with water, it seems probable that a diminution of concentration could be achieved.

One can adopt similar reasoning in the case of other municipal services. In the Federal District these are far greater *per capita* than in other cities, as Yates points out. Here they include such expenses as subsidizing the fuel used by buses and taxis and subsidizing food. In 1958, the *per capita* expenditure of the government of the Federal District was 235 pesos, and that spent by the city governments of Guadalajara and Monterrey was about 50 pesos.[2] (Neither figure includes the cost of supplying water.)

Physical congestion is another problem associated with urban growth. As in the case of supplying water to Mexico City, the continued inflow of migrants and industries will increase the cost of conducting business in the area and the inconvenience of living there. These costs are borne by each individual and firm and the

[1] José Vicente Orozco, 'Plan Hidráulico para el Valle de México', *Problemas del Valle de México*, p. 113.　　[2] Yates, *El Desarrollo Regional de México*, p. 277.

newcomers will not be required to take into account their impact on other people; the only costs they incur are those related to the increased time and inconvenience of their own affairs. In Mexico City, large road building projects and public transportation systems have been provided to help with the problem but these seem to be only temporary solutions. The most recent effort to deal with this problem is the construction of an underground mass transportation system to relieve surface congestion.

Air pollution is also an important problem in Mexico City, worsened by its situation in a valley surrounded by very high mountains. Without controls on the types of fuels in use and with the increasing concentration of heavy industries in the area, the accumulation of pollutants in the air can become quite dense. Prevailing air currents do little to relieve the problem and the atmosphere is often unpleasant.

The costs of providing even those services which are required wherever a person lives are higher in the metropolitan area. Housing is the most obvious of these costs because of the scarcity of land and the higher construction costs in urban areas; in rural areas homes can often be constructed during slack periods when the cost of labour is very small. Higher costs of urbanization will be reflected in the costs of firms in so far as these are reflected in the legal minimum wage and the legal minimum wage is reflected in the actual costs of labour. Here again firms will pay average rather than marginal costs.

In spite of the fact that firms do not pay the full marginal costs of establishment in the Valley of Mexico, it does seem that however much the costs paid underestimate true social costs, they are too high for some firms. In the 1960s there has been some decentralization of industry into towns such as Querétaro and Toluca, that are well served by transport to the capital and other important markets. This decentralization does indeed suggest that if firms were forced to pay the marginal costs they impose, decentralization of industry would have come earlier and more extensively.

Most of the policy discussion of regional development is not carried on in these terms, but is concerned about a lack of industrialization in poorer regions, rather than too much for its own good in the Valley of Mexico. In Chapter 1 some general reasons why governments are likely to be anxious about relative regional incomes were discussed. In the next chapter we shall examine the actual motivation behind Mexico's regional policy—and to do this we must first describe the process of policy-making in Mexico.

3

THE MEXICAN CONCERN
FOR REGIONAL DEVELOPMENT

The decision to allocate scarce investment funds to the several agencies established to develop river basins arose largely from the persistent need to increase agricultural production for both home and foreign markets and to expand supplies of electric power. In other words, the projects resulted from the major aim of economic policy which has been to increase national output as fast as possible. We shall say a little more about this objective later in this chapter. They also resulted from the government's desire for a more even pattern of regional development for its own sake, reflecting various strong political and ideological pressures and also a desire to improve the living conditions of people who may feel that they have been left out of the mainstream of economic progress. The form in which regional development has been promoted itself reflects political forces. In this chapter we present first a brief sketch of the political decision-making process in Mexico to help explain the political and ideological forces at work. Then we examine the reasons for the current anxiety about the pattern of regional development.

DECISION-MAKING IN MEXICO

The role of the President

There is one predominant party in Mexico, the Partido Revolucionario Institucional (PRI), which controls most of the political power in the country without serious challenge from any of the several small parties which are permitted to function. The President of the country is also the real leader of the party and is vested with extensive powers to direct the nation's destiny during his single six-year term of office.

The exact role of the PRI, the President, and functional interest groups in political decisions and, above all, in the selection of the next President, is shrouded in mystery and there exist two different interpretations. The first emphasizes the importance of the bargaining process inside the PRI, which, because of the broad base of the party's organization, embraces most sectors of public opinion.[1] The second interpretation puts much more weight on the role played by a small group of people—called by Brandenburg 'the inner council of the Revolutionary Family'—which has about twenty members. These too may be to some degree responsive to interest group pressures, but this interpretation leaves the PRI on the fringes of the political process.[2] Whichever interpretation of the selection of the President one adopts, the influence of interest group pressures upon the outcome of decisions about economic affairs is significant.

The process of selecting the PRI's nominee begins more than a year before the election, and for several months hidden discussions, consultations, and vetos take place until a consensus is arrived at. The President is elected in July and takes office the following December. But his nomination is announced during the autumn before the election and from that time on, the nominee rather than the incumbent becomes the central political figure in Mexico. The election for the chief executive is almost a formality, but there are occasionally real contests for local offices between the PRI and minority parties.

It is not easy to see any obvious constraints on a President's power once he is elected. He dominates the political scene completely. Not only do ministers and upper civil servants depend on his nomination, but Congress—overwhelmingly consisting of members of the PRI, with a few seats reserved for the opposition —exists merely to rubber-stamp measures initiated by the administration. Since he may constitutionally not be re-elected, the need to ensure personal popularity need not weigh heavily with him. There are, as we shall stress, considerable differences in political emphasis and style between administrations. Nevertheless it is safe to predict that, whoever the next president may

[1] See Scott, *Mexican Government in Transition.*
[2] Frank Brandenburg, *The Making of Modern Mexico* (Englewood Cliffs, N.J.: Prentice-Hall, 1964).

be, he will hold broadly to the ideology of the Revolution, and that he will, to some degree, respond to pressure from economic and social interest groups.

The ideology of the Revolution

The Revolution was no neatly planned affair in pursuit of a consistent and well defined set of objectives. As the political party whose professed rationale is to carry forward the spirit and intention of the Revolution, the PRI and its candidates have no blueprint, Bible, or Marxist–Leninist creed which might supply a political programme. Nevertheless, the nature of the Revolution has dictated some of the directions that policy will take. It will be nationalist—for example foreign investment is accepted, indeed, welcomed, but strictly on Mexican terms. It will seek to improve the lot of the peasant—hence land reform will be stressed. It will promise greater 'social justice', and it will strive vigorously to promote economic development. It can be seen that there may be a potential conflict among some of these goals. One President will resolve this conflict emphasizing one thing—say, less land redistribution and heavier stress on agricultural investment—another will resolve it in another way, putting much more weight on land redistribution. It can be said, however, that ideological considerations have seldom interfered substantially with a desire to promote economic development and the policies adopted are seldom followed in a doctrinaire fashion. Even the particular programmes which have a high ideological content turn out to be pragmatic in operation, and Mexico seems to have avoided being led by ideological considerations to invest large amounts of resources in activities with a relatively low return in terms of promoting economic development.

The best example of this is the Mexican land reform programme. As described in Chapter 2, the demand for land by the landless was one of the most important elements of the Revolution. The redistribution of land held in large estates had been a major programme of successive administrations for more than half a century. The legally permitted maximum size of a holding has varied from time to time and depends on the quality and the use made of the land. In recent years it has ranged from 250 acres of irrigated land to as much as several thousand acres of grazing land.

Land reform has proceeded at a very uneven pace. During the first two decades of land reform—that is from its beginnings in 1915 to the inauguration of President Cárdenas in 1934—land redistribution averaged about a million acres a year. Already before 1934, at least one political leader had pronounced the amount of land available for redistribution to be exhausted—views which several times have been subsequently expressed. But under Cárdenas the redistribution of land took place at a rate never equalled before or since—over 7 million acres a year. Under the next three Presidents, redistribution of approximately 2 million acres a year took place. López Mateos redistributed about 40 million acres between 1958 and 1964 to come closest to Cárdenas and the present rate of land redistribution, though well below the levels of Cárdenas and López Mateos, remains fairly brisk.

Land taken from large estates, usually without compensation, has gone to form the ejido, the landholding village. Sometimes this land has remained collectively managed as well as owned. But collective cultivation has seldom proved practical, so that today less than 3 per cent of the land which has been expropriated is actually worked communally. In the vast majority of cases the ejidatarios have perpetual usufruct rights over a small plot of land which they can pass on to their heirs but cannot alienate in any way. This means, for example, that land cannot be legally rented from an ejidatario. But in practice, the authorities have tended to wink at such abuses, since they ensure the productive use of land. Another abuse which is permitted for pragmatic reasons is the control by private land owners of several plots of land, each of the maximum legal size, under the nominal ownership of relatives or friends. This means that not all large holdings have in fact been broken up—but it also means that there is some assurance that the remaining large holdings will at least be fully utilized. There is no point in breaking the law by owning surreptitiously more land than the permitted maximum if one is not going to use it to make a profit. Leaving land idle is likely to invite investigation by the agrarian authorities and subsequent expropriation, since there is in most areas an unsatisfied demand for ejido land. Ejidatarios must also not allow land to lie idle for more than two years at a time, or they may forfeit their claim to the land.

In spite of the winking at various abuses, the land reform programme has been an important part of every administration's efforts to make the people feel that it is doing its best to implement the goals of the Revolution. The allocation of ejidal plots has been a very visible way of distributing the fruits of the Revolution to large numbers of peasants, some of whom have only tenuous links with the market economy and are only marginally aware of the industrialization efforts of the central government.

This effort to redistribute land has not been accompanied by large-scale investments for the improvement of productive conditions in agriculture in the areas where redistribution has taken place. One of the striking things about the rather successful programme to improve agricultural productivity in Mexico is its concentration in areas and on land which is not predominantly ejidal. This policy has produced a dramatic difference between the development of the private and ejidal agricultural economies; productivity on private lands increased rapidly due to an important programme of public investment in water resources, credit, and marketing facilities, while the ejidos have experienced only small increases in productivity as knowledge has been disseminated and better seeds and fertilizers have become available.

Thus, while the government has been very concerned about its record of distributing land and fulfilling the promise of the land reform programme, it has not found itself bound to limit its investments in the agricultural sector to ejidos. It has, it turns out, placed its agricultural investments in those regions which would have been most productive, and these are primarily in non-ejidal areas, and has been able to appease millions of peasants by giving them parcels of land, much of which had always been of low productivity, often due to its low fertility and the difficulty of irrigating it. In addition to the land redistribution programme, the government is able to point to its very successful programme to improve agricultural productivity, while sidestepping the issue of who is the primary beneficiary of this progress.

This combination of ideology and pragmatism is not necessarily the result of a conscious effort by several Revolutionary administrations to leave the ejidatario in the backwash of progress.[1] Instead, it appears as if this situation has emerged as the product of the mingling of different pressures to increase agricultural output and to redistribute as much land as possible. By placing great stress on this effort to carry out the goals of the Revolution by redistributing land, the government has convinced the peasants of its intention to improve rural incomes. This official concern and interest in the problems of the peasant is constantly stressed in the face of accumulating evidence that the relative standard of living of this group is deteriorating. The substitution of ideology for economic achievements thus permitted the government to divert fewer resources to programmes of social welfare than might otherwise have been necessary.

The land reform programme is not the only instance of a combination of pragmatism and ideology. Mexico's treatment of private foreign investment is similar. With a history of troubled relations with foreign investors, with both real and imagined wrongs on both sides, Mexico has been successful in devising a policy towards foreign investment that enables it both to satisfy strong nationalist feeling and to exploit the benefits that foreign investment can bring. The government recognizes the valuable contribution that foreign investment can make to Mexico. It not only provides important additions to foreign exchange reserves, but it also is a source of external saving for increasing the stock of fixed investment, and, perhaps most important, is often accompanied by scarce technical know-how. Mexico also goes to great lengths to ensure that it maintains a strong position in the international economic community and that it is viewed as an economically and politically stable nation with a favourable environment for investment.

Hostility to foreign capital, however, is a legacy from the Revolution, and from the lengthy dispute with foreign oil companies which culminated in their nationalization in 1938. A

---

[1] These ideas stem largely from many discussions with Clark Reynolds. His own views will appear in his book, *The Mexican Economy: Twentieth-Century Structure and Growth* (New Haven: Yale University Press, 1970).

general dislike of dependence on foreigners, whether as investors, suppliers or customers is widespread—a desire which expresses itself in the rationale for Mexico's import substitution policy, for example.[1] Nationalist feeling is served by a number of regulations which restrict foreign investment activities. Foreign firms are excluded from certain industries regarded as basic, including oil, basic petro-chemicals, electricity, transport, telephone and telegraphic communications. 'Mexicanization'—the selling to Mexican citizens of a controlling interest in a foreign subsidiary—is encouraged by various means, and may be a condition of a new firm's being allowed to operate. It is appreciated that the transfer of control from foreigners to Mexicans is merely symbolic, but it is an important symbol. But there is no legal requirement that foreign firms 'Mexicanize'—and where it is felt that the Mexican national interest is best served by allowing a new foreign subsidiary to be established, in spite of a refusal to sell any shares to Mexicans, such a firm will be permitted to operate.

Interest groups

The Federal Republic has twenty-nine states, two territories (subject to more central control than states) and a Federal District (Mexico City and some surrounding areas). Each has its own political leaders. The governors are the nominal heads of the PRI in each state; they are nominated by the central organization and the choice for each post is apparently carefully considered by the President. The governors serve at the pleasure of the party and, more specifically, of its titular head; past experience indicates that they can and will be removed should their actions conflict strongly with the interests of those at the centre. They do, however, serve as a channel for communicating local feeling to the central authorities. Similarly, there are a great many other organizations in the party which can represent the interests of different groups of the population.

There are three principal interest groups organized within the framework of the PRI which channel opinions to and from their members and the political centre. The largest—the Confederación

---

[1] For further details, see Timothy King, *Mexico: Industrialisation and Trade Policies since 1940* (London: Oxford University Press, 1970), Chapter 5.

Nacional Campesina—was founded in 1938 by Lázaro Cárdenas and retains its original organizational structure. Through this organization more than 2 million ejidatarios can express their views and claim that they are consulted about political decisions through local chapters at the regional and state levels. Similar organizations exist for labour; the Confederación de Trabajadores de México was established in 1936 but its history has been marked by frequent internal struggles which reflect the range of political opinions within the labour movement and it has now less than one-half of the unionized labour force in Mexico as members—about 600,000 workers. Finally, the civil servants have an organization—the Federación de Sindicatos de Trabajadores en el Servicio del Estado—which is a very important member of the PRI and, by its very nature, a staunch supporter of the regime; it has slightly more than 300,000 members.

In addition there are numerous other organizations which exist to make the opinions and political views of their members known at the centre. Several different groups of industrialists and businessmen frequently make pronouncements about economic and political conditions in Mexico. Another organization was created when the PRI itself was shaped from its predecessors (1946) to group together many smaller independent groups including civil servants (who still function independently), co-operativists, small farmers, intellectuals and professionals, taxi drivers, and others not encompassed by other formal representative groups within the party.

The interest groups have a very important function. They provide a means for all people, regardless of their social class and occupation, to feel as though they are actually participating in the political process in spite of the fact that there is only one political party and the results of the national elections are predictable in advance. They do this by providing a formal and relatively open line of communication between individuals and the central decision-making apparatus of the PRI. In other words, there are innumerable channels through which dissent can be expressed and the special interests of a region, social class or economic sector can be mobilized and find some means for communicating their conflicts to the higher reaches of government where they may be given a hearing. In spite of the absence of effective opposition parties and the high degree of centralization of authority in the chief executive, the Mexican decision-making apparatus has managed to retain sufficient flexibility to permit minority views to be channelled up to the highest levels for consideration and response.

Planning

The President's power is further reinforced by the absence of a cabinet system in which ministers can exert their collective power on policy making. All important decisions ultimately are channelled directly to the chief executive who has a final veto on all measures. Although all Presidents are nominated by the PRI, the personality and the views of an individual President largely determine the character of his administration. As a result there have been substantial differences between administrations in the types of programmes undertaken and the emphasis given to different parts of the development programme.

This extreme concentration of power has also meant that most programmes must be designed for completion within a single six-year period—the term of the President who is constitutionally proscribed from re-election. Each administration must work out its own programme and decide its own priorities; there is no planning process which attempts to tie one regime to the programmes of another. Even formal planning within the period of one administration is recent and its influence on economic decisions is highly debatable. From the 1930s on, documents entitled 'Plans' existed, but these were generally political programmes and exhortations prepared by the President or party officials, and they contain little to guide the allocation of national resources or even of public funds.

The spending of public funds became increasingly difficult to control as various so-called 'decentralized agencies' increased in importance. As the Mexican government has increasingly moved into new fields of economic activity—as it has nationalized oil, for example, or bought out electricity companies—it has often seemed easier to create new administrative mechanisms rather than to reorganize the function of a ministry. The result is the existence of more than 300 decentralized agencies, which frequently derive their authority directly from the President. From 1948 until 1962, attempts were made to control and plan public expenditure and, until 1962, most of the so-called 'planning' consisted of various attempts to do this.

The most important agency established during this period was the Investment Commission which was created in 1954 and reported directly to the President. The Commission was responsible for formulating criteria for public investment, selecting projects and co-ordinating them with national development plans. Its annual programmes were subject to scrutiny by the Ministry of Finance while the President continued to examine them closely. Its first attempt at planning consisted of a two-year investment plan drawn up in 1956.

When López Mateos became President, the Commission was integrated into the new Ministry of the Presidency, which was responsible for, among other things, co-ordinating the government's economic activities. The reorganized Comisión Nacional de Inversión Pública was unable to do much in the way of planning, since it was only able to request investment plans from each of the many public agencies receiving funds and try to supervise their outlays. Special care was given to the use of foreign exchange but no comprehensive planning occurred.

The Charter of the Alliance for Progress required recipient countries to formulate a development plan. An Interministerial Commission was established to formulate the new plan and to develop a new planning mechanism. The Commission produced a Plan of Immediate Action covering the period 1962–4 (later extended to 1966), which was submitted to the Organization of American States but which had an extremely restricted circulation in Mexico even at the top levels of government. As a result, the impact of the plan on the people who were making decisions about economic policy can only have been very limited, except in the ministries directly concerned with the plan.

Although this plan has been strongly criticized for its lack of a consistent macro-economic model of the economy on which to base its estimates of investment and their impact on the nation's development, it was the first attempt to include both private and public investment, at least in many basic industries.[1] Since the plan was not widely circulated, however, this co-ordination could not have much impact on actual decision-making, particularly in the private sector.

A second plan also suffered from its lack of exposure to the interested parties. The Interministerial Commission prepared this document during the early years of the Díaz Ordaz administration to cover the period from 1966–70, but even fewer people have had access to the details of this attempt than to the previous one. The Commission projected an overall growth rate of 6·5 per cent per year and also provided detailed analysis of some of the major sectors of economic activity and the balance of payments. This plan has been used for the elaboration of detailed plans for public investment and more stringent controls over investment by de-centralized agencies have been instituted.

Even this limited degree of central planning has been fiercely opposed inside the government, which explains the decision to restrict plan circulation, and limits the effect of the plans to improving the co-ordination and control of public investment programmes. Even within the public sector, the highly placed economic planners do not have the last word on the implementation of investment programmes. Ultimately, the President makes decisions about the allocation of investment funds, and the political need to satisfy sectoral or regional interests must sometimes over-ride strictly economic considerations. The myriad decisions by which the government affects the behaviour of the economy—for example those concerning import licences, price controls, and whether to permit foreign firms to operate—are not taken in the light of the plan, which is unavailable to the officials making the decisions. Aside from the planning of public investment there is little interministerial co-operation; and a great deal of political rivalry among ministers is apparent. This competition is further reinforced by the absence of a cabinet system. Although the Mexican political system has moved some way from *personalismo*—in which the influence of political leaders depended on their own personal following—towards a much more formalized

[1] See Miguel S. Wionczek, 'Incomplete Formal Planning: Mexico' in *Planning Economic Development* (Homewood, Ill.: Irwin, 1963), pp. 156–83.

policy-making process in which functional interest groups play an important part, personal influence of ministers and the heads of government agencies still counts for a good deal.[1]

An example of practical policy-making: the River Basin Commissions.

The River Basin Commissions were created in the same spirit as that of many of the decentralized agencies—to carry out specific programmes which could not be handled by the existing government organizations. Technically, however, they lack the autonomy of decentralized agencies since they are directly answerable to the Minister of Water Resources. Commissions were created to develop and administer large-scale irrigation programmes in a few isolated regions. A very attractive feature of these organizations is their ability to work in several states simultaneously and to co-ordinate the efforts of several different ministries to improve the social overhead capital in a region. As we shall show in the next chapter, River Basin Commissions have been charged with a wide variety of duties, and have proved a flexible tool of regional policy. Sometimes considerable authority over regional investments which were the responsibility of other ministries or state governments have been assumed by Commissions. Sometimes their primary role has been the planning and co-ordination of investment by others. In the first case, the obvious focus on water resources and construction of irrigation, flood control and hydro-electric investment projects, are only part of the Commission's investment— expenditure on roads, schools, urban improvement and public health facilities also takes place. The magnitude of the role played in this respect has depended on the priority placed by the President and his advisers on the particular investment programme elaborated by each Commission. Within the limits imposed by its budget, each Commission could engage in a broad range of measures for comprehensive regional planning. The second type of activity, the co-ordination of the functions of other agencies working in the same region, is more problematical and depends to a much greater extent on the influence and ability of its personnel. The Commission cannot require but only encourage such co-operation and it lacks the resources to carry out itself the functions

[1] See Scott, *Mexican Government in Transition*, pp. 4–33.

of other agencies if these refuse to co-operate. The normal interagency rivalry has naturally made this a difficult task in practice.

In this type of situation the chief executive officer's influence can be crucial in determining the Commission's success, and the extent of his personal political weight may make a significant difference. The choice of the head of each Commission has therefore been an important decision. President Alemán was conscious of this when creating the first two Commissions and selected men with this in mind. As head of the Tepalcatepec Commission, he chose General Lázaro Cárdenas, past president of Mexico and a native of Michoacán where the Commission was to function. This appointment also had the additional feature of giving a prestigious post to a man with a sizable political following who might have sapped strength from the party had he not been fully integrated into the 'Revolutionary effort'. Cárdenas is highly regarded by most people in Michoacán and is a politician who has the ability to obtain political agreement where necessary to achieve the Commission's goals. More recently Cárdenas became head of the Balsas Commission, which in 1960 was formed to extend the work of the Tepalcatepec Commission over a much wider area and which itself incorporated the Tepalcatepec Commission. Although it appears that in recent years Cárdenas has lost some of the political influence he once had, he remains a powerful left-wing political figure and this had no doubt helped him to obtain the resources needed to maintain the impetus of the Balsas Commission.

The Papaloapan Commission's highest post was filled by an engineer, Reynaldo Schega, but it has been suggested that Alemán himself expected to occupy the post upon leaving the Presidency in 1952. The next President, Ruiz Cortines, however, appointed another engineer, Raúl Sandoval Landázuri, who was accidently killed four years later. In his book on the Papaloapan project, Thomas Poleman emphasizes the importance of the person occupying the post of Vocal Ejecutivo (Executive Director): 'the Commission was deprived of a particularly forceful Vocal Ejecutivo through an aeroplane accident, and as the result of a series of high-level decisions its activities were sharply curtailed. It has been on the defensive ever since.'[1] For various political reasons its funds were sharply reduced in the later years of the 1950s, even though the objectives being pursued were, and indeed are, still evidently those of the government. This is not to argue that the director of a Commission need be a leading politician for the Commission to be successful—this is manifestly not the case, since the direction of most of the Commissions has been in the hands of hitherto unknown technicians. But it does suggest that the personal influence of the director of a Commission is a significant factor determining its degree of success in obtaining resources to carry out its work. In other words, investment funds are not allocated simply on the basis of an impartial cost-benefit analysis.

ECONOMIC POLICY AND REGIONAL DEVELOPMENT

National economic objectives

As was pointed out in Chapter 1, some of the objectives of regional development policy will, of course, be the same as national objectives.[2] In Mexico, the major aims of economic policy are to increase income per head as fast as possible, and to provide productive employment for as many of the labour force —now growing at 3·5 per cent a year—as possible. A subsidiary goal that is frequently mentioned is to reduce economic dependence on external events—though Mexico has been much less successful in achieving this than her other goals. Although it is true that import substitution has succeeded in reducing the proportion of imports to final demand, the composition of imports has increasingly come to consist of capital goods, raw materials and intermediate goods. It would in consequence be difficult to cut imports for any prolonged period as a consequence of a balance of payments crisis without leading to a cut-back in the rate of growth of production. In this sense, Mexico remains very dependent on imports. She also maintains complete internal and external convertibility, and has in consequence to try to prevent any situation arising that might lead to a flight of capital. Mexico

[1] Thomas T. Poleman, *The Papaloapan Project* (Stanford, Cal.: Stanford University Press, 1964), p. 98.
[2] For a much fuller discussion of such objectives and achievements, see King, *Mexico: Industrialisation and Trade Policies.*

had devalued twice since the Second World War, but is now determined to maintain her exchange rate. In consequence, a favourable balance of payments situation, and contributing to this, the absence of inflation, is always a much emphasized goal of policy.

The way in which development of regions away from the industrialized urban centres of the country contributes to these national objectives is primarily through the development of agriculture. Agricultural growth has been a significant component of total growth, and the performance here in comparison with several other Latin American countries with broadly similar industrial policies may largely explain Mexico's relative economic success. Mexico has changed from being an importer of certain foods, particularly wheat, into a position where she frequently exports large quantities of wheat, maize and beans, which are her staple foods. This has helped the balance of payments quite directly. It has also meant that without a tendency for increasing population and rising incomes to push up internal food prices (or lead to food imports) it has been easier to control inflation than in many other countries in Latin America, and this indirectly will have helped her to avoid balance of payments crises. In addition, agricultural exports remain much the largest group of commodity exports (though they are now overshadowed by tourist earnings, including expenditures in the border areas) which account for almost 40 per cent of total export earnings.

The search for new agricultural land has been an important motive behind regional development policies. The opening up of new land has been of the greatest importance in explaining the growth of agricultural output since 1940. From 1927 to 1940, the area harvested rose 2·2 per cent a year while yield per hectare rose only 0·5 per cent a year. From 1940–50, the area harvested rose 3·1 per cent a year, and yields 2·6 per cent.[1] From 1951–60, the area harvested rose 2 per cent a year and yields 3 per cent. Settlement of land previously unutilized or used only for rough grazing has been an important goal of several of the river basin

---

[1] México, Sec. de Agricultura y Ganadería, and other government agencies, *Projections of Supply of and Demand for Agricultural and Livestock Products in Mexico to 1970 and 1975* (México, D.F., 1965), pp. 145–6.

projects. So too has been the provision of irrigation facilities—since the availability of water is of great importance in determining the productivity of crop-land.

Another way in which the particular pattern of regional development with which we are concerned in this study has hastened national development has been through increasing electric power supply. In the early 1950s, a shortage of electric power threatened certain industrial areas and placed a potential brake on the pace of growth of manufacturing industry—a threat that has been countered by the rapid growth of electrical generating capacity. Hydroelectric power has been a feature of all of the river basin schemes and has played a part in this expansion. In 1965, installed hydroelectric capacity was nearly four times its 1950 quantity, and accounted for over 40 per cent of the country's installed capacity. Since then the inauguration of large hydroelectric schemes has substantially increased its relative importance. The growth of thermal capacity was greater than that of hydroelectric capacity during the period 1950–65, but growth in actual power generated was greater for hydroelectricity.

The objectives of regional development policy

Apart from the contribution that regional projects can make to national development, and apart from the costs of congestion, which were discussed in Chapter 2, the government is anxious to see a more balanced level of regional development for its own sake. We discussed such motivations of governments in general in the first chapter. The heart of the Mexican political concern for regional development is a desire for social balance. The emphasis on industrialization and import substitution has had its principal impact in the urban areas of the country. New factories are being built and employment opportunities are increasing in the larger cities. Complementary investments in social overhead capital have accounted for a large proportion of the investment budget and left relatively little for rural areas. It is therefore not surprising that people in these rural areas have, through one means or another, been clamouring for more attention and public works.

These demands have not been ignored by policy-makers. The Mexican government is aware of the problems that could arise if wholesale discontent were to erupt in the countryside. Its development programme takes account of such pressures, and attempts to reduce latent dissatisfaction where this could destroy political stability. One of the problems confronting the President is that of finding a proper balance between the requirements of the industrialization programme and the demands for more consumption by the poorest groups. Part of the response to the desire for improvements in rural areas has been the effort in the past decade to increase the redistribution of land under the agrarian reform laws. As already suggested, this has been accompanied by heavy investment in agriculture only in areas where returns promise to be high. Other programmes have been instituted to improve rural road systems, expand the rural electrification programme, increase the number of drinking water systems, and, perhaps most important of all, enlarge the rural educational system. In this way collective consumption of goods is combined with basic investments in rural social overhead capital instead of providing greater quantities of consumer goods and higher disposable incomes for the poor. The only government concession to the desire for greater private consumption is the subsidy on basic food commodities which are distributed through official channels to people in urban slums and in rural areas, but this is not primarily a regional development programme.

These programmes of rural investment are considered essential to minimize the danger of regional disturbances which will upset the delicate balance which has been achieved. In addition, many political leaders are ideologically committed to improve the lot of indigenous communities. These programmes are designed to provide the poorest groups with some tangible evidence of the economic development effort while not diverting an unduly large amount of resources from investment with higher economic return. They are also important to stem the tide of migrants from the rural areas to the urban areas where they are placing heavy burdens on available housing and public services which are offered to urban residents.

As pointed out in the last chapter, the geographic layout of the nation and the cultural diversity of its people produced innumerable pockets of people who still have tenuous links with the rest of the nation. The Instituto Nacional Indigenista directly tackles this problem by working with isolated indigenous groups in various parts of the country. The programme was begun in 1936 by President Lázaro Cárdenas with the formation of a number of 'Cultural Missions' which provided some education and a whole range of other activities to involve isolated communities in the national educational effort.[1] It also was a way of establishing local branches of national political organizations to increase the peasant's sense of participation in the nation.

This effort declined after the Cárdenas era and the present educational and cultural efforts of INI are directed solely to those groups who remain outside the pale of 'Mexican' culture. Although they often offer instruction in the native languages, these programmes are designed to familiarize Indian groups with the range of services and opportunities which are theoretically available to them. Only rarely will the government permit a group to reject explicitly a role of active participation in the nation in favour of the development of a viable but differentiated sub-culture. Concessions are made to surviving traditions and ceremonial patterns but there appears to be a firm insistence on some assimilation with the rest of the nation.

The Indians are not the only ones who are physically and culturally isolated. There are still many areas in the country which have remained untouched by the development efforts. Some of them have become ideal fiefdoms for local politicians hoping to establish their own protectorate or refuges for criminals seeking to avoid the long arm of the law. If such an area becomes especially troublesome, as was the case with the Tepalcatepec river basin, then governmental resources are usually mobilized to reduce the threat to the regime.

Rural expenditure does not go far towards trying to decentralize industry. This does, however, seem to be a general objective of the government—one reason being the costs of congestion. But another seems to be a dislike of over-centralization *per se*, which is expressed by most writers on the subject, though not in

---

[1] For more details about this programme, its objectives, and its accomplishments, see Ramón Eduardo Ruiz, *Mexico: The Challenge of Poverty and Illiteracy* (San Marino, Cal.: Huntington Library, 1963).

economic terms. Zamora likens the Central region to a gigantic, decadent organ maintained at the expense of the healthy parts of the body; López Malo scorns the 'excessive concentration and the defective location of industry'; and Enrique Beltrán comments on the 'absurd centralization' of the country, and Yates compares the capital with Imperial Rome.

In this context it is interesting to ask whether the growth of Mexico City, and the urban areas surrounding it, has been *abnormally* large by international standards.[1] Clearly in many countries the largest city is much larger than the second largest. Some research has been done on the size distribution of cities within a country. H. W. Singer has claimed that Pareto's Law, originally developed to describe the empirical constancy of income distributions, holds also for cities.[2] That is,

$$Y + aX^b$$

where Y is the number of cities with a population of at least X and a and b are constants. If this law holds, it follows that

$$\log Y = \log a + b \log X$$

will be in a straight line. The most complete examination of this law was made by G. R. Allen, who found it generally successful.[3]

Using the distribution of city sizes given in the 1960 Population Census, we find towns with a population of less than 100,000 obey Pareto's Law fairly closely, considerably better than the 17 cities larger than this. Singer also hypothesized that when Y was 1, X would be found to be a value not far from the geometric mean of the size of the two largest towns. Allen found that when conurbations were taken, rather than sticking to the legal boundaries as we have done here, eleven out of twelve cases support the hypothesis. In 1960, however, this was not true even for Mexico City, with a population of 2·8 million, which is 46 per cent larger than the size predicted on Singer's hypothesis and

[1] We obtained the idea of doing this from Benjamin Ward, *Problems of Greek Regional Development*, Research Monograph Series, No. 4 (Athens: Center for Economic Research, 1963), pp. 59–77.

[2] Hans W. Singer, 'The "Courbe des Populations" a Parallel to Pareto's Law', *Economic Journal*, XLVI (June 1936), pp. 254–63.

[3] G. R. Allen, 'The "Courbe des Populations", a Further Analysis', *Bulletin of the Oxford Institute of Statistics*, XVI (May–June 1954), pp. 179–89.

still less true for the Federal District with a population of 4·9 million. A full measure of the population of the conurbation should also include the urban areas in the Valley of Mexico, giving a total population that was in 1960 closer to 6 million than to 5 million. If the hypothesis is accepted as generally valid, then the size of Mexico City and its environs is indeed abnormally large. This does not, of course, prove over-centralization but it at least prevents us from condemning those who plead for de-centralization on the grounds that one always expects the largest city to be several times the size of the second largest.[1]

Different writers who have attacked over-centralization clearly have different views as to what decentralization is desirable. Yates's policy recommendations were concerned with decentral-ization away from the Valley of Mexico to areas on the Mesa Central. It can be argued that this is tending to come about naturally. Zamora, however, saw in the slow growth of the whole Central region a sort of diminishing returns to concentration, and a danger that these may act as a considerable brake on economic growth. Like Yates, he called for decentralization within the Central region, but only as a first step to a more com-plete decentralization to other regions.

The river basin projects have this more radical aim of industrial-izing areas away from the central areas of Mexico. This aim has been quite explicit, and the river basin schemes are one of several steps which have been taken to encourage people and industry to locate outside the three largest cities, and other measures are designed to make it more attractive for people to remain in their rural environments. Perhaps the most important of these have been directed towards the development of agriculture and the improvement of the road and communication networks so that rural markets may function better. It seems that Mexican policy-makers are convinced that one important way to reduce the pressure on the cities is to improve economic opportunities in rural Mexico. In the next chapter we shall say more about the details of such policies. It can be said at this point, however, that although the desire to decentralize industry is no doubt sincere,

[1] For further details of these calculations, see King, *River Basin Projects and Regional Development.*

measures to improve rural infrastructure by themselves—and they have been mostly left by themselves—have not been and are not going to be adequate to counter the tendencies to industrial agglomeration in the central areas of Mexico. We shall show this in some detail in the case study in the latter part of this book.

4

MEXICAN REGIONAL DEVELOPMENT
POLICIES SINCE 1946

RIVER BASIN PROJECTS

In Chapter 2 we described the background to regional development policies since the Second World War, and we have also discussed their political and economic rationale, but we have said little about the policies themselves. This we shall do in the present chapter. We shall be interested primarily in the four river basin projects in which investment has taken place on a large scale and over an extended period of time—representing the bulk of Mexico's regional development efforts since the war. As we showed in the last chapter, River Basin Commissions have offered a way of planning and co-ordinating public expenditure in a region that was difficult to do through already established ministries and state governments, quite apart from the economic desirability of investments made with a view to making the most efficient use of water, which is in such scarce supply in some parts of Mexico and at times is overabundant in others. Indeed, in one instance—the Lerma-Chapala-Santiago project, which has not yet gone significantly beyond the planning stage—the general co-ordinating and planning possibilities associated with integrated planning of a river basin are clearly what has attracted the Mexican government, rather than a desire to plan the use of water resources in a co-ordinated way. Table 7 summarizes expenditure by the River Basin Commissions. In spite of the integrated nature of the work of the Commissions and their role in co-ordinating public investment, these figures do not include all public expenditures inside each basin, but only those channelled through the Commissions themselves. As we shall explain, the proportion of total public investment in a river basin actually controlled by a Commission, has varied from time to time and from place to place.

93

The 'march to the sea' as represented by the River Basin Projects has taken place in the direction of both the Pacific and the Gulf Coasts. The work of the Commissions has been largely determined by the differing nature of hydrologic problems encountered on each coast. On the Gulf, the problems have involved

Table 7. *Expenditures by the River Basin Commissions 1947–1964* (million pesos).

	Papaloapan		Grijalva		Tepalcatepec (incl. Balsas 1962–4)		Fuerte	
	Current prices	1960 prices[a]	Current prices	1960 prices[a]	Current prices	1960 prices[a]	Current prices	1960 prices[a]
1947	7·8	18·6			2·4	5·7		
48	16·0	35·8			11·5	25·8		
49	21·0	43·5			14·1	29·3		
1950	37·5	70·9			16·8	31·8		
51	77·9	122·3			20·7	32·5		
52	111·6	167·4			27·3	40·9	2·9	3·8
53	115·1	174·9	5·5	8·4	27·7	42·0	38·0	57·8
54	99·7	137·6	9·9	13·7	25·7	35·5	111·6	154·0
55	96·6	117·9	13·6	16·6	32·5	39·6	144·1	175·8
56	88·9	103·1	26·3	30·5	30·6	35·5	121·9	141·4
57	89·0	98·8	28·0	31·1	38·3	42·5	60·2	66·8
58	102·8	110·0	34·8	37·2	33·2	35·5	35·7	38·2
59	40·8	42·8	24·3	25·5	19·9	20·9	20·0	21·0
1960	24·3	24·3	57·9	57·9	26·6	26·6	32·9	32·9
61	30·0	29·7	49·4	48·9	10·8	10·8	23·2	23·0
62	21·1	20·5	246·9	239·5	22·3[b]	21·6	25·3	24·5
63	23·7	22·5	412·3	391·7	53·9[b]	51·2	42·0	39·9
64	20·0	19·8	135·0	129·6	54·4[b]	52·2	62·2	59·7
Total	1023·8	1360·4	1043·9	1030·6	468·8	579·9	720·0	838·8

Source: Mexico, Secretaría de Recursos Hidráulicos, *Informe Anual*, various years and information supplied or published by the individual Commissions.

a Current expenditures adjusted by the price index for public investment, *Manual de Estadísticas Básicas*, Banco de México.
b Includes expenditures for the whole of the Balsas Basin. For the Tepalcatepec Basin alone, current expenditures were 1962: 13.9 million, 1963: 13.8 million, 1964: 10.4 million.

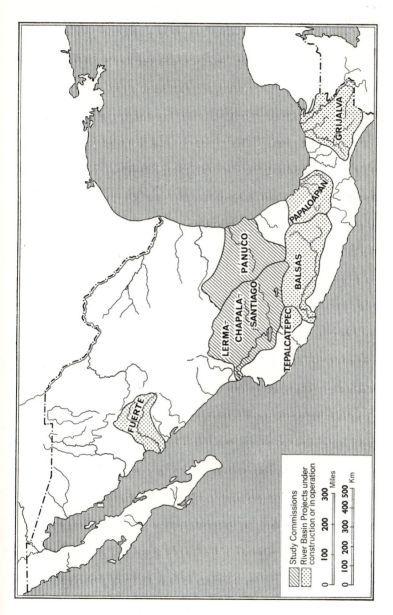

FIG. 2   Mexico: River Basin Commissions, 1963.

periodic flooding and the consequent lack of settlement and isolation of potentially fertile coastal lowland. On the Pacific the problem has been a shortage of rainfall that has restricted development of agriculture unless irrigation is practised. First we shall describe the work of the Papaloapan and Grijalva projects on the Gulf coasts, and then turn to the Tepalcatepec (which later became the Balsas) project and the Fuerte project.

The Papaloapan Commission

In 1947 the Papaloapan Commission was established and charged with the integrated development of the Papaloapan Basin. The basin includes not only the catchment area of the Papaloapan and its tributaries, but also those of a number of smaller rivers that also enter the Gulf of Mexico via the Laguna de Alvarado. Thus defined, the basin has an area of some 18,000 square miles, and contains parts of the states of Veracruz, Puebla, and Oaxaca. Forty-five per cent of the basin is relatively flat. Most of the level land is part of a rolling coastal plain, lying south-west of the coastal strip and enclosed to the north-east by the Sierra de San Martin, and to the south and west by the much more formidable Sierra Madre Oriental. These mountains have an average height of over 6,000 feet, but Orizaba, the highest mountain in Mexico, climbs to 18,700 feet in the north-west corner of the basin. The lower parts of the basin have a humid tropical climate, with temperatures averaging 78°F. and a rainfall of between 60 and 80 inches, concentrated between May and October. The eastern Sierra Madre slope receives an average of some 120 inches and some places receive over 160 inches. During the summer months, saturated masses of air move inward from the Gulf and lose their moisture as they rise and grow cooler over the mountains. Periodically, the area has been visited by Caribbean hurricanes, and the very heavy rainfall that they have brought, mostly in September and October, has been a major source of flooding. Such flooding has a long history, but up to 1944 it seemed to have been increasing due to silting up in the low part of the basin, reflecting in part deforestation in the upper levels of the basin, and in part natural geological events. In 1944 the worst recorded flood inundated some 200,000 hectares (half a million acres), in addition to the 300,000 hectares or so that are flooded annually. Over 100 persons were killed and hundreds of others were made homeless, and still more died from disease in the unhealthy conditions that followed the flood. Though earlier the problem of flooding had been studied and recommendations about control made, nothing had been done. Now a new study, carried out under the auspices of the National Irrigation Commission (the predecessor of the Ministry of Water Resources), suggested in 1946 that flood control by means of five dams on the tributaries of the Papaloapan, levees along its banks, and a by-pass canal, was feasible but expensive.[1]

The 1946 report emphasized the unhealthiness and considerable isolation of the basin. At that time a number of sizable towns with some industry straddled one of the two roads connecting Mexico City with Veracruz, and were served by the Ferrocarril Mexicano that links these cities, but the economy of the rest of the basin was overwhelmingly agricultural, and, in 1946, was served only by the most miserably inadequate transport facilities. There were practically no all-weather roads, and the few ill-equipped railroads were in an appalling state of repair. River traffic had preceded any other form of navigation but had been substantially curtailed by the increased silting of the rivers. Its chief function had become the carrying of sugar cane, which was planted along the banks of the Papaloapan and the Tesechoacan, to the mills, themselves connected by rail with the rest of the country. Sugar cane was, and still remains, commercially the most important crop. For at least fifteen years, the basin has accounted for over a quarter of the total cane production of Mexico. The San Cristobal mill is one of the largest in the world and very markedly the largest in Mexico. Cane is grown in a number of other areas in the basin. Also grown in the lower basin, in places with access to transport, were other tropical crops, of which pineapple was the most important. Bananas and tobacco were also grown but both were in decline.

Higher up, in the cooler but frost-free zone that lies between

[1] José S. Noriega, 'Control del Río Papaloapan: Preparación del plan de estudios definitivos y programa de construcción de las obras', *Ingeniería Hidráulica en México*, 1 (April–June 1947), pp. 5–65 (Part I) and 1 (July–September 1947), pp. 5–48 (Part 2).

four and six thousand feet, coffee was grown, the only commercial crop not grown adjacent to transport facilities. The main subsistence crop was, and still remains, maize, which accounted for over half the harvested area of the basin and about two-thirds of the upper parts of the basin. Here it is still produced with very primitive techniques—largely of the 'slash and burn' variety. The prevalence of primitive techniques reflected the considerable isolation of the basin. So did, even more dramatically, the fact that in 1950 a third of the area's population did not speak Spanish, and among them they spoke nine quite separate Indian languages.

The 1946 Report recommended establishing an organization with some administrative autonomy to undertake investigations and to begin construction. The recommendation was carried out by President Alemán and the Papaloapan Commission was established. The Commission, responsible to the Minister of Water Resources, was given full planning and construction authority for works needed for the integrated development of the basin. Its mandate extended not only to water resource investment—for the provision of flood control, irrigation, hydro-electric power, and drinking water—but also to the establishment of every type of communications network, to all matters of industrial and agricultural development, urbanization, and colonization. It was a further step in the tradition of trying to develop the regions away from the Mesa Central; but it also marked the inauguration of a new approach to the problem of regional development that is still, in a slightly modified way, being followed. At the time the Commission was created, explicit analogies were drawn between it and the Tennessee Valley Authority, and certainly TVA's successes were in large part responsible for the establishment of a programme of integrated river basin development in Mexico. These analogies, however, should not be pressed too far. TVA's autonomy was not adopted in Mexico, since the Commission's President was *ex officio* the Minister of Water Resources. The Commission's area of responsibility was wider than TVA's, although, like TVA, it has never had control over all matters of economic and social development, since other government authorities continue to operate in the basin, and the Commission cannot force them to act or prevent them from doing so.

The Papaloapan Commission was very much Alemán's creature. Its establishment entailed a flamboyant, large-scale gesture that was in keeping with the vigorous but somewhat grandiose style of his administration, and the identification of project with founder has been clearly marked. Alemán is a native of the basin itself and a former governor of the state of Veracruz in which the largest part of the basin lies. The Commission's headquarters were established in a wholly new town to be called Ciudad Alemán, and it was envisaged that although several cities were already established within the basin, Ciudad Alemán would grow to be an industrial city of 150,000 people. The first major work constructed was the Alemán Dam, and one of its functions was to supply water for the Alemán Irrigation Zone. Alemán has remained a controversial and potentially powerful political figure in Mexico. It appears that the identification of the project with the politician has had some effect on the varying political fortunes of the scheme, from the fanfare with which it was launched to its present state of near-suspension.

In its first three years the Commission vigorously started on flood control work. The Miguel Alemán Dam on the River Tonto is one of the largest in Latin America. Its reservoir contains nearly 9 billion cubic metres and covers 50,000 hectares. Because some 22,000 Mazatec Indians lived in this area, a large and difficult resettlement operation was required but only about half of those displaced stayed in the resettlement zones planned for them. In addition to the dam, levees were built to protect the western shore and the more populated areas on the eastern bank. Considerable areas in the north-east of the basin are still subject to flooding but about half of the area previously inundated is now protected.

The other important set of investments carried out in the early stages of the project was the building of a communications network. Two major roads were constructed out of Ciudad Alemán. One of these was constructed as a wide first-class highway in spite of the economic insignificance of the area at that time—a sign of extravagance and lack of planning that characterized other of the Commission's investments of this period. For example, the Alemán Dam was planned to provide supplemental irrigation to 160,000 hectares without adequate study of whether this was desirable or feasible. After the election of President Ruiz Cortines, the administration of the Commission changed, and so did its policy. Irrigation from the Alemán Dam was abandoned as the main canal needed was too expensive to justify the project; work on the dam itself continued but a smaller percentage of the funds went to flood control measures, and there was a general shift away from large-scale spectacular works towards the building of a secondary road network and feeder roads and towards smaller, more direct measures to promote agricultural development. These included two irrigation schemes to irrigate about 34,000 hectares in total. Several colonization schemes were started, together with a programme of agricultural credit, but these were not successful and a great deal of money was lost in credit operations. Poleman, who has studied closely the experience of the colonies, concludes that the principal cause of the failure was misdirection given by the Commission which had not carried out any preliminary experiments with possible crop patterns.[1] The difficulties were compounded by the extreme paternalism and inflexibility of the directions given along with the credit. In 1957, the credit operations virtually came to an end and with them the attempt at supervised colonization.

It cannot be said that the unhappy experiences of 1953–7 were solely to blame for the ending of the schemes. In fact, a 1955 plan called for a very large co-ordinated plan of colonization comprising 430,000 hectares. Rather, the colonies were the first casualties in a more drastic curtailment of activities that was accelerated by the death of the Commission's executive director in 1956. Alleged administrative irregularities may have contributed to the attitude of the López Mateos administration which reduced the budget of the Commission still further. Many of its functions are now performed exclusively by other Federal ministries or by local governments. Even its road building programme, which continued under the Ruiz Cortines administration, was sharply

[1] Thomas T. Poleman, *The Papaloapan Project* (Stanford: Stanford University Press, 1964), pp. 35–42.

reduced by the López Mateos administration and transferred to the Ministry of Communications and Public Works. In no way completed, the project exists today in a state of political suspension with a budget of less than a fifth of that it once enjoyed, scarcely adequate for the maintenance of works already constructed. Plans to construct another dam, much needed to reduce silting of the lower river, have been ready for many years, but no work has been carried out. The Commission still undertakes a considerable amount of long-range planning for a day in which funds may again become plentiful. Table 7 demonstrates in financial terms the extent to which the Commission's activities declined after 1958.

Superficially, the project gives the appearance of having been something of a white elephant, a monument to the inability of the Mexican government to plan anything that would carry over from one administration to future ones, and a perfect example of *proyectismo*, the tendency to proclaim the intention to carry out enormous schemes, but to fail to complete them successfully. Eyler Simpson describes it well:

Thus we have the Mexican who, having glimpsed a far goal, is disposed forthwith to shout, Vámonos! and taking thought of neither his own nor anyone else's past experience, to go galumphing down the road and devil take the consequences. This is one of the most attractive traits of the Mexican character and surprisingly enough, for certain kinds of undertakings, it often leads to success. But quite as often it leads to a cosmic weariness and a stopping by the roadside for a long siesta from which one wakes, forgetful of one's original intention, but rested and ready for another sally at some distant windmill. In either case, this sort of behaviour is of little use for the attaining of objectives which require careful planning and a steady hand over a long period of years.[1]

This is perhaps putting the matter harshly, and it would be unfair to suggest that the treatment of the Papaloapan project was in any way typical of the Mexican handling of large-scale development projects. But it is true that what has been accomplished is rather limited. An extremely rough estimate of the damage saved by

[1] Eyler Simpson, *The Ejido: Mexico's Way Out* (Chapel Hill: University of North Carolina Press, 1937), p. 581.

flood control between 1950 and 1960 (which appears to use 1944 prices) has been made by the Commission and comes to 116 million pesos.[1] In the basin, both the area cultivated and the value of production obtained rose at a very much faster rate than in the Republic as a whole, whereas before the basin's growth rate of agricultural output had been much slower. Between 1947 and 1957, the area harvested more than doubled, and the production of sugar in the basin grew from 167,000 metric tons in 1947–9 to 317,000 tons in 1956–8.[2] In 1958, production was more than a third of national output. Other growth was experienced. A paper factory was established, able to get its electricity from the Temescal plant when that began to operate in 1960. Generating capacity rose from 37,500 kW to 251,000 kW between 1947 and 1960. Most of the power was used outside the basin. The opening in 1963 of an aluminium plant at Veracruz means that the 154,000 kW Temescal plant is now used to full capacity. The project has, therefore, made some contribution to Mexico's economic progress. But in terms of the objective of regional decentralization the results have been disappointing. There has been no significant new local industry. The population of the basin grew between 1950 and 1960 but less fast than that of the Republic as a whole.[3] Part of the reason for this may be in the failure of the overall strategy—the fact that an agriculturally based scheme is unlikely to attract industry in itself, without some much more powerful attraction. But this has not led the Mexican government to abandon the strategy of the Papaloapan project. The Grijalva project, which is at present being vigorously pursued in an area very similar to the Papaloapan Basin some 200 miles to the south, has identical objectives to the Papaloapan project.

The Grijalva project

In June 1951, the Mexican government announced the creation of a Commission to promote the integrated development of the Grijalva and the Usamacinta river basins. These comprise nearly 48,000 square miles of south-eastern Mexico and western

[1] México, Sec. de Recursos Hidráulicos, 'Planificación Integral de la Cuenca del Papaloapan', reprinted from *Ingeniería Hidráulica en México* (1962), p. 36.
[2] *Ibid.*, p. 34.   [3] *Ibid.*, p. 30.

Guatemala, with most lying in the state of Tabasco and Chiapas. This is an area subject to the same climatic forces as the Papaloapan basin, and here too heavy rain falls in high mountains backing a coastal plain that is flooded regularly. The rivers join a few miles from Frontera, Tabasco, where they flow into the Gulf of Mexico. Their combined run-off averages nearly thirty per cent of the Mexican total.

It is believed that the level parts of the basins are very fertile and potentially important producers of tropical agricultural products. But the combination of flooded coastal plain and rugged mountains made land travel in this region virtually impossible until very recently, and the region has remained unhealthy, sparsely populated, and cut off from the rest of the country. Only in 1950 did a railway, keeping slightly above the level of the coastal plain, cross the region and form a land link between the peninsula of Yucatán and the rest of the country. Villahermosa, the capital of the state of Tabasco and the main city in the Grijalva basin, was not connected by land transport with the rest of the country until the construction of the first coastal road in 1958.

Apart from the agricultural potential of this region, the massive water resources hold very considerable promise of hydroelectric power generation for domestic consumption and for export to Central America and the water resource development will naturally continue to concentrate on flood control and hydroelectric power generation.

So far only a relatively small amount of the region's economic potential has been tapped. The Commission has concentrated entirely on the Grijalva basin, which is some 20,000 square miles in area with about one-tenth in Guatemala. Progress has been inevitably slow. Having started work in 1953, the Commission's first years were occupied in carrying out studies, drainage work and a coastal road which itself required considerable drainage and flood defence works. As a result of the studies it was decided to build the extremely large earth-filled Malpaso Dam—in several dimensions, the largest in Latin America at the time it was built, and work started on an access road in 1958.[1] The dam was

---

[1] The name Malpaso is the one commonly used but strictly it refers to the site—the actual name of the dam is Netzahualcoytl.

completed in 1965 at a cost of more than one billion pesos (80 million dollars). The Federal Electricity Commission has since been constructing generating capacity of 760,000 kW which will ultimately be expanded to 900,000 kW and which will eventually be capable of producing nearly 3 billion kW annually. The first power was generated in 1968.

Apart from building the dam and drainage work and a few minor activities such as providing drinking water and sewage systems, the Commission have been mainly involved with the first stage of what is intended to be a very extensive settlement programme coupled with the provision of irrigation and the promotion of tropical agriculture. The first stage of this, the Chontalpa project, begun in 1966 and planned to take about a decade, involves draining and bringing under irrigation some 350,000 acres, less than half of which is presently cultivated. A later stage of the project will develop about 325,000 acres more. In the first stage some 11,000 families will benefit, about 63,000 people, at an estimated cost of about 125 million dollars, about 110 million of which is the cost of basic works of irrigation and agricultural improvement. Only a small proportion will be paid by the farmers themselves, at least in the first ten years. A farmer will pay for his home, perhaps with earnings from labour contributed to the project, pay something towards land clearance and do the internal drainage works himself. Expected returns are said by the Commission to be high now that a great deal of originally planned expenditure on the social amenities of the area has been eliminated.

Those benefited initially were already inhabitants of the area. No doubt later settlers will come from outside the region. The problem that the project seems bound to encounter then is one which reduced the chances of success of the ill-fated Papaloapan colonization schemes and which follows from the fact that agricultural conditions in the crowded highland areas of Mexico from which settlers would come are quite different from the tropical areas of the Gulf Coast. This means that the potential benefits of migrating from the densely populated areas of the Mesa Central must be very great indeed if large numbers of people are to be induced to move to the Grijalva river basin.

Given the present availability of a great many opportunities for enterprising people willing to take risks in areas where irrigation is being introduced without settlement programmes, such people may be repelled rather than attracted by new opportunities in an isolated and unknown region which is being administered by a new government organization with all the bureaucratic problems that this might create.[1] Given the alternative opportunities and the substantial government-provided inducements which the settlement schemes offer, the types of people attracted may not be those most willing to wait the several years that will be required before any returns are visible. In the interim, conditions are likely to be difficult, as in any frontier area. The ability of the colonization project to achieve the expected high returns depends on its success in overcoming this problem.

Even if the settlement project is as fully successful as its sponsors hope, the impact that such schemes can possibly have in shifting the locational balance of the agricultural population of Mexico and in relieving the pressure on land in the crowded central regions is obviously limited. In the first five years of the 1960s the national labour force in the agricultural sector rose by about 170,000 people a year. The scheme will benefit about a thousand families a year with two to three members of the labour force in each—i.e. roughly 3,000 members of the labour force a year are affected at a cost of over 3,000 dollars each, not including the cost of flood-control provided by the Malpaso Dam. To absorb 170,000 people annually at 3,000 dollars a head would involve an annual investment of over 500 million dollars—something over one-eighth of Mexico's total investment. It should be noted that this may not be very expensive compared with the cost of employing a person in industry, but available data does not permit any direct comparison of the costs of creating a job in the industrial sector and in the agricultural sector. The 1961 Industrial Census of Mexico indicated that there was at least 5,000 dollars of capital invested for every worker in the manufacturing sector. Unfortunately little reliance can be placed on the Industrial Census. This estimate is much lower than the probable cost of

[1] This was suggested to us by several people connected with various actual and proposed colonization schemes.

employing an additional man in industry with modern techniques, since census figures include figures from much older, small-scale industry. For example, a UN study of the optimal technology for Latin American textile plants estimated that investment per employed person was 20,659 US dollars in 1965, in plants working three shifts.[1]

Employment on the supervised settlement project is not of course the only permanent employment the project will create. Other land will become more intensively utilized once protected from floods, and the provision of generated electric power will contribute to greater industrial employment, though much of this is likely to be outside the basin. Gulf Coast petro-chemical complexes are being established, and these will require electric power. Malpaso power is also to be fed into a national grid. In his fourth annual Presidential Report delivered on 1 September 1968, President Díaz Ordaz linked the construction of hydro-electric power facilities at Malpaso to the expansion of aluminium, steel, car, fertilizer, paper and phosphorous factories.[2] But what was involved in each instance was not divulged.

Attempting to assess the combined effects of the Papaloapan and Grijalva projects, it is clear that two decades of heavy investment in the Gulf region have had only very limited effect in terms of decentralizing the location of economic activity. Hydro-electric schemes have not proved a marked attraction to labour intensive industry, though the Gulf Coast's petro-chemical and aluminium industries have benefited from the abundance of local power. Agricultural development has taken place at only a moderate pace and has not led to much migration into the area. A good deal of the investment carried out in communications may no doubt be justified in terms of the political desire to bring scattered communities a sense of integration with the Mexican nation, even if it would not be justified by more purely economic criteria.

In the details of the investment in the Gulf Coast projects it appears, *prima facie*, that economically there has been a great deal

[1] Quoted in W. Paul Strassman, *Technological Change and Economic Development: The Manufacturing Experience of Mexico and Puerto Rico* (Ithaca N.Y.: Cornell University Press, 1963), p. 154.
[2] *El Mercado de Valores*, 9 September 1968, p. 595.

of waste though we have not been able to test this rigorously. In the early years of the Papaloapan project much of the expenditure was needlessly extravagant, but it appears unlikely that the switch from the Papaloapan project to the Grijalva could have been justified in economic terms.

The Tepalcatepec and Balsas projects

The Tepalcatepec project, whose activities we shall describe in much greater detail in the next part of this study, was the first of the river basin projects to develop the hot dry area of the Pacific Coast. The Tepalcatepec Commission was created by presidential decree in May 1947, with a mandate very similar to that of the Papaloapan Commission established three months earlier. It was charged with the integrated development of the Tepalcatepec river basin. To this end it was to have 'the fullest facilities for the planning, proposing, and construction of works for irrigation and for the development of sources of energy, for sanitary engineering, for establishing communications, including roads, railways, telegraphs and telephones, and for the creation and expansion of population centres'.[1] It was also to have power over industrial, agricultural, credit and colonization affairs, and might intervene in agrarian matters.

The Tepalcatepec basin, some 7,000 square miles, located mainly in the state of Michoacán, with a small area in the state of Jalisco, is less than 40 per cent of the size of the region developed by the Papaloapan Commission, and the whole scale of the project has been much smaller. Between 1947 and 1960, for example, the Papaloapan Commission spent 927 million pesos, and the Tepalcatepec Commission, 323 million (both unadjusted for price changes).

The Tepalcatepec basin flows into the much larger River Balsas. The 43,000 square miles of the Balsas became the responsibility of a new River Basin Commission in 1960 and this Commission then absorbed the Tepalcatepec Commission. Initially it made little difference to the work of the Tepalcatepec Commission, and

[1] Quoted in Vincente Fernández Bravo, *Estudio Económico Social de la Cuenca del Río Tepalcatepec* (México, D.F.: U.N.A.M., Escuela Nacional de Economía, Tésis por Lic. en Economía, 1959), p. 231.

at first the most active area of the new Commission remained the Tepalcatepec basin. The personnel was little changed; the executive director of the Balsas Commission is ex-President Lázaro Cárdenas who personally served in the same capacity for the Tepalcatepec Commission. Under Cárdenas, the administration of the Commission has had much more continuity than the administration of the Papaloapan Commission, and it would appear that the changing ideas of successive Mexican governments have had less effect on the work carried out. There has been some diminution of its activities in the Tepalcatepec basin in recent years as greater attention has been paid to the development of other areas of the Balsas basin, and further development remains to be undertaken, but there has been no drastic slowdown with critical parts of the project as yet unstarted, as in the case of Papaloapan. This fact and the relatively small size of the project make it somewhat easier to assess the impact of the scheme upon regional development, and this assessment, accompanied by a much more detailed account of the Commission's activities, will form Chapter 6.

The strategy being adopted in the Balsas basin is likely to be much the same as that adopted for the Tepalcatepec basin. The Balsas, with a run-off of nearly 14,000 million cubic metres, is Mexico's largest river flowing into the Pacific. It rises in the volcanic area and in the Oaxaca mountains to the south-east of Mexico City and for most of its length flows west. The basin is very mountainous, but its flatter parts, lying to the north of the river, offer scope for irrigation. Like similar low-lying plains in Mexico, these hot, dry areas are known as the Tierra Caliente. In the Tierra Caliente near Ciudad Altamirano, two dams have been constructed, the first stage in plans to irrigate eventually some 80,000 hectares. The similarity between this region and the one chosen for a case study in Michoacán will lead us to say more about it when we assess the Commission's investments.

To the west of Ciudad Altamirano the river joins the Tepalcatepec and turns sharply south to flow through the Sierra Madre del Sur into the Pacific. On this final stretch of the river the Commission has constructed two large dams. El Infiernillo, the largest, is now generating power for Mexico City with a capacity of 600,000 kW. A smaller dam below it at La Villita will eventually be used to produce electricity for a projected steel mill which is to be constructed on the coast. The electric furnaces will utilize iron ore from the nearby Las Truchas deposits and will be linked to the rest of Mexico by a new railway and a port to be built near the mouth of the Balsas. The Tepalcatepec Commission and later the Balsas Commission have played a vigorous part in the promotion of the steel complex. In spite of the fact that the iron ore deposits lay outside the Tepalcatepec basin and studying them was far from the normal range of expertise possessed by a River Basin Commission, initial studies were made by the Tepalcatepec Commission, later aided by the Krupp Company. In the 1960s when the Las Truchas site was only one of a number of possible sites under consideration for new steel development—and in many ways by no means the most promising, since although the iron ore deposits are rich there were no facilities of any kind and virtually no population there—the Balsas Commission became something of a pressure group in official circles urging steel development there rather than elsewhere.

The work done by the Tepalcatepec and Balsas Commissions in this area illustrates both the flexible use which the Federal government has been able to make of such a decentralized body with broad powers whose authority cuts across other administrative boundaries, and the fact that once established such an agency tends to make itself into a pressure group for regional development. If it remains politically in favour, as has the Balsas Commission, it may be very effective. If, like the Papaloapan Commission, it becomes associated with politicians who are out of favour, then the project will do badly irrespective of its economic merits.

Other work done by the Balsas Commission has been primarily social investment in the Oaxaca mountains, very much on the lines of the work by the Papaloapan Commission in similar conditions and, earlier, by the Tepalcatepec Commission in the mountain areas of Michoacán.

The Fuerte Project

The progress of irrigated agriculture in the north-western valleys of the Pacific Coast has been the brightest event in Mexican agricultural development since the war. One of these, the basin of the River Fuerte, became the responsibility of a River Basin Commission, formed in June 1951 along the lines of the Papaloapan and Tepalcatepec Commissions, to promote its integrated development. With an annual run-off of between 5 and 6 billion cubic metres (though this has varied between less than 2 and more than 12 billion) the Fuerte is the largest river in the north-western region of Mexico in terms of flow. It drains an area of some 12,000 square miles in the states of Sinaloa, Sonora, Durango, and Chihuahua. The Commission is active, however, only in the irrigable lower part of the basin, entirely within the state of Sinaloa, and not, as yet, with the sparsely populated areas of the Sierra Madre Occidental or the plateau, where there are unexploited timber and mineral resources. The principal function of the Commission has been the improvement, conservation and expansion of the Fuerte irrigation district. Indeed it has been criticized for its failure to carry out integrated development in the manner envisaged by the Alemán administration, and for its concentration on the irrigation possibilities and the serious flood problems of the lower basin. It is not therefore a good example of an attempt to promote regional development by integrated river basin investment, but its contribution to north-western agricultural development is itself interesting and important. The basin and its development, therefore, deserve a brief description.

Irrigation in the basin goes back to the 1890s when the first canal was dug by an American Owenite socialist community which pumped water from the southern bank of the Fuerte river.[1] Shortly afterwards, the lands and the canal passed into the hands of one Benjamin F. Johnston, who built a sugar mill in the tiny community of Los Mochis in 1903, to be operated by his United Sugar Company. The company dominated the entire cultivated area of the lower basin from that time until its land and water rights were expropriated in 1938 and became the property of the newly created SICAE (Sociedad de Interés Colectivo Agrícola Ejidal). By a 1943 presidential decree, however, the ejidatarios

---

[1] The history of the basin's development may be found in Mario Gill, *La Conquista del Valle del Fuerte* (México D.F., 1957).

were compelled to continue growing cane for the mill; they did so under protest, since it was argued, not without reason, that sugar was a relatively unprofitable crop at such a northern latitude.[1] At the time of the expropriation, irrigation water was still pumped out of the river. In 1947, however, the SICAE canal (later, Canal Valle del Fuerte) which could potentially irrigate 40,000 hectares, about twice the then irrigable area, started to operate. The Commission later greatly enlarged this canal. Another canal, which pre-dated the Commission's work, was constructed on the right bank to irrigate some 25,000 hectares. Under the Commission the irrigable area has expanded impressively to some 230,000 hectares and, as can be seen from Table 8, so has the total area irrigated, except for occasional setbacks due to flooding.

Table 8. *River Fuerte Commission: cultivated area by major crops, 1952/3–1965/6, selected years ('000 hectares)*

	1952–3[a]	1955–6	1959–60	1962–3	1965–6
Cotton	12·2	12·7	48·7	28·6	50·3
Rice	—	0·9	55·7	26·3	—
Sugar cane	8·4	7·7	11·0	11·2	22·3
Safflower	—	—	1·7	7·1	21·5
Grain sorghums	—	0·4	0·5	15·1	15·4
Wheat	0·9	17·6	1·5	32·1	17·8
Other	26·3	21·0	37·3	31·7	51·1
Total	47·8	60·3	156·3	152·3	178·4

[a] 1 June 1952 to 31 May 1953, and so on for the other years.

Sources: Comisión del Río Fuerte, *Boletín Valle del Fuerte.*

The most important step in this development was the building of the earthfilled Miguel Hidalgo Dam between 1953 and 1956. A major objective, apart from irrigation, was to control floods which had been serious in the lower basin. Unfortunately the

[1] Mario Gill, *La Conquista del Valle del Fuerte*, pp. 156–63; Centro de Investigaciones Agrarias, *Los Distritos de Riego del Noroeste: Tenecia y Aprovechamiento de la Tierra* (México D.F.: Instituto Mexicano de Investigaciones Económicas, 1957), pp. 78–81.

original planned size of the dam was reduced before it was built and the dam was clearly too small, a fact demonstrated by serious floods in 1955, 1958 and 1960. The latter destroyed crops on some 40,000 hectares and destroyed irrigation facilities. In consequence the dam had to be enlarged between 1962 and 1964.

The Federal Electricity Commission built a plant with a capacity of 60,000 kW at the dam, contributing to the rapid growth of a thriving agricultural area whose chief town is Los Mochis. In addition to the sugar mill, a number of cotton ginneries and other processing and service activities have been established. A long-postponed railway reached the area in 1961 and has helped the export of winter vegetables, particularly tomatoes, to the United States. The main growth has come in cotton, wheat and rice although both of the latter have declined again below their former peak output.

The ownership of land in the irrigation district is roughly equally distributed between ejidal and private ownership. Ejidos here have made an important contribution to the growth of most of the major cash crops of the region, and are far from behaving as the tradition-bound subsistence crop producers which many people associate with ejidos, an idea derived from ejidal performance in poorer agricultural areas of the central region. Ejidatarios do, however, plant a much larger proportion of subsistence crops than do private farmers and a smaller proportion of wheat and tomatoes. Where the risks involved are high, as with perishable tomatoes exported to a very competitive and unstable United States winter market, private farmers appear more prepared to take them, and the fact that they, unlike ejidatarios, can mortgage their land makes them better credit risks.

The future of this area seems bright. Salinity has been a serious problem giving rise to the need to improve the drainage of the area to combat salinity, but this has been tackled. There are various plans to expand the area irrigated, increase power generation and improve flood control. One such scheme, the El Sabino project, is designed to irrigate a further 60,000 hectares. The first stage of this, to bring under irrigation some 40,000 hectares, mostly not cultivated at all at present, would benefit 3,700 farmers and about 2,000 of these would come from outside the project zone. As with the Grijalva project, however, such settlement is expensive; the project requires an initial investment of 48.3 million dollars or about 13,500 dollars per family, which is even more expensive than the Grijalva project, and even this figure makes no allowance for any contribution made by the Miguel Hidalgo Dam to the control of the whole river. Work done outside water resource investment has been slight, though the Commission has done some on local roads, helped in the town planning of Los Mochis, installed drinking water and sewage facilities there, and provided medical service for its employees. It has also, in what is an interesting development that may become more general throughout Mexico, built a number of facilities with ejidal money. All people who receive irrigation pay a water fee of 100 pesos per year, but the ejidatarios also pay 'cuotas de cooperación' of a similar amount for ten years. These quotas are spent through the Commission on educational facilities and public facilities and services in the ejidos. In this area, however, most of the investments complementary to the water resource investment have been made by other agencies. It does not appear that this has in any way detracted from the efficiency of the Commission's investments in the region.

The Lerma-Chapala-Santiago project

The largest river basin wholly obtained within the borders of the Republic of Mexico is the Lerma-Chapala-Santiago basin. The River Lerma rises in the state of Mexico near Toluca. Leaving the Toluca basin, the river drops sharply into the basin of Guanajuato. Descending more gently, it then crosses the important agricultural area of the Bajío in Guanajuato, northern Michoacán, and Jalisco, and enters Lake Chapala. This area is all on the densely populated Mesa Central. Out of Chapala flows the River Santiago whose sub-basin is quite different. It plunges through gorges in sparsely populated mountainous country, flowing out to the sea in Nayarit. In addition to the five states mentioned above, parts of Aguascalientes, Durango, Querétaro, and Zacatecas are in the basin. The 50,000 square miles of the basin are 6·6 per cent of the area of the Republic but in 1960 about 6·7 million people, almost 18 per cent of the total population, lived there.

The upper part of the basin, including most of the area drained by the River Lerma, is very different from the other river basins developed by other Commissions because of its long history as a rich agricultural area and an industrial centre with high rates of economic growth. The lower basin, drained by the River Santiago, contains many isolated and backward Indian communities. In the upper basin, the Bajío is an important source of fruit and vegetables, including the valuable strawberry crop which is almost entirely exported to the United States at a time when American growers have no product to market. Although its commercial agricultural output has been recently overshadowed by rapid growth in other regions this area continues to be an important source of food for the capital city. Manufacturing industries in the whole basin have experienced fast rates of growth in recent years (9·6 per cent annually). Finally, communications and other social overhead facilities are as well developed as in any area of the Republic. Regional output was nearly 16 per cent of the national product in 1965 and was growing faster than that of the nation as a whole.

This short description of the basin indicates how different in character it is from the ones that we have been discussing, and it is clear that the objectives we considered for the other projects are not quite in keeping here. The potential for water resource development is fair. The annual run-off of the Santiago into the Pacific is about 6,000 million cubic metres. There are already hydroelectric generating schemes on both rivers, but the Santiago, in particular, offers scope for much more. Less than 3 per cent of the cultivable area of the basin is now irrigated; future irrigation projects have been proposed but most are small. Though water is an important and scarce resource in the basin, shared water resources problems hardly seem to constitute a suitable focus for the economic planning of the region through which the River Lerma flows. This is partly because, as also occurs in the Balsas basin to a lesser extent, what is in the basin is so diverse, and even more because of what the basin leaves out. Except for Guanajuato, Aguascalientes, and Nayarit, less than half of each state is included in the basin, and often the portions of a state omitted share common problems with the parts included. The

Valley of Mexico is not in the basin but, as we have seen, it quite dominates the economy of the whole Mesa Central. As a unit for regional development, the basin appears at once too big and too small. It is too big because it is so varied, and therefore lacks any focal common problem. It is too small because the problems it has are shared equally with surrounding areas. It is so big that it offers all the difficulties attendant to planning a large region but it is too small to solve the manifest problems of the Mesa Central. Nevertheless, it is clear that river basin planning is a politically acceptable way of obtaining the co-operation of state governments and government agencies who might refuse to surrender authority to other agencies.

The Lerma-Chapala-Santiago Commission was established in November 1950. It is not a River Basin Commission like the others, and it has operated on a much smaller budget. It consists of a representative of the Ministry of Water Resources, one of the Federal Electricity Commission and one each of the five principal states—México, Guanajuato, Michoacán, Jalisco, and Nayarit—plus technical advisers. Also on the Commission is a representative of the Federal District which, although not in the basin, draws part of its water from the basin through the Lerma aqueduct. The Commission's principal function has been the study of the problems of the basin and the making of recommendations to other agencies of the Mexican government. Occasionally, however, it has been permitted to carry out small irrigation, flood control, and water supply projects of its own in co-operation with local authorities. From 1963 to 1967 its staff was engaged in an extensive study of regional development inside the basin, financed by a loan from the Inter-American Development Bank. It is quite possible that the economic objections to the use of a River Basin Commission for planning on the Mesa Central are outweighed by the political advantages of being able to do any planning at all.

Other regional development policies

Apart from the River Basin Projects, the Federal Government has had little in the way of a regional development policy. A frequently heard criticism of its programme of tax exemptions to encourage the establishment of manufacturing industries under the so-called Law of New and Necessary Industries is that among a long list of criteria which must be considered by the Ministry of Industry and Trade in deciding whether to grant exemption no mention is made of the location of industry concerned.[1] The ministry also takes no overt account of locational considerations when deciding whether an industry merits protection under the import licensing system. Locational factors may, however, sometimes be taken into account when direct negotiations take place between individual firms and the government, just as when a foreign-owned firm is seeking permission to operate. An offer to locate outside the Valley of Mexico may be a useful bargaining weapon of a firm; the government may be able to make location outside the Valley of Mexico a condition of granting some particular concessions. Instances where political pressure has clearly influenced the location of a firm can be found. But there is no way of knowing how widely and with what force such pressure has been applied.

There are two other exceptions to the Federal government's relative lack of activity in the sphere of industrial location. The first was the establishment of a heavy industrial complex in Ciudad Sahagún, Hidalgo, in an old and exhausted mining area with heavy unemployment. The main investments here took place during the 1950s, largely with Nacional Financiera funds. The second exception has been the policy towards the areas of Mexico which border the United States.

In the 1930s, when communication between the western border areas (i.e., those bordering on California and Arizona), and the rest of the country were still very bad, these areas were permitted to import with very much less in the way of import restriction and duties than the rest of the country. Quintana Roo, an even more isolated part of the Yucatán peninsular bordering British Honduras (now Belize), also received similar concessions. Certain towns further to the east along the US border were given some rather less generous concessions in the early postwar years. The persistence of these import concessions, as communications have

---

[1] For further details see Timothy King, *Mexico: Industrialisation and Trade Policies since 1940*, Chapter 4.

improved, and at a period when many people in Mexico have been worried about whether the domestic market is large enough to permit the exploitation of industrial economics of scale, reflects the political impossibility of repealing the concessions. The concessions do however deprive Mexican manufacturers of quite a large market for certain products, since the areas have very high incomes per head, and they make smuggling into the rest of the country considerably easier. Mexican manufacturers are given a subsidy of 25 to 30 per cent on rail freight to all border areas (whether imports are admitted freely or not). Nevertheless those areas receiving import concessions still tend to be dominated by US goods.

The border areas raise other problems for the Mexican government. Incomes are higher in this area, helped by the fact that many residents have been absorbed into the US economy and cross the border daily to work. The high incomes and the possibility of eventually entering the United States attracts substantial net in-migration and causes a continual employment problem. Because the areas are visited by millions of American visitors high unemployment is embarrassing to the Mexican government and since 1961 there has been a programme to improve the amenities of the border towns. Since 1966, firms have been entitled to import raw materials free of duty without needing to add a specified minimum percentage of value domestically, provided that the entire production so assisted is re-exported. Wage differentials between the United States and the Mexican border towns are sufficient to make this scheme very attractive to US firms which carry out labour intensive operations, and considerable interest has been expressed by, among others, electronics firms. Just what this is likely to mean in terms of long-term employment, however, is not clear and the amount of labour involved in actual or planned projects was (up to the autumn of 1967) only a few thousand. The success of the programme depends to a considerable degree on the willingness of the United States to charge duty only on the amount of value actually added in Mexico, and it is not very surprising to find that the programme has already attracted some US opposition. As the programme grows, so presumably will this opposition, and it must therefore be doubtful how much impact this programme can hope to have on total Mexican employment problems.

Apart from these limited policies of the Federal government to alter industrial location, most state governments try independently to attract industry. This they do by offering exemption from state taxes, which are not themselves very important, to newly established manufacturing industries, often for a considerable period. This is now so widely practised that differences between state laws in this respect can scarcely be an important factor influencing industrial location. Even before its practice became so widespread, it seems unlikely that tax exemption had much effect on location. A study of the Federal District concluded that for only a small group of industries were taxes a significant element in costs, and that the attraction of the market appeared to be a much greater influence on location.[1] Zacatecas has had industrial promotion laws that include tax exemption since 1930, Colima since 1934, Aguascalientes since 1935, Chiapas since 1939 and Tlaxcala since 1940.[2] These states have not experienced significant industrialization.

Another device used by state governments has been industrial parks. A number of cities, within the Central region but outside the Valley of Mexico, have these. Usually this has involved making land, well supplied with social overhead capital, easily available to manufacturing firms. The existence of such parks may have facilitated the industrial growth of areas on the Mesa Central away from the Valley of Mexico. There is no evidence that it has caused any further decentralization of industry, and this certainly seems unlikely.

In summary, the River Basin Projects have been the only serious systematic attempt to develop the regions away from the Mesa Central. They are not, of course, the only places away from the Mesa Central where development is taking place or public investment going on, but the River Basin programme is the only programme which counts among its explicit objectives regional development and the decentralization of industry. In the last

[1] Gustavo Romero Kolbeck and Victor Urquidi, *La exención fiscal en el Distrito Federal como Instrumento de Atracción de Industrias* (México D.F. 1952).
[2] Ernesto López Malo, *Ensayo sobre Localización de la Industria*, p. 216.

chapter we shall summarize its collective achievements in this respect. Before that, however, we shall first discuss the work of the Tepalcatepec Commission in much greater detail as a case study of the impact of one project in the region in which it is situated. We shall do this in the next part of this book.

5

THE TEPALCATEPEC RIVER BASIN

The Tepalcatepec river basin is located in the states of Michoacán and Jalisco, about two hundred miles west of Mexico City. In 1947, the Comisión del Tepalcatepec was established to develop this area on an integrated basis. This part of the book describes the Commission's activities and its results. This chapter presents a general description of the region's natural resources, its economic and social structure, and the Commission's regional development programme. The next chapter traces the economic progress of the region since large-scale irrigation works built by the Commission started to operate.

PHYSICAL CHARACTERISTICS

The basin's 7,000 square miles extend over four distinct geographic zones. Following terminology commonly used in Mexico, we shall describe them as the Tierra Fría, the Tierra Templada, the Tierra Caliente, and the Costa Sierra. The Commission defined its area of activity to extend beyond the hydrologic basin so as to include parts of the two mountain ranges between which it lies: The Meseta Central to the north and the Sierra Madre del Sur to the south.[1]

The highest part of the Meseta Central is known as the Tierra

---

[1] As is true of most geographical areas, there are many ways to define the limits of the Tepalcatepec basin. This study uses the Tepalcatepec Commission's definition which is based on a hydrologic basin. In the course of its work, the Commission enlarged the zone to include some municipios (the basic unit of local government) not properly in the hydrologic basin. Of the thirty-two municipios in Michoacán which are in the basin, wholly or in part, only twenty-seven have more than one-half of their territory in the basin, as defined by the Tepalcatepec Commission; the other five municipios are not generally included in discussions of the Commission's impact on the region, and this practice was followed in this study. A list of the municipios included in the basin can be found in Table 10.

Fría (cold country) because of its inhospitable climate. Temperatures often descend to freezing and more than 50 inches of rain falls annually (Table 9). The Tierra Fría is a volcanic belt on the southern edge of the Mesa Central. It lies above 5,250 feet and generally to the north of Uruapan, the largest city in the basin. The highest point in this mountainous area is nearly 13,000 feet above sea level and was formed by the volcanic cone named Tancitaro. The most recent volcanic action formed the Paricutín mountain between 1943 and 1952 and had widespread repercussions throughout the basin. As a result of the volcanoes (there are about 800 in the region) and dense forests, there is a highly permeable soil which rests on top of an impermeable layer of volcanic rock to form a large natural storage area for the heavy rains common in this zone. The vast underground reservoir supplies about 1,824 million cubic metres of water annually to springs and rivers at an almost constant rate of 57·8 cubic metres per second. In spite of these ample water resources, the Tierra Fría is the poorest part of the basin in other physical features. Since it is a mountainous and densely forested zone, its soil has been rendered thin and infertile by volcanic action and centuries of primitive agricultural techniques. The soil is so permeable that surface streams are absent and irrigation prohibitively expensive.

South and to the west of the Tierra Fría lies the Tierra Templada (the temperate zone) extending from about 5,250 feet down

Table 9. *Meteorological data in the Tepalcatepec basin*

	Tierra Caliente	Tierra Templada	Tierra Fría	Costa Sierra
Temperature (°F)				
Average	80	60	50	60
Average—May	90	70	63	70
Average—January	77	60	54	60
Rainfall (inches)				
Average	20	45	55	50

Source: G. Aguirre Beltrán, *Problemas de la Población Indígena de la Cuenca del Tepalcatepec* (*Memorias del Instituto Nacional Indigenista*, Vol. 3, México, 1952).

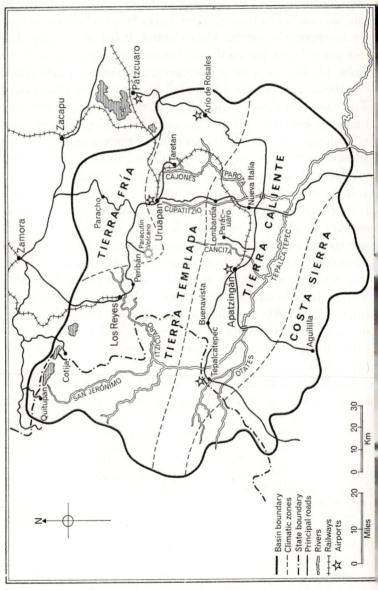

Fig. 3   The Tepalcatepec river basin.

to about 2,000 feet. Much of this land is steeply sloping and even in some cultivated areas the soil is stony and far from level. The zone is generally both drier and warmer than the Tierra Fría, and parts of the region are both cultivable and irrigable, making this area much more important from an agricultural standpoint than the Tierra Fría. In the north-west of the basin are several valleys that were once small lakes, but which have long since been drained and irrigated. Small-scale irrigation is also possible near the urban centres of Uruapan and Ario de Rosales.

The principal rivers of the basin originate in springs in the Tierra Templada. The River Tepalcatepec itself is formed by the union of the Itzícuaro and San Jerónimo which irrigate the north-western part of the basin. Their flows are controlled by two storage dams, one of which was constructed and an earlier one improved by the Commission. The Tepalcatepec flows down into a valley known as the Tierra Caliente (hot country). Here it is joined on its left bank by its three main tributaries, the Cancita (Los Bancos), the Marques, formed from the union of the Cupatitzio and the Cajones, and the Casilda (La Parota). At the south-eastern end of the basin the Tepalcatepec joins the River Balsas as that river turns southward to flow into the Pacific.

The three main tributaries have a combined flow of about 43 cubic metres per second, about three times the run-off of the Tepalcatepec. Although the volume of this flow is not large when compared to other river basins, its economic impact is important because of the constancy of the flow which eliminated the necessity of constructing large storage dams to regulate the supply of water for hydroelectricity or irrigation. In addition, sudden changes in altitude along the Cupatitzio provide a naturally suitable geographic setting for the location of three sets of hydro-electric turbines. These same geographic features would have made it difficult, if not impossible, to construct the dams necessary to control the waters had the flow not been constant.

These rivers flow down into the Tierra Caliente which is about 45 miles wide and 75 miles long. The valley is about 1,300 feet above sea level and without irrigation it would be a barren land with rocky soil; high temperatures and low rainfall (Table 9) add to its steppe-like appearance. This part of the basin has fertile, in part alluvial, flat lands which are quite suitable for mechanized agriculture once the stones are cleared away. The winter-free climate here permits two crop cycles a year.

To the south of the Tierra Caliente lies the Sierra Madre del Sur (Costa Sierra) which rises to 8,000 feet. The climate of the area in these mountains is very much like that of the Tierra Templada; but since it has fewer trees than the Meseta Central to the north, its soil is more eroded and agricultural yields are lower. A few rivers, of which the most important is the Otates, descend to the right bank of the Tepalcatepec during the summer when torrential rains fall in the Costa Sierra; natural conditions preclude subterranean storage of the waters.

THE SOCIO-ECONOMIC STRUCTURE OF THE REGION BEFORE 1950

Differences in environment and in history have produced distinct settlement patterns in the four parts of the basin, whose origins antedate the arrival of the Spanish.[1] At the time of the Spanish conquest, Tarascan speaking people lived in the Tierra Templada and parts of the Tierra Fría while the Tierra Caliente and the Costa Sierra contained scattered groups of Tarascans as well as people who were predominantly Nahuatl-speaking. The Tarascans submitted to the Spaniards without war and consequently were not enslaved. In the mountain areas, Tarascan culture was almost undisturbed, except for some adaptation of their former religion to Christianity. Of course, like all Indians of the western hemisphere, the Tarascans suffered from epidemics of recently introduced European diseases, but, unlike the Nahuatls of the Tierra Caliente and of the Costa Sierra, they were not virtually wiped out.[2]

[1] Aguirre Beltrán examined the influence of the conquerors on the basin's population in great detail. His colourful account of this material is only suggested in the broadest outline in this section. Cf. *Problemas de la Población Indígena de la Cuenca del Tepalcatepec* (*Memorias del Instituto Nacional Indigenista*, Vol. 3, Mexico, 1952), Part 2.

[2] Aguirre Beltrán estimated that the population of the southern part of the basin dropped from 50,000 to only 4,000 between 1520 and the end of the century whereas that of the Tierra Fría and the Tierra Templada dropped from 58,000 to 30,000.

Part of the devastation in the southern parts of the basin was due to disease. Until the Commission drained the swamps near Apatzingán, the Tierra Caliente was always unhealthy, and only the immunity of the inhabitants to familiar diseases had permitted survival. The introduction of new diseases tipped this precarious balance. The enslaving of the native population to work in cacao plantations and in the gold and copper mines of the Costa Sierra and on the western fringes of the Tierra Caliente also led to a drastic reduction in population.

In the early years of the seventeenth century, Negro slaves were brought to work in the copper mines and the sugar mills of the Tierra Caliente and the Tierra Templada. As the population slowly increased, miscegenation virtually eliminated the pure Tarascan from the lower parts of the basin. In the nineteenth century, Apatzingán gained fame when the Constitution of 1814 was signed there; this provoked an armed attack by the Spaniards who destroyed most of the town in their search for the Mexican rebels.

By 1900 the population had risen to more than 175,000 people and, in spite of a setback during the Revolution, rose to more than 300,000 by 1950 (Table 10).[1] The population of the Tierra Fría, however, declined slightly. This area continued to depend, as it does today, on subsistence agriculture with maize overwhelmingly the most important crop. Techniques are most primitive. Ox-drawn ploughs, not all of metal, are used, but little if any artificial fertilizer is applied. A two-year rotation system with a period of rest after each cultivation remains in general use. In the Tierra Fría, the only non-subsistence products of importance are from the pine forests which are owned communally by the villages. The wood is used locally for firewood and for shingles, and is sold to sawmills to make other construction items. Sap is collected from living trees to make turpentine and tar. In addition, the many communities in the region specialize in different products and have done so for centuries. Paracho, for example, is well-known for its guitars and other stringed musical instruments

[1] Aguirre Beltrán's figures differ from those in Table 10 because of differences in definitions of the size of the region. His regions were determined by cultural characteristics, while those used in this study are based on those of the Tepal-catepec Commission which were based on geo-economic considerations.

Table 10. *Population in the Tepalcatepec basin, 1900–1960*

	Area of unit[a] (km.²)	Population				Population density[b]		Population change 1950–60 (% change)
		1900	1930	1950	1960	1930	1960	
Tepalcatepec basin	22,518	177,202	214,278	308,958	424,436	8·1	18·8	37·4
Tierra Caliente	6,038	35,256	43,887	63,067	119,411	3·8	19·8	89·3
Apatzingán	806	8,707	7,480	15,283	30,975	3·2	38·4	102·7
Buenavista[c]	713		3,314	6,246	14,100	2·8	19·8	125·7
Gabriel Zamora[d]	211				7,895		37·5	
La Huacana	1,648	15,240	9,139	11,295	17,073	2·4	10·4	51·2
Parácuaro	370	5,962	8,145	5,742	11,360	11·4	30·7	97·8
Tepalcatepec	714	5,347	6,030	9,502	15,040	7·1	21·1	58·3
Zaragoza[e]	50			7,427	15,142		23·1	103·9
Jilotlán, Jal.[f]	1,526		9,779	7,572	7,826	3·8	5·0	3·4
Tierra Templada	6,370	86,246	109,954	171,103	204,229	16·2	32·1	19·4
Ario de Rosales	623	15,487	15,953	19,668	24,236	13·3	38·9	23·2
Cotija	543	9,109	7,929	12,384	16,035	14·3	29·5	29·5
Nuevo Urecho	402	6,119	6,472	5,096	5,186	29·3	12·9	1·8
Peribán	435	4,881	5,034	4,860	7,288	20·1	16·8	50·0
Los Reyes	524	3,088	11,047	16,533	19,298	14·8	36·8	16·7
Tancítaro	753	10,737	11,152	14,481	16,232	24·1	21·6	12·1
Taretán	352	7,789	3,810	4,241	5,178	13·1	14·7	22·1
Tingüindín	272	12,471	4,918	8,574	10,036	14·0	37·0	17·1
Tocumbo[g]	294		5,912	7,276	9,943	17·3	33·9	36·7
Uruapan	830	16,565	23,976	52,587	61,221	18·0	73·7	16·4
Ziracuaretiro[h]	144		3,702	4,170	5,225	16·8	36·4	25·2

	Area[a]	1900	1930	1950	1960	Density[b]	Density[b]	
Quitupan, Jal.[f]	365		6,517	11,793	13,721	9·5	37·6	16·3
Valle de Juárez, Jal.[f]	208		3,532	4,448	6,553	14·3	31·5	47·3
Tierra Fría	1,528	43,270	35,575	41,509	56,923	24·7	37·3	37·1
Charapan	102	8,696	3,849	4,003	5,516	31·8	54·0	37·8
N. Parangaricutiro[j]	431	5,095	4,058		4,167	13·4	9·7	
Paracho	278	8,377	6,885	10,924	13,464	20·7	48·4	23·3
Santa Clara	460	11,505	13,324	17,176	21,177	33·1	46·0	23·3
Tangamandapio	257	9,597	7,459	9,406	12,599	31·0	48·8	33·9
Costa Sierra	8,582	12,430	24,862	33,279	43,873	3·7	5·1	31·8
Aguililla	1,630	6,445	8,004	12,984	16,100	9·4	9·9	24·0
Arteaga	3,935	5,985	11,808	14,389	12,570	2·3	3·2	—14·5
Churumuco[k]	1,390		5,050	5,906	8,428	6·1	6·1	42·7
Tumbiscatio[l]	1,627				6,775		4·2	

[a] Area of municipios and regions is given for 1960.
[b] Population densities are based on the 1930 and 1960 areas respectively.
[c] Buenavista was part of Tepalcatepec in 1900.
[d] Gabriel Zamora was part of Uruapan until 1955.
[e] Zaragoza was part of Parácuaro until 1942.
[f] Jilotlán de los Dolores, Quitupan, and Valle de Juárez, Jalisco, were formed after 1900.
[g] Tocumbo was part of Tingüindín in 1900.
[h] Ziracuaretiro was part of Taretán in 1900.
[i] Manuel M. Diéguez, Jalisco was part of Jilotlán de los Dolores until 1939.
[j] Nuevo Parangaricutiro was part of Uruapan in 1950; figures for Parangaricutiro are presented prior to 1943 when the county was incorporated into Uruapan because of the disappearance of its county seat as a result of the action of the volcano, Paricutín.
[k] Churumuco was part of La Huacana in 1900.
[l] Tumbiscatio de Ruiz was formed from parts of Aguililla, Arteaga and Apatzingán in 1955.

Source: México, Secretaría de Industria y Comercio, Dirección General de Estadística, 2, 5, 7, 8 *Censos de Población (1900, 1930, 1950, 1960): Jalisco and Michoacán* (México).

while other communities produce woollen garments and blankets.

The Tierra Templada, more accessible than the Tierra Fría and healthier than the Tierra Caliente, has long contained most of the major centres of population. Uruapan has the largest market-place of the basin, which provides the population of the surrounding areas with an opportunity to sell their handicrafts and buy supplies. Within the town itself, there is also a wooden handicraft industry, specializing in lacquered goods. There are several turpentine factories. Two cotton textile factories, which both spin and weave and send their cloth to be finished in Mexico City, date from around the turn of the century, and were the first industries in the basin to take advantage of the Cupatitzio's water power. Uruapan's other activities—bottling plants, construction firms, automotive agencies, *tortilla* factories and the like, exist to meet the needs of the population of the town and surrounding rural areas. Los Reyes and Ario de Rosales are other important market towns in the zone.

The commercial crops of the Tierra Templada include avocados and a small amount of coffee, but the main commercial crop for several decades has been sugar cane. Irrigation and drainage preceded the establishment of the Commission, and there are several long established sugar mills, especially in the north-west of the basin. Food crops are also grown on irrigated land.

Since the Commission was established, the Tierra Caliente has become unquestionably the zone of the greatest economic importance in the basin. At the turn of the century there were at least two irrigation systems already functioning in the Tierra Caliente. But because of its isolation and the low value of its agricultural production, the region was not of economic importance until in 1907 Dante Cussi, an Italian emigré, settled there. He established the haciendas of Nueva Italia and Lombardía under a colonization contract from the Porfirio Díaz regime. Despite the serious disruptions of the Mexican Revolution after 1910, Cussi completed a series of irrigation works agreed to in the colonization contract by 1915, some of which are still in use today. They provide an example of the skill which the Cussis brought to the region. During the ensuing years, the Cussis expanded their holdings until 61,449 hectares of the richest land in the Tierra Caliente were expropriated in 1938 by General Lázaro Cárdenas in one of the most famous agrarian reform measures of his administration;[1] the Cussis sold the land remaining in their possession and other assets to the new ejidal communities that were formed to work the lands collectively. Communal agriculture concentrated on the crops which had been profitable for the Cussis: maize, rice, and lemon orchards, as well as livestock. The Banco Nacional de Crédito Ejidal provided financial assistance for all of these activities. Internal problems of administration led to a breakdown in the collective system of work and the accumulation of a large debt at the bank. Modified systems based on smaller groups did not resolve these problems. Finally, in 1956, the land and livestock were divided among the ejidatarios.[2]

The Cussis' holdings were not the only improved lands in the Tierra Caliente at the time the Commission was formed. The National Irrigation Commission estimated that 4,550 hectares were irrigated by 1939, almost all on land taken from the Cussis, and that 10,000 additional hectares were made irrigable during the following nine years. These new projects were in the western part of the Tierra Caliente on land that was privately owned. Rapid development of the area, however, was held back by the lack of adequate communications and by the generally unhealthy conditions. Poisonous spiders, malaria and vitiligio or *mal de pinto*[3] were the principal threats to human beings in the region. Remedial work was quickly undertaken by the Commission, but not all steps in this development waited for this. In particular, a railway linking Uruapan and Apatzingán was inaugurated in 1940. This was used for the export of lemons, rice, and sugar, the main non-subsistence crops of the pre-Commission era.

---

[1] Salomón Eckstein, *El Ejido Colectivo en México* (México: Fondo de Cultura Económica, 1966), pp. 157–63.

[2] For details of the expropriation and subsequent history of these *ejidos*, see Emilio Romero Espinoza, *Antecedentes de la Reforma Agraria: Lombardía y Nueva Italia, una Realización Ejidal* (México: UNAM, Escuela de Economía, Tesis for Licenciado en Economía, 1950), and Javier Hernandez Segura, *Estudio de la Condiciones Económicoagrícolas de Las Sociedades de Nueva Italia*, Michoacán (Chapingo, México: Escuela Nacional de Agricultura, Tesis, 1959).

[3] A skin disease caused by a fungus which leaves blotches on the skin.

The Costa Sierra has never been a region of economic importance. More isolated and sparsely populated than the other zones,
it remained even more dependent on primitive agriculture.

1950 Census data, shown in Tables 10, 12, 13, 14 and 15 (discussed in greater detail later in this chapter and shown at that
point) summarize the population, labour force and industrial and
agricultural output as they were soon after the Commission
started to work. The area was much more agricultural, of course,
than the nation generally—as evidenced in the labour force
figures. This is true for each climatic zone, though there were
marked differences between the zones. The industrialization of
the Tierra Templada was more advanced than that of the other
zones. There was a similar difference in regional literacy rates
(Table 17). In the basin as a whole the proportion of literate people
was not very different from that of the nation as a whole, excluding Mexico City, but the average in the mountain areas in
particular and also in the Tierra Caliente was well below the
national average.

In summary, it would be unfair to characterize the basin in the
years before the Commission was formed as a stagnant backwater.
Some development had already taken place and undoubtedly
would have continued without the Commission. On the other
hand, there were considerable areas that were economically backward, while the development of the most important resource—
the fertile but unirrigated land—was held back by unhealthy
conditions and poor communications as well as by lack of investment in water resource facilities. To entrust the integral development of such an area to a River Basin Commission was an obvious
strategy to adopt.

THE TEPALCATEPEC COMMISSION'S INVESTMENT PROGRAMME

President Miguel Alemán formed the Tepalcatepec Commission
in 1947 with the 'integral development of the region's natural
resources' as its goal. It was endowed with authority to work
with other ministries for the 'harmonious development' of agriculture, education, health and welfare, and communications

programmes, to produce benefits 'not only for the inhabitants of the basin, but also for the national economy'.[1]

The Commission has been working in the Tepalcatepec basin for almost two decades and during this period has constructed facilities at a cost of nearly 400 million pesos. These expenditures were intended to improve the productive conditions in the area and provide social infrastructure for the improvement of living conditions, the raising of educational levels, and the development of more efficient communication with the rest of the nation. In 1960, the Tepalcatepec Commission was absorbed by a new organization, the Balsas Commission, which now performs similar functions in a much larger area encompassing eight states. There were no changes in the organization of the work within the region although it became obvious that relatively more attention would be devoted to other parts of the Balsas river basin than to the Tepalcatepec area. This shift manifested itself in declining appropriations for the Commission's investment and operations programme in the Tepalcatepec area (Table 11).

In the course of this section, we shall examine the expenditures of the Commission to determine the costs of the projects under consideration so that they may later be compared with the benefits they brought. In accordance with the Comisión del Tepalcatepec's objectives, the major expenditures (Table 11) were 'economic' investments to irrigate newly cultivated areas in the Tierre Caliente and to improve and expand existing irrigation systems in other parts of the basin. Irrigation and drainage expenditures needed to be supplemented by roads to carry the increased production to market. Agricultural development was also promoted in co-operation with the Ministry of Agriculture.

Efforts to improve living conditions and raise the level of literacy were also important goals of the 'social' investments of the Commission. Drinking water and sewage systems and schools were constructed. Subsidies financed health campaigns and education. Urban improvements were part of the effort to improve the environment, although they undoubtedly also had a beneficial

---

[1] Adolfo Orive Alba, *La Política de Irrigación en México* (México: Fondo de Cultura Económica, 1960), pp. 114–15. The author was Minister of Water Resources in Mexico and *ex officio* President of the Tepalcatepec Commission from 1947 to 1952.

Table II. Expenditures of the Tepalcatepec Commission, 1947–1965 ('000 pesos)

	Economic				Social			Total investment		Total current expenditures	Totals	
	Irrigation and drainage	Communications	Agriculture	Education	Drinking water and sewage	Urban facilities[a]	Misc. investment	Current prices	1960[b] prices		Current prices	1960[b] prices
1947	1,454	1		208	184	6	514	1,975	4,700	416	2,391	5,691
1948	2,972	4,380		34	98	177	1,471	9,392	21,038	2,091	11,483	25,722
1949	6,385	3,865		3	156	397	1,049	11,828	24,602	2,251	14,079	29,284
1950	8,043	5,500		55	202	433	583	14,718	27,817	2,089	16,807	31,765
1951	10,448	6,052	64	397	199	760	912	18,493	29,034	2,203	20,696	32,493
1952	16,382	4,997	167	32	276	1,277	877	24,296	36,444	2,981	27,277	40,916
1953	18,775	3,431	280	57	109	604	1,255	24,653	37,473	3,004	27,657	42,039
1954	18,182	3,418	181	221	530	560	495	23,002	31,743	2,713	25,715	35,487
1955	21,269	5,447	134	817	501	243	1,379	29,223	35,652	3,275	32,498	39,648
1956	16,423	6,285	161	3,535	242	2,443	717	27,347	31,723	3,224	30,571	35,462
1957	18,722	6,468	820	2,153	1,539	2,143	2,379	34,309	38,083	3,982	38,291	42,503
1958	12,059	10,526	267	681	631	1,877	766	29,187	31,230	3,991	33,178	35,500
1959	5,789	6,640	377	467	107	1,184	1,182	16,484	17,308	3,397	19,881	20,875
1960	14,795	3,538	261	72	58	1,255	941	21,364	21,364	5,196	26,560	26,560
1961	4,141	394	163	1,231	628	273	318	5,419	5,365	5,490	10,909	10,800
1962	72	2,934	58	1,575	406	593	647	6,163	5,978	6,916	13,079	12,687
1963	259	2,352	92		420	200	715	5,599	5,319	8,283	13,882	13,188
1964	480	2,621	250			230	3,020	7,021	6,740	6,760	13,781	13,230
1965	655		242				730	1,627	1,546	8,729	10,356	9,838
Total: Current prices	177,305	78,849	3,517	11,538	6,286	14,655	19,950	312,100		76,991	389,091	
1960 prices	238,260	106,052	4,004	12,740	7,464	18,127	26,512		413,159	90,529		503,688

a Includes expenditures for hospitals, disease-control campaigns, and electrification.
b Deflated with Index of Public Investment of Secretaría de la Presidencia; Dirección de Inversión Pública.

Source: Comisión del Río Balsas, Gerencia del Bajo Balsas, Accounting Department.

effect on the political stability of the region. Most construction programmes have been completed, reflecting a shift in emphasis to other parts of the Balsas river basin where the Commission is now active.

Administrative and operational expenses replaced economic and social investments as the Commission's staff grew and as the tasks changed from the construction to the operation of an irrigation system.

Economic investments

These are the investments of the Tepalcatepec Commission which enabled the farmers to increase their production and change to more valuable crops. They include investments in irrigation and drainage systems, the road network and the agricultural experiment stations which will be described in turn.

Irrigation. More than half of the total investment was for irrigation and drainage works (Table 11). To facilitate the construction and administration of the works, three irrigation districts were established. Two of them, the Cupatitzio-Cajones and the Tepalcatepec districts, are located in the Tierra Caliente, while the third, the Cotija-Quitupan district, is located in the north-western corner of the basin and is independent of the other two. According to a recent estimate of the Balsas Commission, canals can provide water to 92,000 hectares in the two districts in Tierra Caliente while an additional 11,500 hectares are irrigable in the Cotija-Quitupan irrigation district. In addition, a number of small irrigation projects affecting another 6,000 hectares were constructed throughout the basin. When allowance is made for the land already under irrigation in 1947—about 15,500 hectares— the net addition to the irrigable lands in the basin was about 94,000 hectares.

Most of the additional irrigable area is dominated by canals constructed by the Commission. Part of the land in the Cotija-Quitupan district was reclaimed by drainage canals. In addition, a small proportion of the land, especially in smaller irrigation projects, depends on pumps to supply water for irrigation.

The Commission's total expenditures on the development of the irrigation systems up to 1965 was about 180 million pesos in current prices or about 240 million pesos when converted to 1960 prices.[1] This resulted in a cost per hectare for irrigable land of about 2,550 pesos in 1960 prices. The average investment in Mexico per hectare for irrigated land was about 5,230 pesos (in 1960 prices) up to 1958.[2] The favourable physical characteristics of the area account for this relatively low average cost per hectare to improve the productivity of the land by using available water supplies for irrigation in the Tepalcatepec river basin.

Communications. Roads were the second most important item in the Commission's budget; almost one-fourth of the investment was for this purpose. In addition to the road system, expenditures for four landing strips and numerous small bridges built in connection with the canal system are included. Two roads, the bridge-siphon[3] Barranca Honda, and the road section built on top of the Piedras Blancas Dam in the Tepalcatepec Irrigation District, were not included here because the data were not sufficiently detailed to separate out the road component.

The most important road built by the Commission, both in terms of its cost and its economic significance, was the Uruapan-Apatzingán road. Construction began on this road as soon as the Commission was created. Until then the only means of communication between the Tierra Caliente and the highland areas was a dirt road which required about one day's travel (depending on the time of the year) to reach Apatzingán from Uruapan instead of the present hour and one-half. This road, about sixty miles long, was opened in 1952 and since then it has constituted the primary route between the Tierre Caliente and the rest of the nation. It cost approximately 26 million pesos to build.

[1] These expenditures include those classified as hydroelectric development costs by the Commission since, according to its records, they were used for the construction of canals whose main purpose was irrigation. Expenditures were divided between the CdT and the Federal Electricity Commission according to the principal purposes for which the funds were to be used, and the section financed by the CdT supplies water to a part of the Cupatitzio-Cajones Irrigation District. Since the hydroelectric plant is completely separate from the irrigation system, there is no need to take it into account in the present analysis.

[2] A. Orive Alba, *La Política de Irrigación* pp. 161, 177. Such comparisons should be used with caution because most irrigation projects include the cost of large (and expensive) storage dams which were usually not needed in the Tierra Caliente. In 1965 the cost was more than 10,000 pesos a hectare.

[3] A dual purpose structure to transport vehicular and pedestrian traffic and water across a chasm.

A network of secondary roads, including some with all-weather gravel surfaces was also a part of the programme. Approximately 30 miles of roads were paved in the Tierra Caliente in addition to the main road described above. Inadequate maintenance, however, has led to the disappearance of any trace of paving along many of the routes. In addition, about one thousand miles of unpaved roads were constructed in the basin; of these about one hundred have gravel surfaces, three hundred have finished embankments, and the rest are no more than vehicle tracks. Most of the roads in rural Mexico are of the last two types and might be compared to farm-to-market roads in the United States. The road programme is dependent, in part, upon the co-operation of the people who were to benefit directly from the roads. The villagers were expected to contribute, in cash or in kind, about one-third of the cost of constructing the farm-to-market roads; actual experience has shown that this contribution is somewhat less than one-third and that the only help most of the villagers can offer is their labour. About 50 million pesos were spent on these secondary roads by the Commission through 1965.

Scores of communities in the Tierra Caliente could never have flourished without this network of secondary roads. From an economic point of view, these may be considered as a necessary supplementary investment to the irrigation works because they reduce transportation costs for the increased agricultural produce. Other roads, however, especially those in the Tierra Fría, did not have an economic function as their primary purpose; instead, they were designed to facilitate communication between communities which previously had only marginal contact with other population centres. The impact of these roads on the area's continued development will be examined below.

Agricultural development. The Tepalcatepec Commission worked closely with the Ministry of Agriculture and Livestock to help improve farming techniques. Its efforts were directed towards the development of a number of experiment stations which tested possible changes in cultivation methods and disseminated the results to the farmers in the area. The Commission co-operated in the construction of an experiment station for agriculture, livestock, and poultry in the Tierra Caliente; a bee station, a zoological post and artificial insemination unit in Uruapan, a fish breeding station, and a small sugar mill. The total investment in these activities is much larger than the 3 million pesos indicated in the Commission's reports because the Ministry of Agriculture provided an equal, if not larger, part of the funds for the construction and operation of these facilities. In recent years a large part of the Commission's expenditures for agricultural development has been for the expansion of tree nurseries and a continuing programme of reforestation in the basin.

Social investments

Social investments are usually made to improve the environment in which people live. They do not directly increase the products which are available for consumption but may contribute to the greater efficiency of factors of production by increasing the stored knowledge and capabilities of human beings through education or health measures. They may also provide collective consumption opportunities through such things as drinking water or rural electrification programmes. One common feature of these investments is that they cannot simply be evaluated in terms of their effects on productivity. This does not mean that they have no such effect, but rather that this is only a part of the reason for undertaking the investment.

In Chapter 3 we pointed out that the expenditures on social investments have been restricted in Mexico to conserve resources for the development effort. In the Tepalcatepec river basin they accounted for less than 10 per cent of all the Commission's investments through 1965. The expenditures provided a minimum of services to people in all parts of the basin and were concentrated in those areas where the cultural and physical isolation was greatest. Much fanfare was given to the projects which improved social welfare, but in the final analysis they appear to be a rather inexpensive way of demonstrating the government's interest in the people. Many problems of evaluation arise in connection with social investments; they will be considered at the time we evaluate the Commission's work.

School construction was the most important of these social investments, although it accounts for only three per cent of the total expenditures. Four large technical schools, several secondary schools and many primary schools were constructed. Two of the technical schools train students for work in agriculture and one requires only a third grade education for admittance. The other technical schools are for the preparation of teachers and forest rangers.

Drinking water systems, rural electrification, and urban improvements were all part of a co-operative effort with the communities directly involved. Villagers from the communities which received the improvements were expected to contribute at least the necessary labour for the projects, enabling large numbers of villages to benefit at low cost. About eighty-five drinking water systems were installed, and important urban improvements in Apatzingán and Uruapan included streets, markets, monuments and a national park which harnesses the headwaters of the Cupatitzio river (River of the Singing Waters) in a most imaginative way. Estimated electricity consumption increased twice as fast as the national average between 1950 and 1960.

The Commission also built health facilities and provided some small financial assistance to malaria-eradication jointly sponsored by the United Nations and the Mexican government. It constructed several hospitals and community clinics in the basin and in surrounding areas where the Balsas Commission is now active.

Although the bulk of the economic investments took place in the Tierra Caliente, most of the social investments were made in other parts of the basin. As suggested in Chapter 3, the government appears to have used their programmes to reduce feelings of resentment towards those areas which were benefiting economically from the river basin development investments.

ECONOMIC PROGRESS IN THE
TEPALCATEPEC RIVER BASIN, 1950–60

The ways in which the Commission's work affected growth in the Tierra Caliente are described in detail in the following chapter. It is possible in that chapter to use adjusted figures for the output of major crops in the Tierra Caliente (this is explained in

Appendix A). No such adjustments can be made for the whole basin and the following broad description of the changes that took place between 1950 and 1960 is drawn from the census data, presented in Tables 12–15. It must be stressed that much of the irrigation and the increase in agricultural output that can be attributed to the work of the Commission has taken place since 1960 and consequently does not appear in the census statistics.

Apart from its agricultural and related investments in the Tierra Caliente and its social investments dispersed throughout the basin, the Commission carried out drainage and irrigation in the sugar cane-growing areas of the Tierra Templada, particularly in the north-western part of the basin. In this area the Commission constructed one dam and rehabilitated another in the early years of its activities. It also operates an irrigation district in this region. The area of cane cut each year in the Tierra Templada has more than doubled since the Commission was established. As yet the Commission has not been influential in increasing the cultivated area in the Costa Sierra. One of the still unfinished projects of the Tepalcatepec Commission is the construction of a storage dam to capture and utilize the waters from this source for irrigation during the dry months.

Population and labour force growth

Population growth during the 1950–1960 decade varied from one part of the basin to another. The most rapid increase was in the Tierra Caliente, where the population more than doubled in the decade following the creation of the Tepalcatepec Commission. The average increase in the entire region was about 40 per cent; the slowest growth occurred in the temperate zones of the Uruapan Sierra and in the southern mountain ranges.

The Tepalcatepec basin's natural rate of population growth (births less deaths) increased by about 18 per cent from 1950 to 1960 (Table 12); in both years it was greater than the national average. This was the result of both a higher birth rate and a lower death rate than the average rates for the nation. With the exception of the Tierra Caliente, all parts of the basin had lower death rates than the national average in 1950. By 1960 even the death rate in the Tierra Caliente had fallen below the national

Table 12. Migration in the Tepalcatepec basin, 1950–1960

| | 1950 | | 1960 | | Natural growth rate (5) | Expected 1960 population (6) | Imputed net migration | |
	Births (1)	Deaths (2)	Births (3)	Deaths (4)			1950–60 (7)	% of 1950 population (8)
Mexico	45·6	16·2	46·0	11·5	3·19	35,321,572	− 398,443	− 1·5
Tepalcatepec basin	48·0	14·1	49·2	9·6	3·68	442,472	− 18,036	− 5·8
Tierra Caliente	59·0	16·5	55·5	10·6	4·37	96,720	+ 22,691	+ 36·0
Tierra Templada	46·7	14·6	48·9	10·5	3·53	241,931	− 37,702	− 22·0
Tierra Fría	47·1	13·3	49·3	9·3	3·69	59,634	− 2,711	− 6·5
Costa Sierra	36·3	9·1	33·9	3·6	2·87	44,183	− 310	− 0·9

Sources and method of computation:

Column:

(1)–(4) Rates per 1,000 population; Secretaía de Industria y Comercio, Dirección General de Estadística, Oficina de Nacimientos y Difunciones.

(5) Geometric mean of 1950 and 1960 natural rates of increase of the population (Birth-rate − death-rate).

(6) 1950 population (Table 10) × (Column 5)[10].

(7) Actual 1960 population (Table 10)—Column 6.

(8) Column 7 as a percentage of 1950 population (Table 10).

Methodology based on Aguirre Beltrán, *Problemas de la Población Indígena de la Cuenca del Tepalcatepec*, pp. 130–1.

rate. The birth rate was also higher than the national average in all regions except in the Costa Sierra.

Estimated natural population growth was greater than that observed on the basis of the 1950 and 1960 Censuses. That is, there were fewer people reported to be residing within the basin in 1960 than would have been expected by an extrapolation of natural population growth (Table 12). The estimated emigration from the basin during the 1950s was about 6 per cent of the 1950 population. The inter-regional differences in migration patterns were large; the Tierra Caliente was the only zone with immigration, estimated at almost 40 per cent of the base year population. Emigration from the other areas was a reflection of the relative lack of economic opportunities in the Uruapan Sierra.[1]

As is true for most of Mexico, a little less than one-third of the basin's population were in its work force according to the 1960 Census. The regional differences within the basin were very small, with the range extending from a low of 29 per cent in the Tierra Caliente and in the Meseta Tarasca to a high of 33 per cent in the Costa Sierra. The average for the basin was 31 per cent in 1960.

Economic structure

The basin's economy is still fundamentally agricultural. Even the Tierra Templada, the most industrialized zone, has a smaller proportion of people working in industry than the nation as a whole (Table 13). The Tierra Caliente's agricultural labour force grew even more rapidly than its total labour force, which itself grew about 75 per cent during the decade. This growth was a response to the greatly increased economic opportunities which resulted from the Tepalcatepec Commission's investments. Apatzingán's population more than doubled in the ten years following the Commission's creation. The growth of agricultural employment opportunities induced a further growth of employment needed to introduce and maintain a more complex agricultural technology.

---

[1] Since the 1960 Census the immigration into the Tierra Caliente probably increased as a result of increasing prosperity. Thus, over a longer span it is possible that the net flow into the basin as a whole was positive.

	Mexico		Tepalcatepec basin		Tierra Caliente		Tierra Templada		Tierra Fría		Costa Sierra	
	1950	1960	1950	1960	1950	1960	1950	1960	1950	1960	1950	1960
Labour force												
Total			95,687	132,006	20,295	35,335	52,400	65,653	12,680	16,341	10,312	14,677
Relative[a]			1·1	1·2	21·2	26·7	54·8	49·7	13·1	12·4	10·8	11·2
Activities[b]												
(1) Agriculture, etc.	58·3	54·2	73·0	73·1	77·6	79·3	67·7	65·7	77·6	79·3	84·9	84·5
(2) Industry	15·9	18·9	10·7	10·7	7·4	6·4	12·7	13·7	11·7	10·8	5·6	7·8
Extractive	1·2	1·2	0·2	0·4	0·2	0·4	0·2	0·4	0·2	0·3	0·1	0·8
Manufacturing	11·7	13·7	8·4	7·6	5·0	4·0	9·8	9·7	10·5	9·2	5·0	4·9
Construction	2·7	3·6	2·0	2·4	2·1	1·8	2·5	3·1	1·0	1·2	0·5	2·0
Electricity, Gas, etc.	0·3	0·4	0·1	0·3	0·1	0·2	0·2	0·5	e	0·1	e	0·1
(3) Commerce	8·3	9·5	7·1	7·7	6·3	6·5	8·6	9·6	5·3	6·5	3·9	3·5
(4) Transport	2·5	3·1	1·5	2·1	1·0	1·7	2·1	3·0	0·8	0·6	0·4	0·3
(5) Services	10·6	13·5	5·2	6·1	5·8	5·9	5·7	7·7	3·0	2·6	4·2	3·6
(6) Others[d]	4·3	0·7	2·4	0·2	1·9	0·1	3·2	0·3	1·7	0·1	0·9	0·3

[a] Figure for the Tepalcatepec basin refers to the percentage of the national labour force in the region. Those for the other zones are their relative share of basin total.

[b] Expressed as a proportion of the total labour force in each area. Totals may not add up to 100 % because of rounding.

[c] Includes livestock, hunting, forestry, and fishing.

[d] Activities not sufficiently specified for classification.

e Less than 0.1%.

Source: Population Census: 1950 and 1960.

Table 14. *Industrial activity in the Tepalcatepec basin,*[a] *1950*[b] *and 1960*

	Number of establishments		Value of production		Capital investment[d]		Number of employees	
	1950	1960	1950	1960	1950	1960	1950	1960
Tepalcatepec basin[e]								
Number	609	715	32,324,000[f]	100,081,000[f]	19,947,000[f]	140,735,000[f]	2,789	5,434
%	0·8	0·7	0·7	0·2	0·5	0·3	0·4	0·6
Tierra Caliente	14·8	24·6	12·5	23·3	13·7	23·7	8·8	38·8
Tierra Templada	61·1	47·8	84·8	75·2	81·9	74·8	77·1	49·9
Tierra Fría	19·5	24·9	1·8	1·3	2·1	1·2	5·5	9·7
Costa Sierra	4·6	2·7	0·9	0·3	2·3	0·3	8·6	1·6
Industrialized municipios								
Uruapan	21·3	27·7	42·1	40·9	29·0	41·2	46·1	36·5
Apatzingán	6·1	16·8	7·9	20·8	1·5	21·5	3·8	35·8
Taretan	2·1	0·8	6·3	9·5	11·4	15·7	3·2	2·4
Others	70·5	54·7	43·7	28·8	58·1	21·6	46·9	25·3

Table 14 (contd.)

Principal industries[e]			
Sugar refining	32·6	30·3	4·3
Chemical products	19·9	17·0	6·9
Ice plants	10·8	8·1	25·6
Textiles	7·6	3·0	5·3
Rice mills	1·9	1·4	0·6
Other industries	27·2	30·2	57·3

[a] Expressed as the relative share of industry in each region as censused.
[b] Data for 1950 omit the four counties in Jalisco. In 1960 these counties represented less than 0·1% of the total value of production within the basin.
[c] Tepalcatepec basin as a percentage of the total for Mexico. The other regions are shown in terms of their relative importance within the basin.
[d] Includes both fixed and working capital.
[e] Data for 1950 by industry in the basin not available.
[f] Pesos.

Sources: 1950: México, Secretaría de Economía, and Michoacán, (State), *Proyecto de Programa de Gobierno del Estado de Michoacán* (México, 1957), pp. 202–4. Based on data from the 1950 *Industrial Census.*
1960: México, Secretaría de Industria y Comercio, Dirección General de Estadística, *7° Censo Industrial,* 1960 (México, 1965). Based on unpublished worksheets on municipal level.

The Tierra Fría also experienced an increase in the relative importance of its agricultural labour force. In spite of an increasing demand for many of the handicraft products for which the region is well-known, the proportion of people involved in manufacturing declined by almost 20 per cent during the decade of the fifties. The Costa Sierra continued to offer few economic activities outside agriculture. Mining has become more important in recent years but still occupies less than 1 per cent of the labour force.

The industrial censuses provide a measure of the relative importance of the basin's industrial production.[1] Although the basin's industrial production increased from 1950 to 1960, its proportionate share of national industrial output fell. In both years it represented less than 1 per cent of the total (Table 14), but by 1960 it had declined from about 0.7 to about 0.2 per cent. Of this product, more than three-quarters of the value was produced in the Tierra Templada. The relative share of industrial production in the Tierra Caliente almost doubled from 1950 to 1960. Apatzingán, the second most important town in the basin, increased its relative contribution to regional industrial production from less than 10 to more than 20 per cent of the total during the period. Uruapan is still the most important town in the region, but its growth has slowed down in recent years and during the decade 1950 to 1960 emigration to other parts of the basin and nation was noted.

In 1960 the most important industry in the basin was sugar refining. Although not a new industry, it accounted for almost a third of the basin's industrial production. It employed a very small share of the industrial work force. The chemical industry was second in importance. Included among its products are turpentine and tar, which along with other wood derivatives represented about 75 per cent of the value produced by this industry.[2] More

---

[1] No absolute figures are given for industrial production in each municipio because of the incompleteness of the industrial censuses. In spite of the fact that such figures are provided for the basin totals, these numbers can only provide a general idea of the order of magnitudes involved rather than a precise estimate in each category. The relative numbers are probably more informative.

[2] In 1967 a new plant to produce turpentine and tar products was opened in the municipo of Paracho. This plant, which was constructed with governmental assistance, is owned collectively by members of a local ejido and provides a vivid demonstration of the continued importance of the forest resources in the area.

than one-third of the industrial production and more than one-fifth of industrial employment stemmed from the forest resources in the area. At one time there were plans for the construction of a paper plant to be financed by Nacional Financiera, the Mexican development bank, but other regions have been selected for this investment.

Since the 1960 Industrial Census, several cotton gins have been constructed in Tierra Caliente to process the growing harvest. They are an important source of employment during a part of the year. They may, in fact, constitute the largest industry in the basin at the present time. Their role in the regional economy is discussed below. A barium processing plant is another recent addition to the Tierra Caliente's industrial base. In the rest of the basin there has been little change in the structure or size of industry.

Although agriculture was the most important economic activity in the basin, the zone produces little more than 1 per cent of the nation's agricultural production (Table 15).[1] As in the case of industrial production, this share declined during the last decade, although not as precipitously. During that decade the relative geographical importance of the zone changed dramatically. The Tierra Caliente's relative share of the basin's harvested area rose from 30 to 43 per cent, and its share of the value of production from about one-third to almost one-half. The construction by the Commission of a distribution system for irrigation water from the rivers flowing down from the Tierra Templada led to an increase in the cultivated area in the Tierra Caliente from about 42,000 hectares to 109,500 hectares in 1965; the irrigated area jumped from about 15,000 hectares to almost 72,000 in 1960 and 89,500 in 1965. Thus, in the first fifteen years of operation the Commission could claim credit for a growth in cultivated land of about 250 per cent and a substantial change from about one-third to four-fifths in the proportion of this land which was irrigated. According to the censuses, however, the area harvested in the other three parts of the basin actually declined during the decade.

[1] This section is based on data from the agricultural censuses, in spite of the many deficiencies of this source. Some of these are referred to in Appendix A. Although absolute figures are presented, it is more likely that the relative orders of magnitude are a better reflection of the actual situation.

Table 15. *Agricultural, livestock and forest production, Tepalcatepec basin, 1950 and 1960*

	Tepalcatepec basin		Tierra Caliente		Tierra Templada		Tierra Fría		Costa Sierra	
	1950	1960	1950	1960	1950	1960	1950	1960	1950	1960
Agricultural[a]										
Area cultivated (hectares)										
Total	142,076	142,739	41,589	61,415	59,910	49,769	17,404	12,148	23,173	19,407
Relative[b]	1·5	1·2	29·3	43·0	42·2	34·9	12·2	8·5	16·3	13·6
% Change	0·5		47·7		−17·9		−30·2		−16·3	
Value of production ('000s 1960 pesos)										
Total	81,978	139,347	28,288	68,060	36,264	50,887	8,566	9,143	8,860	11,257
Relative[b]	1·2	1·1	34·3	48·8	44·3	36·5	10·4	6·6	10·8	8·1
% Change	7·0		140·6		40·3		6·7		27·1	
Yield (pesos/hectare) (1960 pesos)										
Total	577	976	680	1,108	605	1,022	492	753	382	580
Relative[b]	79	87	118	114	105	105	85	77	66	59
% Change	69·2		62·9		68·9		53·0		51·8	
Corn area as % of total area	68·7	67·2	60·1	53·5	73·0	69·0	86·9	95·5	57·5	87·9

Table 15 (*contd.*)

Livestock

Animal production ('000s 1960 pesos)

Total	49,432	45,996	16,830	18,278	24,027	16,395	4,492	3,046	4,083	8,277
Relative[b]	1.6	0.8	34.0	39.7	48.6	35.6	9.1	6.7	8.3	18.0
% Change		−7.0		8.6		−31.8		−32.2		102.7

Head of cattle[c]

Total	314,648	318,437	130,272	135,969	118,297	111,119	20,831	17,057	45,248	54,292
Relative[b]	2.3	2.0	41.4	42.7	37.6	34.9	6.6	5.4	14.4	17.0
% Change		1.2		4.4		−6.1		−18.1		20.0

Forest products

Value of production ('000s 1960 pesos)

Total	2,497	7,528	458	610	1,292	1,517	703	1,159	44	4,242
Relative[b]	1.4	0.7	18.4	8.1	51.7	20.1	28.2	15.4	1.8	56.4
% Change		201.5		35.2		174		64.9		864.1

[a] Total of production of crops and fruits.
[b] Relative Tepalcatepec basin figures are a proportion of total for Mexico. In the other zones the figures are the region's contribution to the basin total.
[c] 1960 figures based on census of livestock conducted by Apatzingán Office of Agriculture and Livestock Ministry (see text).

Source: Agricultural Censuses, 1950 and 1960 (preliminary figures), except as noted.

Agricultural yield per hectare harvested in the basin was lower than that of the nation. Although some progress was made towards closing the gap between the national and regional averages, in 1960 the basin's figure was still 13 per cent lower than the nation's. The Tierra Caliente was the only zone where yields even approached the national average. The great importance of subsistence production accounts for these low yields. In 1960, more than 65 per cent of the cultivated area in the basin was planted in maize, with a much higher proportion of maize in the Tierra Fría and the Costa Sierra. In the Tierra Templada a greater diversity was noted in the 1960 Census. Sugar cane, wheat, chickpeas, and various fruits occupied important places in the region's production. The Tierra Caliente's agriculture is the most varied of the regions. In 1960, sesame, rice and maize were the principal crops. In contrast with other regions, there have been significant changes since that time. As will be described in Chapter 6, cotton, melon, and watermelon have grown in importance as irrigation facilities have been completed and credit and technical knowledge have become available.

According to the Agricultural Census of 1950, the value of animal products sold in the basin was about 60 per cent of the value of crop and fruit production (Table 15). During the 1950s the importance of animal products reportedly declined both absolutely (in constant prices) and relatively. The 1960 Census indicated that there was an absolute decline in the number of cattle in the region. The Tierra Caliente is the most important cattle-raising zone in the basin. Many residents of the Tierra Caliente claim that the cattle industry has been declining as irrigation usurped much of the pasture land for cultivation. A census conducted by the head of the livestock experiment station in the zone indicated, however, that this is not the case; a comparison of this source with the census of 1950 shows that the livestock population remained almost constant in the Tierra Caliente and declined slightly in the rest of the basin.[1] There probably was no

[1] The one-third decline in the cattle population registered in the 1960 census is not a good reflection of the actual situation in the basin. It is also probable that the census seriously understated the value of the animal products produced in 1960, but no additional information is available on this subject. The data collection methods for livestock data were the same as for agricultural information and, therefore, subject to the same problems discussed in Appendix A.

significant change in the number of cattle in the region, and the value of animal products probably increased in absolute terms, even if the relative share of the basin's production in the nation declined.

Timber production is also important in the regional economy. There is much unscientific exploitation of the forests in the Meseta Central, and, since most of it is illegal, it does not get reported in the value of forest products produced in the region. The agricultural censuses indicate a large increase in the value of forest production but a drop in the relative share of the regional product in the national (Table 15). The most important change in the distribution of production within the basin was the increase in importance of forest production in the Sierra Madre del Sur. This is due almost exclusively to the opening up of sizable areas of the Costa Sierra to commercial exploitation techniques. This production represented more than one-half of the value of agricultural production in 1960 as contrasted with the negligible forest production in 1950.

In summary, the economy of the Tepalcatepec river basin is dominated by agricultural activities. These activities provide employment for the majority of the labour force and produce most of the region's income. The structure of agricultural and livestock production has not changed much in the zone; there were important changes in the agriculture of the Tierra Caliente but they occurred after the 1960 Census was conducted. The only other change was the increase in the importance of forest products in the Costa Sierra. The basin provides only a small proportion of the total agricultural, livestock, and forest production in Mexico. In terms of monetary yields, its agriculture is less productive than the nation's as a whole. It remains a small mineral producer. Some copper mines are operated and barium mining and processing started in 1962.

SOCIAL SERVICES

The supply of social services in the Tepalcatepec basin includes most of the essential elements although they are not as abundant as in other parts of the country. Its road system now includes about 225 kilometres of paved roads. A complementary network of secondary and farm-to-market roads has been extended throughout the basin. There is postal service in every town while there are telegraph offices in sixteen communities. The principal towns have telephone service, including access to long distance lines.

Although there were fewer miles of paved road per square mile of area in the basin than the national average in 1958 and this is unlikely to have changed since, the present roads are adequate for most of the present needs and there are no plans to enlarge the length of the area's paved roads. The basin also has a rail line connecting Uruapan and Apatzingán with the capital. This line was completed in 1942 and is an important commercial link for the region. There is also a line from Los Reyes to Guadalajara which connects this sugar producing region to its market.

About one-quarter of the people in the basin have drinking water in their homes; the national average is about 30 per cent. However, as one might expect, most of these people are concentrated in the temperate zones of the Uruapan Sierra. Almost none of the people in the Meseta Terasca or in the Costa Sierra have this facility. During the 1946–63 period, about fifty drinking-water systems were constructed in the basin.[1] These benefited communities have a combined population of about 160,000 people or about 38 per cent of the basin's population.

According to a study by the Ministry of Health and Welfare, only five municipios did not have doctors in residence in 1961, and there were ninety-four doctors then practising in the basin, but eleven municipios were without institutionalized medical services such as clinics or hospitals.[2]

More than one-half of the children of primary school age enrolled for school in 1964 (Table 16). About two-fifths of the students in primary school were enrolled in first grade, while only 5 per cent were in their last year of primary school attendance. The number of students per classroom and teacher was 20 per cent higher than the national average of fifty students per

[1] México, Secretaría de Recursos Hidráulicos, *Agua Potable y Alcantarillados* (*1 de diciembre de 1946–31 de diciembre de 1963*) (México, 1964).
[2] Information on doctors and medical services is from the files of the Balsas River Commission.

Table 16. *Primary education in the Tepalcatepec basin, 1964*

	Tepalcatepec basin	Tierra Caliente	Tierra Templada	Tierra Fría	Costa Sierra
Number of students enrolled in school					
Total	75,529	21,691	38,502	9,321	6,044
Relative	100	28·7	51·0	12·3	8·0
Proportion of school-age population enrolled in school[a]	58·7	58·3	63·0	54·7	45·2
Proportion of students in first grade	43·3	47·6	41·2	39·0	47·7
Proportion of students in sixth grade	5·1	3·9	5·8	5·9	3·6
Students/classroom	58	66	57	53	55
Students/teacher	66	77	62	55	71

[a] Based on number of children between six and fourteen years old in 1964, using 1960 Census figures and assuming no deaths or migration.

Source: México, Secretaría de Industria y Comercio, Dirección General de Estadística, Departamento de Estadísticas Educativas.

Table 17. *Proportion of literate people*[a]

	1930	1950	1960
Mexico[b]	24·9	42·0	47·0
Tepalcatepec basin	26·0	43·0	45·4
Tierra Caliente	18·6	37·2	43·0
Tierra Templada	31·9	48·6	49·6
Tierra Fría	20·5	36·7	41·4
Costa Sierra	19·7	34·6	37·8

[a] Literacy is defined as ability to read and write. The proportion is the percentage of inhabitants above six years old (ten years in 1930) who were literate.
[b] Does not include Mexico City.

Source: Population Censuses: 1930, 1950 and 1960.

primary school teacher. Although the rate of literacy increased from 43 per cent to 45 per cent between 1950 and 1960, it rose less fast than in the nation as a whole (excluding Mexico City) whose average is now higher than the basin's average (Table 17).

In spite of the large effort to improve social services, they are less available in the basin than in the nation as a whole and the social infrastructure is less complete than in the rest of Mexico. However, essential public services are available in the basin and with an adequate geographic distribution so that no region is completely cut off from the benefits that these services provide.

6

THE TEPALCATEPEC COMMISSION'S
IMPACT ON THE TIERRA CALIENTE

The investment programme discussed in the last chapter had a significant impact on the development of the social and economic environment in the Tierra Caliente. In addition to the sizable increases in the land under cultivation, the value of agricultural production, and the working population alluded to above, the region's industrial sector was enlarged to include new cotton-ginning firms and there was some increase in other non-agricultural activities. The main efforts of the Tepalcatepec Commission's activities, however, were devoted to agriculture, and the second part of this chapter deals with developments in that sector. The Commission continued and enlarged the investment programme begun in the Tierra Caliente Irrigation District by its predecessor, the National Irrigation Commission. Although new investments are still being made in the area, the creation of the River Balsas Commission resulted in a new emphasis on developments in other nearby zones which were neglected until recently; the remaining projects in the Tierra Caliente are small in comparison with earlier ones.

A discussion of industrialization and its relation to this agricultural development follows together with a more general description of the region's economic structure and its prospects for the future. These economic variables relating to a more balanced development of the region were of paramount importance to the decision-makers, as we pointed out earlier, and a discussion of them is necessary to prepare the way for the assessment presented in the next chapter. Finally, the improvements in social welfare are outlined.

THE COMMISSION'S INVESTMENTS IN THE
TIERRA CALIENTE

The Tepalcatepec Commission's principal programmes in the Tierra Caliente were designed firstly to raise agricultural productivity and secondly to improve living conditions. This region includes seven municipios which were the object of most of the field investigation for this study because of their preponderant position in the activities of the Commission since 1947.

In Table 18 the investment expenditures in the Tierra Caliente are set forth by function and year, as was done in the previous table for all of the Commission's expenditures. Almost 90 per cent of the expenditures on irrigation were for structures in the Tierra Caliente. This investment in irrigation facilities represented more than two-thirds of the expenditures in the Tierra Caliente.

In contrast to expenditures on irrigation, road construction in the Tierra Caliente required less than three-quarters of the total expenditures for communications in the basin. This lower proportion is, in part, a reflection of emphasis placed on building roads in the upper part of the basin, to provide a link among the isolated communities of that region and with the rest of the country. The smaller proportion of the 'social' investments spent in the Tierra Caliente reflects the general need for these services throughout the basin.[1]

An overwhelming share of the expenditures in the Tierra Caliente, as in the whole basin, were for the construction of facilities to provide irrigation for lands that had previously been poorly irrigated or cultivated only during the rainy season. This emphasis on the Tierra Caliente, which accounted for three-quarters of the total investment budget of the Commission, produced an increase in agricultural production much larger than might have been expected had the Commission not intervened. This effect is the subject of this chapter.

[1] *Cf.* Henry Steiner, *Criteria for Planning Rural Roads in a Developing Country: The Case of Mexico* (Stanford: Institute in Engineering-Economic Systems, Stanford University, 1965), Chapter 5. For a fuller treatment of social investments see the last section of this chapter.

AGRICULTURAL DEVELOPMENT

This section presents a quantitative description of the changes that occurred in the Tierra Caliente; it identifies and measures that part of the change attributable to the Commission's intervention. The increase in the net value of agricultural output since the Commission's creation provides a measure of the primary benefits of the new irrigation system. Although this requires an adjustment to allow for the progress that might have taken place without the Commission's activities, we postpone this step until the next chapter when we reduce the net value of output by the same proportion that agricultural production increased in a control region. Some of the qualitative changes in the agricultural economy and in the lives of the farmers which resulted from these changes are included to make the discussion more complete.

The agricultural situation in 1950

In 1950 agricultural production in the Tierra Caliente had not yet reflected the Commission's presence in the area. 1950 was selected as the base year because, although several projects were under construction, no additional land was placed under irrigation until 1951 and 1952. In addition, the choice of 1950 facilitated the use of the regular decennial agricultural and population censuses which provide the most complete description available of the area's agriculture; it was necessary to adjust these figures with data obtained during the field investigation.[1]

During the 1949–50 agricultural cycle, more than 42,000 hectares were cultivated (Table 19), of which 36 per cent was irrigated (Table 20). Cotton, lemons, melon, rice, sugar cane, and watermelon were grown only on irrigated land, while the subsistence food crops were not. Only 12 per cent of the maize and 19 per cent of the sesame areas were irrigated in that year (Table 20).

Some 78 per cent of the land was planted only during the rainy season (Table 21), but even then cultivation was precarious because rainfall, according to local estimates, was insufficient to

A fuller description of the adjustment process and its significance is the subject of Appendix A.

Table 18. *Investments of the Tepalcatepec Commission in the Tierra Caliente, 1947–1965* ('000s pesos)

	Economic			Social				Total investment	
	Irrigation and drainage	Communica-tions	Agriculture	Education	Drinking-water, sewage	Urban facilities[a]	Other	Current Prices	1960[b]
1947	1,452	1		159	158	69	74	1,527	3,634
1948	1,706	4,303		2	5	241	681	7,076	15,850
1949	3,435	3,726				109	379	7,788	16,199
1950	7,521	5,281				591	169	13,080	24,721
1951	10,215	5,853		15		923	226	16,900	26,533
1952	16,068	4,820		45		234	50	21,906	32,859
1953	18,375	3,078		23		84	157	21,867	33,238
1954	17,893	2,902		8		7	30	20,917	28,865
1955	19,905	3,588		1		171	93	23,594	28,785
1956	13,420	4,172		221		654	557	18,541	21,508
1957	14,447	2,076		2,772	56	489	646	20,651	22,923
1958	9,346	4,586		897	982		116	16,416	17,565

Table 18 (*contd.*)

1959	5,647	3,525	95	463	456	546	26	10,758	11,296
1960	14,045	1,117		125	86	476	39	15,888	15,888
1961	4,131	21	55	31		129	53	4,420	4,376
1962	69	737	21	23	205	398	92	1,545	1,499
1963	844	575	76		43	167	280	1,985	1,886
1964	180							180	173
1965	41						280	41	39
Total:									
Current prices	158,740	50,361	247	4,785	1,991	5,288	3,668	225,080	307,837
1960 prices	212,430	75,004	247	5,456	2,282	6,824	5,594		

[a] Includes expenditures for hospitals, disease-control campaigns, and electrification.
[b] Deflated with Index of Public Investment of Secretaría de la Presidencia; Dirección de Inversión Pública.

Source: Comisión del Río Balsas, Gerencia del Bajo Balsas, Accounting Department.

Table 19. *Area cultivated in the Tierra Caliente, Michoacán, 1949/50–1964/5*

Crops	Area cultivated (hectares)				% Increase in area cultivated			Relative distribution of crops (%)			
	1949–50	1954–5	1959–60	1964–5	1954–5	1959–60	1964–5	1949–50	1954–5	1959–60	1964–5
Total	42,317	63,314	105,664	109,500	53.2	149.7	158.8	100.0	100.0	100.0	100.0
Beans	587	1,100	1,608	500	87.4	173.9	−14.2	1.4	1.7	1.5	0.5
Maize[a]	22,310	33,000	55,292	20,000	47.9	147.8	−10.4	52.7	52.1	52.3	18.3
Cotton	12	500	4,099	42,000	4,066.7	34,058.3	349,000.0		0.8	3.9	38.4
Lemons	3,146	4,458	8,380	8,000	41.7	166.4	154.3	7.4	7.0	7.9	7.3
Melon	256	1,335	4,552	6,000	421.5	1,678.1	2,243.8	0.6	2.1	4.3	5.5
Rice	6,852	11,661	13,828	12,000	70.2	101.8	75.1	16.2	18.4	13.1	11.0
Sesame	7,887	8,000	10,690	12,000	1.4	35.5	52.1	18.6	12.6	10.1	11.0
Sugar cane	658	129	553	b	−80.4	−16.0	n.a.	1.6	0.2	0.5	
Watermelon	79	131	3,964	5,000	65.8	4,917.7	6,229.1	0.2	0.2	3.8	4.6
Others	530	3,000	2,698	4,000	466.0	409.1	654.7	1.3	4.7	2.6	2.7

a Includes maize and beans sown together.
b Less than 100 hectares.

Sources: 1950, 1960: Appendix A.
1955, 1965: Comisión del Río Balsas; Department of Agriculture, Mexico.

Table 20. *Irrigated area in the Tierra Caliente, Michoacán 1949/50–1964/5*

	Irrigated area (hectares)				Increase in irrigated area over 1949-50 (%)			Relative distribution of irrigated area (%)				Proportion of cultivated area irrigated (%)			
	1949-50	1954-5	1959-60	1964-5	1954-5	1959-60	1964-5	1949-50	1954-5	1959-60	1964-5	1949-50	1954-5	1959-60	1964-5
Total	15,368	31,515	71,994	89,500	105.1	368.5	482.4	100.0	100.0	100.0	100.0	36.3	49.8	68.1	81.7
Beans	0	133	1,107	0				0	0.4	1.5	0	0	12.1	68.8	0
Maize[a]	2,600	10,204	33,537	12,500	292.5	1,189.9	380.0	16.9	32.4	46.6	14.0	11.7	30.9	60.7	62.5
Cotton	12	500	4,099	42,000	4,066.7	34,058.3	349,000.0	0.1	1.6	5.7	46.9	100.0	100.0	100.0	100.0
Lemons	3,146	4,458	5,674	6,000	41.7	80.4	90.7	20.5	14.1	7.9	6.7	100.0	100.0	100.0	75.0
Melon	256	1,335	4,552	6,000	421.5	1,678.1	2,243.8	1.7	4.2	6.3	6.7	100.0	100.0	67.7	100.0
Rice	6,852	11,661	13,828	12,000	70.2	101.8	75.1	44.6	37.0	19.2	13.4	100.0	100.0	100.0	100.0
Sesame	1,500	1,464	3,331	4,000	-2.4	122.1	166.7	9.7	4.6	4.6	4.5	19.0	18.3	31.2	33.3
Sugar cane	658	129	553	0	-80.4	-16.0	-100.0	4.3	0.4	0.8	0	100.0	100.0	100.0	0
Watermelon	79	131	3,964	5,000	65.8	4,917.7	6,229.1	0.5	0.4	5.5	5.6	100.0	100.0	100.0	100.0
Others	265	1,500	1,349	2,000	466.0	409.1	654.7	1.7	4.8	1.9	2.2	50.0	50.0	50.0	50.0

[a] Includes maize and beans sown together.

Sources: 1950, 1960: Appendix A.
1955, 1965: Comisión del Río Balsas; Department of Agriculture, Mexico.

permit profitable harvests in more than three out of five years.[1] Any production estimate, therefore, should be reduced by about 40 per cent of the potential output to reflect adequately its expected value in any one year.

More than 70 per cent of the cultivated area was devoted to four crops that yielded little in monetary terms: beans, maize, rice, and sesame (Table 22). Maize, the principal crop, covered more than one-half of the cultivated land and was planted on small plots. Sesame accounted for the second largest area and was closely followed by rice, which had been grown in the region for several decades. Beans took up very little of the total area.

Only 10 per cent of the area cultivated during the 1949–50 agricultural cycle was planted with crops having a gross yield of 1,000 pesos or more per hectare. All of this land was irrigated and most was used for lemon trees which require little effort to obtain a valuable harvest. Melons and watermelons had been gradually introduced into the region since 1943, but did not occupy an important part of the land in 1950. At that time cotton was an experimental crop planted in only one part of the zone. Sugar cane was being withdrawn from production as more profitable uses for the irrigated land were found. Despite their low acreage, these five crops accounted for more than one-quarter of the irrigated land and a similar proportion of the total value of agricultural production.

The net returns to the farmers for their principal crops were very low. Production costs for 1950, obtained during the course of the field investigation, were deducted from the gross monetary yields to obtain the net yields (Table 23).[2] The four principal

---

[1] De la Peña commented that 'from 1942 to 1947 [the region] experienced alternatively a good year and a bad one, and previously, a good one for two bad ones over a long period according to the farmers. For maize based on rainfall . . . there are those who are of the opinion that two bad years, two average years and one good year is the normal expectation during a five-year cycle.' *Problemas y Posibilidades de la Cuenca del Tepalcatepec y Costa Michoacana* (México, 1951, unpublished manuscript), p. 32. During the field investigation, it was ascertained that 1950 could be considered a good year in terms of the agricultural harvest.

[2] The costs of production referred to here and elsewhere in this chapter include the rent of the land, the labour and material costs, an allowance for interest on working capital, and administration. Charges for fixed capital assets used in production are based on their rental values. These figures do not include the

Table 21. Area cultivated in the Tierra Caliente, Michoacán (by seasons)

Crop	1949/50 (hectares)			1959/60 (hectares)			1949/50			1959/60		
	Dry	Wet	Both	Dry	Wet	Both	Dry	Wet (%)	Both	Dry	Wet (%)	Both
Total	5,650	32,863	3,804	25,341	74,096	6,227	13·4	77·7	9·0	24·0	70·1	5·9
Beans		587		1,032	576			100·0		64·2	35·8	
Maize	1,950	20,360		10,736	44,556		8·7	91·3		19·4	80·6	
Cotton		12			4,099			100·0			100·0	
Lemons			3,146		2,706	5,674			100·0		32·3	67·7
Melon	256			4,552			100·0			100·0		
Rice	2,100	4,752		3,664	10,164		30·6	69·4		26·5	73·5	
Sesame	1,000	6,887		44	10,646		12·7	87·3		0·4	99·6	
Sugar cane			658			553			100·0			100·0
Watermelon	79			3,964			100·0			100·0		
Others	265	265		1,349	1,349		50·0	50·0		50·0	50·0	

Source: Appendix A.

crops all had monetary returns of less than 350 pesos: maize yielded 97 pesos per hectare; sesame, 206; rice, 317; and beans only 26.[1] The relatively high return for rice was due to its low cultivation costs once the initial investment in the layout of the land was made. Since this investment was made in this region before 1940, cultivation costs included only the maintenance work. The most profitable crop was watermelon which yielded 1,952 pesos per hectare followed by cotton with 1,421 pesos.

The production costs of commercial crops were relatively low

Table 22. *Agricultural production in the Tierra Caliente, Michoacán, 1949–1950*

Crop	Area hectares (1)	Physical yield kgs/ hectare (2)	Production metric tons (3)	Rural price pesos/ ton (4)	Monetary yield pesos/ hectare (5)	Value	
						'ooos pesos (6)	Relative (7)
Total	42,317				495	20,929	100·0
Beans[a]	587	300	196	730	244	143	0·7
Maize[a]	22,310	898	19,994	322	288	6,427	30·7
Cotton	12	2,070	25	1,530	3,167	38	0·2
Lemons	3,146	3,951	12,430	348	1,375	4,324	20·7
Melon	256	5,195	1,330	400	2,078	532	2·5
Rice	6,852	1,954	13,389	348	680	4,659	22·3
Sesame	7,887	470	3,704	905	425	3,352	16·0
Sugar Cane	658	52,161	34,322	28	1,460	959	4·6
Watermelon	79	8,082	638	400	3,233	255	1·2
Others[b]	530				452	240	1·1

[a] Maize area includes 200 hectares of land planted in maize and beans. The products have been added to columns 3, 6, and 7 but not taken into account in physical yields (column 2).
[b] See text.

Source: Appendix A.

payment of taxes, water fees, and insurance premiums as explained in Appendix II of Barkin, *Economic Development in the Tepalcatepec River Basin* (unpublished Ph.D. dissertation, Yale University, 1966).
[1] Farmers persisted in planting maize and beans in spite of their low profits because of their predominant place in their diet. Since they were fearful of price fluctuations for agricultural goods which were controlled by local merchants, many planted subsistence rather than cash crops.
At that period the exchange rate was 8.65 pesos to the dollar.

compared with similar costs in other parts of Mexico. The fertility of the little-used soil accounts for this fact. Only natural animal wastes were used as fertilizers. There were few plagues or diseases so that no fumigants or insecticides were necessary, and there were no local suppliers of these products. Horses and oxen, which could be cheaply maintained because of the abundance of pasture land, provided the principal source of power. No rent was imputed to the land used in dry farming, since there was much vacant land available for planting and pasturing.

The net value of the harvest was converted to 1960 prices using an index of rural prices constructed by the Office of Agricultural Projections of the Bank of Mexico (Table 23, Column 4).[1] These figures were then adjusted to take into account the expected losses in crops planted without the aid of irrigation (Column 6). As explained above, it was assumed that there would not be sufficient production to warrant a harvest in two of every five years.

The figures in the preceding paragraphs refer to the Tierra Caliente's nine principal products during the 1949–50 agricultural season. According to the census, the value of other production amounted to 12 per cent of the total production although the area devoted to the cultivation of these other products represented only 1·5 per cent of the total area in the Tierra Caliente. Most of this was fruit production (especially of bananas, coconuts, and mangoes) which yields a highly valued crop and occupies relatively little space. In adjusting the totals of Tables 18 and 21, we used the conservative estimates of this production shown in the census, whose data show a definite downward bias for the more valuable products. The net value of these products was obtained by assuming that their production costs were two-thirds of their gross value. It was further assumed that one-half of the area planted in these products was irrigated, and the expected value of the

[1] It should be emphasized that these are average net returns based on estimated average production costs and yields. The dispersion of actual receipts is probably wide. Figures of this are obviously not easy to obtain without extensive sample surveys. An indication, however, can be obtained from results published by the Banco Ejidal giving details of its cotton operations for the year 1961–2. The Bank pays living expenses as well as other production costs, gins and markets the cotton, pays all taxes and returns the net profit to the ejidatario. Almost one-quarter of all ejidatarios made net losses, the average profit per hectare was 1,529 pesos and 8.5 per cent of the borrowers made a profit per hectare exceeding four thousand pesos.

production was estimated to be 80 per cent of a good year's harvest (Table 23, Columns 4 and 6).

Table 23. *Net monetary yields in the Tierra Caliente, Michoacán, 1949–1950*

Crop			Total costs pesos/ hectare (1)	Net monetary yields pesos/ hectare (2)	Net value of harvest			Expected value of harvest '000 1960 pesos (6)
					'000 pesos (3)	'000 1960 pesos (4)	% (5)	
Total					7,768	12,792	100·0	10,638
Beans			218	26	15	25	0·2	15
Maize	D	191[b]	178	97	2,145	3,532	27·6	2,285
	W		290					
Maize and beans			203	17	3	6	0	4
Cotton			1,746	1,421	17	28	0·2	28
Lemons			978	397	1,249	2,057	16·1	2,056
Melon			1,254	824	211	347	2·7	347
Rice			363	317	2,173	3,577	28·0	3,577
Sesame	D	219[b]	198	206	1,625	2,676	20·9	1,809
	W		309					
Sugar cane	P	1,314[b]	2,096	146	96	158	1·2	158
	S		923					
Watermelon			1,281	1,952	154	254	2·0	254
Others[a]					80	132	1·0	105

[a] See text. [b] Weighted average.

W = Irrigated farming.
D = Dry farming dependent on rainfall.
P = Original plant.
S = Subsequent growths.

Sources:

Column 1: Barkin, *Economic Development in the Tepalcatepec River Basin.*
2: Table 22, Column 5—Table 23, Column 1.
3: Table 22, Column 1 × Table 23, Column 2.
4: Column 3 converted to 1960 prices by index of rural prices of the Bank of Mexico, Office for the Study of Agricultural Projections, *Projections of Supply of and Demand for Agricultural and Livestock Products in Mexico to 1970 and 1975* (Mexico, 1965), Table III–34, p. 182.
5: Derived from Column 4.
6: Based on a 60% expectation of a harvest under dry-farming conditions.

In the rest of the Tepalcatepec basin agriculture was not as commercialized as in the Tierra Caliente. Most of the area was devoted to maize and its yield per hectare was about 20 per cent lower than in the Tierra Caliente. According to the 1950 Agricultural Census, nearly 94,000 hectares of land planted during the 1949–50 agricultural cycle produced about 37,500,000 pesos of produce value at 1950 prices.[1] That is, the other eighteen municipios of the state that are in the Tepalcatepec basin cultivated an area 120 per cent larger than in the Tierra Caliente but produced only 80 per cent more in value terms.

Livestock was an important source of income for many people in both areas.[2] More than 417,000 hectares were used for pasture in the Tierra Caliente according to the census. The cattle population was about 111,000 head. In the other eighteen municipios there were only 268,000 hectares of pasture land, but there were almost 155,000 head of cattle on this land. Cattle were raised much more extensively in the Tierra Caliente where land was presumably less in demand for other purposes than in the rest of the basin where conditions required a more intensive use of the land. More than twice as many head of cattle were on each hectare of pasture land in the eighteen Michoacán municipios outside the Tierra Caliente than in the six in the area.

A larger proportion of the working population was in agriculture in the Tierra Caliente than elsewhere. In 1950, according to the Population Census, there were about 62,000 people working in agriculture and forestry in the Tepalcatepec basin (Table 13). They represented about 70 per cent of the work force and 22 per cent of the population. In the Tierra Caliente more than three-quarters of the work force was in agriculture. The proportion of the labour force in agriculture was lower in the remaining eighteen municipios because the area had larger cities which claimed a greater number of people for the commercial and service sectors. However, the proportion is not as low as one might otherwise suppose because of the greater labour intensity of agricultural

[1] Census figures are used for the rest of the Tepalcatepec basin because time and resources did not permit a detailed investigation of the agricultural economy of the other municipios.

[2] *Cf.* de la Peña, *Problemas y Posibilidades de la Cuenca del Tepalcatepec*, p. 36 and Chapter 6.

exploitation outside the Tierra Caliente. If we assume that all the people enumerated in this sector were working cultivated land (that is, that they were not occupied on the pasture land or in the forests), then each man in the Tierra Caliente was farming 50 per cent more land than his peer in the rest of the basin. This ratio would be even larger if we could make adjustments for the number of people employed in livestock and forestry production.

These figures further confirm the judgment that agriculture in the Tierra Caliente was more land intensive and probably less costly per hectare than that in the rest of the basin. They also indicate that the upper area was plagued by the problem of smaller holdings of agricultural land which may have been one of the causes of the lower productivity observed in this area. The difference in the size of the agricultural holdings is, in part, the result of the different geographical features of the two regions. The rest of the basin, described in Chapter 5, is at higher altitudes and is more mountainous than the Tierra Caliente; the large holdings characteristic of the lower regions before the Mexican land reform were not found in the higher reaches. Population density was also greater in the upper part of the basin because the climate was more hospitable. There was also pressure for the breaking up of those large holdings that did exist once the land reform was promulgated. The result of the land reform in the Tierra Caliente was the division of large holdings into individual parcels which were considerably larger than those in the other zones because there were fewer claimants for the land. Some landowners had not yet had their land expropriated and were cultivating large expanses, at times illegally.

The higher land–labour ratio in the Tierra Caliente was also a reflection of its relatively scarce labour supply. In spite of the markedly higher wages prevalent in the Tierre Caliente, reported to have been almost twice as high as in the Tierra Fría, poor health conditions and lack of communications combined to make agricultural day-labour sufficiently unattractive to create a labour scarcity. Construction activities by the Commission, which began in 1947, aggravated this problem; the guarantee of a fixed wage attracted many people from agricultural occupations to construction jobs, thereby creating additional pressures on the labour supply during the harvest seasons. This situation improved in later years when the new job opportunities in agriculture and construction attracted large numbers of new workers to the Tierre Caliente and reduced pressures on the wage rate.

Agricultural developments since 1950[1]

As might be expected, there have been significant changes in the agricultural economy of the Tierra Caliente since the initiation of the construction programme to provide irrigation for a large part of the zone. Productivity has increased and the cultivated area has rapidly grown. Traditional crops have given place to export-oriented crops whose annual value more than equals the programme's total foreign exchange costs. In this section we shall examine the changes that have occurred during the first eighteen years of the Commission's existence.

Growth of cultivated and irrigated area. The most direct effect of the Commission's investment programme was the increase in the area that can be cultivated throughout the year by means of irrigation. During the fifteen-year period 1950–65, there was a 160 per cent increase in cultivated land (Table 19). Even more spectacular was the growth in irrigated area, which was 480 per cent greater in 1965 than fifteen years earlier (Table 20). The area is now much less subject to the vagaries of rainfall than in 1950, in spite of the large increase in total area under cultivation.

As irrigation became more widespread, there was a gradual tendency to substitute more valuable crops for the traditional crops. Irrigation canals reduced the risk of insufficient moisture and made the use of new agricultural inputs more effective. However, this change took place very slowly as illustrated by the fact that maize still dominated the Tierra Caliente's production in 1960 (Table 19). Most of the changes occurred during the 1960s. By 1965 cotton covered more land than maize. Melons and watermelons accounted for one-tenth of the harvested land. Maize

---

[1] The errors in official statistics of agricultural production seem to grow with time. Under-reporting appears to be worse when a change from traditional subsistence to higher-valued cash crops is going on. Substantial corrections were introduced in order to arrive at the figures used in this section. See Appendix A for a discussion of this problem.

declined in relative importance, occupying only one-fifth of the crop land.

The adjustment of the cultivation pattern is more marked when only the irrigated land is considered (Table 20). The relatively small changes between 1950 and 1960 are sharply contrasted with those observed in the subsequent five years. In spite of the almost fivefold increase in irrigated land during the 1950s, there was no significant shift to new crops; on the contrary, there was a relative increase in the amount of irrigated maize land and significant declines in the relative acreage of lemons, rice, and sesame. During the next five years, the situation was dramatically reversed. Cotton displaced maize as the most important of the irrigated crops. Melon and watermelon production continued to occupy one-eighth of the irrigated land as they did in 1960.

One of the most notable things about the shift from traditional to commercial crops in the Tierra Caliente was its slow pace. It was not until the 1962–3 agricultural cycle that cotton production covered more than one-quarter of the zone's cultivated land. The change came about as more credit became available from private and public sources for production loans to finance the crops. Public institutions were severely limited in the amount of credit that they could provide, and their entrepreneurial efforts to encourage the planting of higher valued export crops were limited by the degree of private co-operation.

Once private sources of agricultural working capital observed the financial success of the expansion of cotton lands and the established market for the melon crop, they were quick to help fill the demand for credit.[1] The changes in the crops planted on the irrigated lands in the Tierra Caliente, therefore, were observed to be a function of the supply of inputs into the production process. Profitable production of commercialized crops requires relatively large amounts of working capital to buy seeds, fertilizers, insecticides, and to rent machinery. The supply of new credit was not forthcoming as fast as the availability of irrigated land. The adjustment process was long because there had been

---

[1] For a more detailed discussion of the relation between public and private sources of crop financing and their effect on agricultural production, see the section on entrepreneurship and finance below.

relatively little experimentation and because the technical level of the region's farmers was so low that investors considered that risks were high.

Supply factors have now been joined by demand factors in determining the distribution of crops over the available crop land. The weakening of the cotton market, combined with rising production costs in the Tierra Caliente, has reduced the attractiveness of this product. Melon sales are subject to demand in the United States market, and since this has not increased significantly during the months in which the Mexican growers can supply this highly perishable good, there is a limit on the area that can be profitably planted with this fruit. Recently there have been other changes in the demand picture to indicate that there will probably be further adjustments in the relative importance of various products in the Tierra Caliente; these will be discussed in the part of this chapter which discusses the outlook for the coming years.

The seasonal pattern of cultivation. The increase in cultivated area was accompanied by a change in harvest time. The availability of irrigation water made possible a tremendous growth in the acreage under cultivation during the dry season. This benefited the melon and watermelon crops, since their success depends upon the heat and absence of humidity. Maize, which gradually gave way to cotton in the rainy season, was planted during both agricultural seasons; more than one-fifth of the total production was harvested during the dry season in 1960 and about 50 per cent in 1965 (Table 21).[1]

Technological and productivity changes. Production techniques changed dramatically during the period because of both the availability of irrigation water and the more intensive cultivation of the irrigated land. The introduction of cotton farming in the region brought with it many new problems of pest and disease control which had been ignored in the region until that time. Unlike other cotton-growing areas, the Tierra Caliente does not have a period of frost during the year to kill dormant insects and

---

[1] Although cotton extends beyond the wet season, it is usually counted during that season; and there is usually sufficient time between one harvest and the next season for a maize crop if the farmer wishes to plant it.

fungi which, consequently, have a cumulative influence. An increasing quantity of fumigants and insecticides is used every year to protect the cotton, lemon, melon, and watermelon crops. Their use is less frequent for the more traditional crops, but the farmers planting sesame are resorting to these control chemicals with increasing frequency.

The greater intensity of cultivation increased the need for artificial fertilization and it is becoming almost a necessity for any of the commercialized crops; it is used less frequently in maize and sesame cultivation. Tractors were introduced on a large scale for the application of these chemicals, as well as for the working of the land. Horses are still used on many farms, especially in those areas where traditional crops prevail. Aeroplanes are commonly used for the application of insecticides.

Cultivation techniques were taught to the people of the Tierra Caliente by immigrants from other regions, including those contracted by the banks to supervise the agricultural credit. Little agricultural extension work was carried out by government agencies because they lacked funds and trained personnel. One agricultural training school was established in the region to train the sons of farmers in new techniques of farm management and animal husbandry. These programmes have not been as effective as the assistance given to the borrowers by the various public and private lenders of credit to protect their investments. They charge the borrower for this service through a 'supervisory fee' which is standard in many credit contracts.

One notable change in production techniques occurred in recent years: there was a switch from the broadcast to the transplant method of seeding rice. As a result of this change, imposed on the farmers by the administration of the irrigation district to minimize the use of water for rice production, yields increased two and threefold without the addition of fertilizers. This change was, and still is, opposed by many of the farmers because of the higher costs of production and the more intensive work required to obtain a harvest. At the same time, however, increased yields, which range up to eight metric tons a hectare, and higher prices for rice, made rice cultivation more attractive to many. As a result, rice remains an important crop in the region.

The productivity of the region's land increased with the changes in production techniques and the addition of irrigation water. The increase in physical yields (Table 24, Column 3) was not large in any crop, with the exception of beans which were declining in importance. Changes in the productivity of rice did not appear until 1964. Monetary yields did increase, however, as more valuable crops occupied a greater proportion of the total area; the share of the land dedicated to the four most valuable crops (cotton, lemons, melon and watermelon) grew from 8 per cent in 1950 to 20 per cent in 1960 and to 56 per cent in 1965. These crops represented 20 per cent of the value of production in 1950 and more than 40 per cent of the value in 1960.

Table 24. *Agricultural production in the Tierra Caliente, Michoacán, 1959–1960*

Crop	Area hectares (1)	Physical yield kgs/ hectare (2)	% Change in yield 1950–60 (3)	Produc- tion metric tons (4)	Rural price pesos/ ton (5)	Monetary yield pesos/ hectare (6)	Value '000s pesos (7)	% (8)
Total	105,664					1,714	181,067	100·0
Beans	1,608	700	133	1,669	1,260	882	2,103	1·2
Maize[a]	55,292	1,049	17	57,393	700	734	40,175	22·2
Cotton	4,099	2,436	18	9,985	2,250	5,481	22,467	12·4
Lemons	8,380	5,000	27	41,900	800	4,000	33,520	18·5
Melon	4,552	6,956	34	31,600	500	3,478	15,830	8·7
Rice	13,828	1,959	0	27,094	870	1,704	23,572	13·0
Sesame	10,690	685	46	7,322	1,900	1,302	13,912	7·7
Sugar cane	553	54,898	5	30,359	50	2,745	1,518	0·8
Watermelon	3,964	9,937	23	39,392	550	5,465	21,666	12·0
Others[b]	2,698					2,337	6,304	3·5

[a] Includes 1,603 hectares of land planted with maize and beans. The products have been added to Columns 4 and 6 but not to the physical yields (Column 2).
[b] See text.
Source: Appendix A.

The Tierra Caliente as part of the Tepalcatepec basin. The progress of the Tierra Caliente was not matched by the rest of the basin. The census, which can only provide a minimum estimate of production in the rest of the basin, registered monetary yields per hectare about 55 per cent as high in this area as the adjusted figures indicate was obtained in the Tierra Caliente.[1] The census reported

[1] This comparison between census data and figures which significantly altered the census data is, in principle, unjustified. Although supplementary evidence

about 76,000 hectares under cultivation in the twenty municipios of the basin outside the Tierra Caliente during the 1959–60 agricultural cycle which yielded a harvest worth almost 71 million pesos. This indicated an absolute decline in the area of cultivation of 19 per cent and a fall in the value of production, in constant prices, of 7 per cent.[1] In this larger area there was 72 per cent as much land reported under cultivation as in the Tierra Caliente, but it produced only 30 per cent as much in value terms. It is obvious that the Tierra Caliente clearly dominated the Tepalcatepec basin's agricultural production by 1960.[2]

The livestock population remained stable from 1950 to 1960 in both areas. According to the estimates by the experiment station in the area, the number of cattle rose slightly to 115,000 in the Tierra Caliente and fell to about 150,000 head in the rest of the basin.[3] Land classified as pasture in the census increased by about

---

indicates that there were large omissions in the census figures from the twenty municipios, as in the Tierra Caliente, the relation between the area and the production figures for those farms which were enumerated is probably an accurate reflection of the actual situation. If the census figures for the Tierra Caliente were used in place of the adjusted figures for monetary yields, then the yields in the rest of the basin would be about seventy-six per cent of those in the Tierra Caliente.

[1] The design of the 1960 Agricultural Census data gathering mechanism is probably the cause of these low figures. It is improbable that results such as these would be wholly caused by under-reporting on the part of those enumerated. Although the totals are probably low, the yields are likely to be representative of those enumerated (see Appendix A).

[2] An analysis of the 1950 and 1960 Agricultural Censuses (Appendix A) indicated that the data recorded in the former are a better representation of the facts than the latter. An intensive field investigation conducted in the Tierra Caliente suggested that under-reporting was likely to be higher when a region was undergoing changes from traditional crops to higher-valued crops. The twenty municipios under discussion, however, were not experiencing structural changes in agriculture during the fifties. The only conclusion which might be drawn from the reported results when they are compared with the actual situation is that there were significant omissions in the enumeration process which were overlooked by field workers.

These data provide sufficient information to support the inference that agricultural production conditions did not change noticeably during the inter-censal period in the twenty municipios outside the Tierra Caliente. Consequently, no analysis was made of the changes that took place in this part of the basin for inclusion in the benefits to be attributed to the Commission's investments in irrigation.

[3] These estimates, available only in the local office of the Ministry of Agriculture, were used instead of those from the census because the latter indicate a drop of about thirty-seven per cent in the livestock population in both zones since 1950. This is not plausible.

one-quarter during the ten-year period in the twenty municipios while it fell 7 per cent in the Tierra Caliente. As might be expected, the number of hectares per head decreased as land pressure increased in the Tierra Caliente. With relative yields declining in agriculture in the rest of the basin, the opportunity cost of pasture land was also declining and the ratio of pasture to livestock increased by almost one-third. However, cattle raising was still more land-using in the Tierra Caliente, where there was almost 50 per cent more pasture per head than in the rest of the basin.

The agricultural labour force in the Tierra Caliente grew faster (89 per cent) than the working population (82 per cent) in the 1950s (Table 13). In the rest of the basin agricultural employment grew at about the same pace as the whole labour force (30 per cent). Labour intensity in the Tierra Caliente declined by 30 per cent because of the sizable increase in cultivated land (150 per cent); there were four hectares of land under cultivation for each man in the agricultural labour force in 1960, when ten years earlier there had been only three. It is likely that labour intensity remained stable or increased slightly in the rest of the region, but it is improbable that it increased by 30 per cent as indicated in the census data.[1]

That rising yields could be obtained at the same time as increasing cultivated land per head of the labour force demonstrates the importance of the considerable capital investment in the Tierra Caliente during this period, in contrast to its relative absence elsewhere in the basin. Outside the Tierra Caliente the problems of small land holdings and low agricultural incomes intensified during the 1950–60 period. In the Tierra Caliente, net agricultural incomes rose rapidly and so did the demand for labour, which pushed up wages. There were, however, serious problems of increasing income inequalities which accompanied this growth.

Costs and the net value of the harvest. The additional requirements of the new technology and the new crops increased the costs of production (Table 25). Because the labour supply did not grow as fast as the demand for agricultural workers (Chapter 5), especially during the cotton, melon, and watermelon seasons,

---

[1] This is further proof of the judgment that the 1960 Agricultural Census seriously understated the area under cultivation and, by implication, the value of agricultural production.

labourers had to be brought in from other regions. High wages were necessary at planting and harvest time to attract these workers to the Tierra Caliente. At these times, often more than one-third of the year, wages in the zone were substantially higher than could be obtained for agricultural work in other nearby regions. During the 1965–6 cotton harvest, approximately 15,000 men were attracted from outside the region to satisfy the labour needs.

The inadequate supply of unskilled-day labourers residing in the zone was due, in part, to the region's unattractive climatic conditions and the lack of permanent job opportunities in the area which could absorb idle hands during slack periods. Skilled farm labour to work mechanical equipment such as tractors and to serve as foremen to direct the unskilled labour was in even shorter supply. This shortage reflected a lack of trained people throughout the nation. As the irrigated land expanded with the completion of new canals and the improvement of old irrigation systems, the demand for labour increased and the upward pressure on wage rates resulted in higher real earnings for many of the workers.[1] This problem was not as acute as it had been in earlier years because migrant farm workers had begun to include the Tierra Caliente on their itinerary during those parts of the year when they knew that unskilled labour would be in demand. It is through this mechanism that the large pool of under-employed labourers in Mexico are able to find sufficient work and ease the pressure on wages during periods of heavy demand.

The very increase in the land under cultivation accounted for part of the higher production costs. The price of land increased as irrigation became more generally available. Idle lands which could be cultivated almost disappeared. Larger differentials in rents were observed between irrigated and non-irrigated land, and it became increasingly difficult to find unclaimed land without irrigation for which a rent should not have been paid, or imputed, to the cost of production.

The increasing area under cultivation led to external diseconomies for the cotton growers as the increase in the number

[1] During the 1965–6 harvest, cotton pickers earned up to four times the normal daily wage in the region.

and intensity of attacks by plagues and insects necessitated the introduction of aerial fumigations for pest control. The increased costs of production as a result of these aerial sprayings exerted greater pressure on the farmer to improve his cultivation techniques to obtain a profitable harvest. The experiment stations pointed out that there was a great deal of waste in the application of fumigants due to ignorance which 'makes cotton production unprofitable.'[1]

As in the case of cotton, melons and watermelons have high costs of production because of the expense of pest control. During the first part of this decade, costs of some producers reached unacceptably high levels, because crops were heavily damaged by insects or fungi. The melon growers suggested that the relatively long history of melon growing in the region will soon come to an end. There is an optimum period during which melons and watermelons can be cultivated profitably before costs become prohibitive as the soil becomes less fertile and pest control more expensive. The Americans in the Tierra Caliente said that their past experience indicated that this period is about seven years.

As a consequence of these factors, the net value of production in 1960 represented a lower proportion of gross production value than it did ten years earlier; it dropped from 37 per cent in 1950 to 33 per cent in 1960 (Table 25). Watermelon continued to be the most profitable crop followed by lemons, cotton, and melon (Table 25, Column 2).

Estimates of the expected net value of production were arrived at by assuming that a profitable harvest can be gathered in three out of every five years on unirrigated land (Table 25, Column 5).[2] The increase in the value of net production over the 1949–50 agricultural cycle was the basis for the estimates of the net agricultural benefits arising from the availability of irrigation water in the zone (Tables 26 and 29).

These production data refer only to the nine principal crops in the Tierra Caliente during the 1959–60 agricultural cycle; an

[1] Instituto Nacional de Investigaciones Agricolas, Secretaría de Agricultura y Ganadería, *El Cultivo del Algodonero en la Cuenca del Río Tepalcatepec* (Antunez, Michoacán, México, 1963), p. 8.
[2] As in 1950, farmers claimed that the 1960 harvest was good.

adjustment was made for the other products grown in the region by using the preliminary figures of the 1960 Agricultural Census. These products were reported to cover 5 per cent of the cultivated area and 10 per cent of the region's gross production value. As in 1950, these products were primarily fruits and were the most productive, per unit of land. Tables 19, 20, 21 and 24 were adjusted, as before, by adding the census figures to the adjusted area and production figures already discussed. Corrections were

Table 25. *Net monetary yields in the Tierra Caliente, Michoacán, 1959–1960*

Crop		Total costs pesos/ hectare (1)	Net monetary yields pesos/ hectare (2)	Net value of harvest '000s pesos (3)	Net value of harvest % (4)	Expected value of harvest '000s pesos (5)
Totals				59,654	100·0	54,085
Beans	Dry	683[b]	552			
	Wet		742	199	320	0·5	280
Maize	Dry	595[b]	491			
	Wet		663	139	7,463	12·5	6,291
Maize and beans		551	356	571	1·0	343
Cotton		3,829	1,652	6,772	11·4	6,772
Lemons		2,269	1,731	14,506	24·3	12,635
Melon		2,222	1,256	5,717	9·6	5,717
Rice		1,477	227	3,139	5·3	3,139
Sesame	Dry	641[b]	592			
	Wet		748	661	7,066	11·8	5,123
Sugar cane	P	2,541[b]	4,189			
	S		1,718	204	113	0·2	113
Watermelon		2,334	3,131	12,411	20·8	12,411
Others[a]				1,576	2·6	1,261

P=original plant; S=subsequent growth.

[a] See Text.   [b] Weighted average

Sources:

Column 1: Barkin, *Economic development*, Appendix II.

2: Table 24, Column 6—Table 25, Column 1.

3: Table 24, Column 1 × Table 25, Column 2.

4: Derived from Column 5.

5: Based on a 60% expectation of a harvest under dry-farming conditions.

made in Table 25 by assuming that three-quarters of the gross value of the additional products represented costs of production and that one-half of the area was irrigated and this not subject to the vagaries of rainfall.

Net agricultural production. In order to make a judgment about agricultural development it is necessary to measure the value of production after its costs have been subtracted. The net value of production is presented in this subsection while the next discusses future developments in the region as a prelude for the estimation of the net benefits from agricultural production which can be attributed to the Commission's investment programme.

Our quantitative picture of the evolution of the basin's agricultural structure since the creation of the Tepalcatepec Commission points out two measurable changes in the agricultural economy of the Tierra Caliente up to 1960: firstly an increase in area under cultivation of 150 per cent; and secondly, a rise in the gross monetary yield per hectare of 108 per cent. Production increased 412 per cent during the first decade of development in the Tierra Caliente.

This progress is the result of an increase in area, a shift from traditional crops to commercialized export crops, an increase in physical yields, and an increase in the prices of some of the products. The availability of irrigation facilitated the expansion of cultivated area and the switch to more valuable products. Technological changes, stimulated by irrigation, permitted a more effective use of modern inputs, such as fertilizers, insecticides, and mechanized equipment, to arrest and even reverse the negative influence of declining soil fertility and the increasing incidence of plagues on physical yields. Nevertheless, irrigated lands needed improved inputs and farmers had to be responsive to market conditions if the potential was to be realized.

The increase in the value of agricultural production was disaggregated to determine how it was achieved.[1] The change in

---

[1] The disaggregation of the gross increase in production was achieved by utilizing the following identity: (A = area, P = price, Y = physical yield)

$$\frac{\Sigma P_{60} Y_{60} A_{60}}{\Sigma P_{50} Y_{50} A_{50}} - 1 \equiv \frac{\frac{\Sigma A_{60}}{\Sigma A_{50}} \Sigma P_{50} Y_{50}\left(A_{60}\frac{\Sigma A_{50}}{\Sigma A_{60}}\right)}{\Sigma P_{50} Y_{50} A_{50}} - 1 + \frac{\Sigma P_{60} Y_{50} A_{50}}{\Sigma P_{50} Y_{50} A_{50}} - 1$$

$$+ \frac{\Sigma P_{50} Y_{60} A_{50}}{\Sigma P_{50} Y_{50} A_{50}} - 1 + \frac{\Sigma(P_{50}\Delta Y \Delta A + Y_{50}\Delta P \Delta A + A_{50}\Delta P \Delta Y + \Delta P \Delta Y \Delta A)}{\Sigma P_{50} Y_{50} A_{50}}$$

area and the concomitant adjustment in the composition of the products accounted for the lion's share of the increase. Together, these two factors accounted for 67 per cent of the increased production,[1] while the rise in prices received by the farmers explained about 8 per cent of the change, and increase in physical yields 5 per cent. These three factors interacted among themselves to induce a further increase in production during the decade of about 20 per cent of the total change. Most of this interaction (15 per cent) was due to the shift in the composition of the products towards products whose physical yields rose.

These improvements were accompanied by similar changes in the net value of agricultural production (Table 26). During the 1950s, the net value product increased more than fourfold. It is expected to double between 1960 and 1970. Measurement of this progress depends on the data discussed in the previous sub-section. Information from four benchmark years—1950, 1955, 1960 and 1965—provided a base for the determination of the amount of cultivated area throughout the period (Tables 19 and 20 and Appendix B); the projections to 1970 were made with the help of information summarized in the next sub-section. Information on market conditions was combined with cost data to obtain profit estimates and to determine the net value of the region's agricultural production (Table 26, Column 2). Agricultural production in the rest of the basin was not included, as explained above, because it did not appear that there were important measurable changes which could be attributed to the Commission's intervention.[2]

Conceptually, the terms of the identity represent (in the following order): (1) the increase in area multiplied by the change composition of the products; (2) the change in prices; (3) the changes in physical yields; and (4) the interaction among all of these factors. We are indebted to Drs Shane Hunt and Walter Hettich for their help on this approach.

[1] Unfortunately, it was not possible to separate out the influence of the change in composition from the increase in area because the two are multiplicative in the identity shown above.

[2] As was noted in the last chapter, the Commission invested in irrigation works in the north-eastern part of the basin where wheat, chickpeas, and sugar cane are important crops. Although no attempt was made to include the benefits from these investments in the total, the changes in the Tierra Caliente heavily outweighed those in the north-eastern part of the region. Table 24 is, therefore, an understatement of the benefits from the Commission's investments in irrigation

The value of net agricultural production rose rapidly from 1961 to 1962 reflecting the change to cotton cultivation. Previously, there had been a steady upward trend in the net value with a spurt in 1957. There was another significant increase in 1965 when the new technique of rice cultivation began to make its influence felt. The decline in the net agricultural product projected during the rest of this decade reflects deteriorating market prospects for cotton and melons, to which we now turn.

Table 26. *Net agricultural production in the Tierra Caliente, Michoacán, 1947–1970*

Crop year ending	Area cultivated (hectares)	Net agricultural production ('000 pesos)
1947	42,317	10,637
1951	42,842	11,375
1952	45,350	13,200
1953	51,625	15,777
1954	55,625	17,653
1955	63,314	20,804
1956	67,300	26,994
1957	76,150	44,622
1958	82,600	47,429
1959	92,450	53,784
1960	105,664	54,483
1961	106,600	68,851
1962	107,400	91,578
1963	106,500	103,971
1964	107,700	108,990
1965	109,500	139,064
1966	109,000	138,218
1967	103,000	131,039
1968	108,000	134,918
1969	114,000	122,003
1970	109,000	113,743

Source: Appendix B.

because of this omission; although this was thought to have had a minimal influence on the results, the quantitative conclusions about the project might have been even more favourable had this data been included.

The future of the Tierra Caliente. The recent history of the Tierra Caliente is characterized by a change from traditional crops to four important commercial products: cotton, lemons, melons, and watermelons. This reorientation of the agricultural endeavours has made the Tierra Caliente a major contributor to Mexico's exports of cotton and melons. The prospects for these crops, or others that can take their place, will determine whether the region will continue to prosper, to stagnate, or to decay.

Cotton is Mexico's most important export crop and now the Tierra Caliente's as well. It was virtually unknown in the basin when the Commission began its operations there in 1947, although the crop had been cultivated in prehispanic times by the inhabitants of the region.[1] Cotton area expanded from 12 hectares in 1950 to 4,100 hectares in 1960 and then jumped to 42,000 hectares in 1965. Several factors limit the expansion of this important crop: the availability of credit to cover production costs is limited, the costs of cultivating cotton are continually rising because of the increasing need for pest control, changing world market conditions have caused its price to fall, and the search for markets has become more difficult. The first two of these problems are discussed elsewhere, but the latter concerns us now.

The softening of the world market is due to a faster growth in the supply than in demand and a change in American marketing policies. As a result, the Mexican farmer received no increase in the money price paid for his crop between 1959 and 1965. Declining world prices,[2] rising costs, and political pressures combined during the 1965–6 season in the Tierra Caliente to press the government to provide subsidies for some farmers by fixing prices paid by the Banco Ejidal to the ejidatarios above the prevailing world market prices.[3]

This situation has produced a group of people who argue that cotton should be discouraged in the Tierra Caliente. There are some who assert that cotton never should have been encouraged in the zone and that the sooner it disappears the better. They point out, rightly, that if sesame was well-cultivated with irrigation to

[1] Aguirre Beltrán, *Problemas de la Población Indígena de la Cuenca del Tepalcatepec*, p. 146.
[2] Banco Nacional de Comercio Exterior, *Comercio Exterior*, November 1965, p. 835.
[3] *El Día* (Mexico), 11 and 22 January 1966.

supplement the rains, the farmers could obtain the same profit per hectare with an investment of less than half that required for cotton. This group, composed principally of agronomists and technical personnel working in the region, also points out that livestock raising could be a potentially important use for the land. Both of these suggestions are possibilities that we will return to shortly.

On the other hand, there is a considerable number of people who have vested interests in the continuing cultivation of cotton. Most obvious among these are the owners of the cotton gins who reportedly reap handsome profits from their operations even when world market conditions are not up to their expectations. They are joined by businessmen who sell and service agricultural machinery, provide aerial fumigations, and distribute seeds, fertilizers, and other inputs. These groups have a strong influence over cotton production because they are a major source of production credits when farmers cannot obtain them from banking sources. They also cultivate sizable amounts of land under rental contracts.

The present subsidy programme for cotton is unlikely to be continued for many years, and high-cost cotton producers in the Tierra Caliente will have to find profitable alternatives. The principal barrier retarding the shift to other crops is a lack of other sources of credit to replace the funds presently supplied by the ginning plants. Thus, the government or other private interests will have to provide additional agricultural credit and some technical assistance to facilitate the shift if the subsidy programme is to be discontinued with a minimum of disruption.

Recent experience suggests that there will be a gradual decline in the area planted in cotton as the high-cost producers change to other products. During the five agricultural cycles following the 1964–5 season, the cotton area will probably fall to about 30,000 hectares.[1]

Melon and watermelon production are also faced with limitations imposed by the demand for the product. Because of their perishable nature, these products must be sold soon after harvest.

---

[1] This reduction in cotton planting will probably be accompanied by a reduction in the total cultivated area in the region as well as a return to some of the more traditional crops.

The only market, up to this time, has been the United States and Canada during the period from January to April when Mexico supplies almost all of the melons consumed in the United States.[1] Demand, according to those in the Tierra Caliente, fluctuates with the weather and the number of conventions in New York City. The Tierra Caliente is the most important Mexican melon producing region, although its share of the market is falling as melon growers move into new areas. In 1963 the Tierra Caliente accounted for about three-quarters of the American imports of Mexican canteloupes but by 1965 it supplied only 60 per cent of Mexican exports to the US.[2] Prices often fluctuate widely for the export crop; during a recent harvest, the price for the same quality fruit varied from 60 to 20 pesos a crate. Even this bottom price, however, is above the normal domestic price, which, at its highest, is about 20 pesos per crate for the farmer.[3]

With these conditions, there is a strong incentive to control costs because the growers, and even the suppliers, have little influence over the market prices.[4] In addition, these producers do not have the political leverage necessary to obtain a government income stabilization programme for their products. Consequently, production and income in the Tierra Caliente fluctuate sharply and this has proved disastrous for some growers. There is now discussion of moving to other areas where disease control would be less costly and of adopting a pattern of rotation based on the

[1] *Cf.* US Department of Agriculture, Agricultural Marketing Service, *Fresh Fruit and Vegetable Shipments* (AMS–36, 1963) (Washington: Government Printing Office, May 1964), pp. 19–20.

[2] US Department of Commerce, Bureau of the Census, *US Imports of Merchandise for Consumption* (Washington: Government Printing Office, April 1963 and April 1965).

[3] There are two prices for melon depending on the market in which it is sold. Domestic prices are considerably lower than export prices, and the quality of domestic fruit is correspondingly inferior.

[4] Producers have little control over melon prices because of the organization of the market. Individual farmers seek credit from the lender-distributor who is the intermediary between producers and buyers. There are about ten competing distributors acting under conditions of imperfect competition; each has to consider his impact on the total supply, but no one can control the total quantity of melons on the market.

Growers view the market as perfectly competitive. Expected demand is a function of last year's actual demand and supply also depends on the amount of credit available. Market clearing often results in a cobweb cycle whose fluctuations are held in check by the imperfectly competitive distributors.

seven-year cycle to minimize damage from disease. The probable result of the current consolidation moves will be a slight diminution of the area under cultivation to about 10,000 hectares for melon and watermelon within the Tierra Caliente and a system of rotation within the zone. At the same time, there will be a growth of new melon producing areas as suitable areas are located and as the necessary roads are constructed and agricultural experiments are carried out. There is a great potential market for these fruits within Mexico which has not been developed because the fruit available domestically consists of rejects from export production.

Lemon production is currently being encouraged by the Banco Ejidal as a result of a long-term contract to export lemon products which the Bank's processing plant recently signed. Production was very low, and only a small part of the plant's capacity was being used prior to the signing of the new contract. Bank officials expect to authorize sufficient credit to increase the area dedicated exclusively to lemon trees to 10,000 irrigated hectares in the near future.

The area under rice cultivation will probably not increase from its present level of 12,000 hectares during the next few years. The requirement that all production be done with the Chinese or transplant system and the limited amount of water available for rice production discourage its expansion. The change to the transplant system was necessitated by increasing demands for irrigation water (the new system makes more efficient use of water), but even under this method of cultivation, rice requires about three times as much water as other crops. As a result, the irrigation district's administration was unwilling to permit further expansion of rice cultivation.[1] Recent experience indicates that rice yields can be raised to an average of five tons a hectare with some yields of eight or more tons; these changes will come about as cultivation techniques improve through observation, experimentation, and instruction by agronomists in the use of water and the application of fertilizers.

[1] The irrigation district administration controls the planting of rice and other crops by issuing permits for specified crops after water charges are paid. The water fee for rice cultivation is three times as high per agricultural cycle as for other crops.

Sesame is the only other crop that is likely to experience an important change in its relative importance. When new techniques for the production of this product are accepted by the farmer, and this is just beginning to occur, yields may rise to one and one-half tons per hectare. Rural prices for sesame have also risen, and the crop is therefore becoming more attractive. Agricultural department officials think it likely that 20,000 hectares will be sown with sesame by 1970, and that a large proportion of this land will be irrigated.

One further aspect of the agricultural picture remains to be discussed: livestock. It was noted earlier in this chapter that the number of head of cattle in the Tierra Caliente remained constant during the 1950–60 period, although the area dedicated to pasture decreased as the demand for crop land increased. This trend did not continue because, as indicated, the amount of land under cultivation has not increased very much since 1960. On the contrary, it is possible that there will be small increases in pasture land as intensive cattle-raising becomes more common.

At present the two government agricultural credit banks are encouraging the development of the intensive approach to cattle-raising on a pilot basis. Their combined operations do not involve more than 5,000 head, but there is great hope that these projects will stimulate similar enterprises by others. The banks are financing the maintenance of artificial pasture lands and the upgrading of the cattle stock. Preliminary results confirm the faith the banks had in this project and indicate that the net profits per hectare from cattle operations will be between 1,000 and 3,000 pesos. In spite of this auspicious beginning, it is improbable that there will be any significant move to this type of enterprise in the near future. Such a programme would require a large investment in fixed and working capital, as well as a relatively long gestation period before the investment produced a return.

The combined effects of all these tendencies is that there will be little change in the variety of products planted in the Tierra Caliente before 1970. By that time, there will be more than 80,000 hectares planted in cotton, lemons, melons, rice, sesame, and watermelons.

Maize will certainly not disappear from the scene, and there may be some small quantities of new crops, especially high-valued vegetables, and renewed emphasis on the region's fruit producing potential. There may even be some drop in the area under cultivation, but this will be relatively small and will come from the non-irrigated parts of the zone. The benefits from the irrigation works were calculated for the coming years on the basis of this analysis and added to those actually observed (Table 26) for an estimation of the total benefits from the availability of irrigation water in the region.

Entrepreneurship and finance

The developments which we have just described were strongly influenced by the availability of agricultural credit in the Tierra Caliente. The institutions, businesses, and individuals who provide agricultural credit have played an important role in shaping the progress of the region and in determining the beneficiaries of the public investment programme. Most commercial agricultural production cannot continue without the assistance of credit for such out-of-pocket expenses as seed, fertilizers, machinery, and labour even if the farmer is able to pay for his own living expenses during the growing season.

The striking thing about agricultural development in the Tierra Caliente is the influential role played by suppliers of credit in determining which products were introduced and the timing of these changes. Several different credit sources played this role for varying reasons which we shall explore below, but in assessing agricultural development it is important to note that the initiative for innovations in the Tierra Caliente has often been taken by outsiders seeking to stimulate the region's contribution to their other business activities rather than by the farmers in the area. Past experience suggests that any groups wishing to introduce innovations into the region usually try to persuade farmers to accept credit from them to plant new crops.

Credit is not, however, important only when new products are being cultivated. Most crops require it to some extent and the ease of access to financial assistance is an important determinant of the prosperity of the farmer. In a developing country credit is likely to be scarce and even more so in a prosperous region like the Tierra Caliente where the demands for credit increased dramatically in a very short period of time. Given this situation, it is not surprising that the people who controlled credit could determine not only which crops would be planted but also who would plant them.

In this section we explore the influence of credit on the agricultural sector during its initial years of growth by grouping lenders according to the motives for supplying credit. After describing the entrepreneurial activities of the public banking institutions in the region we discuss those of the American melon growers. Another group which entered the picture later is the private cotton-ginning interests anxious to ensure a steady and reliable supply of raw cotton so that its other investments would be profitable. A third group, the local merchants, was interested in expanding its sales of agricultural supplies and other goods while a fourth group, the private banks, participated in the financing of agricultural development as an extension of its normal lending functions.

Two of the government's agricultural credit banks operate in the Tierra Caliente and have tried to serve an entrepreneurial function in addition to serving their more traditional role as a vehicle for channelling funds to the ejidatarios and small farmers on private lands. The former group is served by the Banco Nacional de Crédito Ejidal (Banco Ejidal) which is practically the only source of credit to the ejidal sector which, under the law, does not have the right to mortgage its land in order to obtain the working capital necessary for commercial crop production. Another bank, the Banco Regional de Michoacán, serves the small non-ejidal farmer in the Tierra Caliente; it is a branch of the Banco Nacional de Crédito Agrícola.

The Banco Ejidal lends money to cover producing and living costs and maintains constant supervision over the borrowers. The bank has been operating in the Tierra Caliente for more than two decades with its most important operations located in Lombardía and Nueva Italia, the co-operative ejidos on the Cussi land. It experienced large losses because of crop failures and mismanagement during its first fifteen years in the region and, as a result, has become more selective in its lending operations. It withdrew from several ejidos as a result of high losses and only lends to the most successful farmers in the communities in which it is currently working.[1] The Ejidal bank's operations have concentrated on maize, cotton, lemon orchards, and rice; it also played an important entrepreneurial role in stimulating cotton production and rebuilding the lemon orchards which had begun to decay.

The Banco Ejidal's influence was of great importance in encouraging the expansion of cotton production in the Tierra Caliente. The bank built a cotton-ginning plant in 1956 from used components of other plants which were no longer in service in other parts of the country and began to finance the production of cotton. In 1956 it provided credit for 197 hectares of cotton[2] and expanded its operations to more than 2,000 hectares in the following year.[3] By 1960 it had further expanded its operations to cover more than 3,000 hectares. In 1964, it lent money for almost 12,000 hectares (Table 27) and was operating a second ginning plant with high-speed machinery to process the increased production; this accounted for more than one-fourth of the total planted area.

The Banco Ejidal oversees the cultivation of cotton from the earliest stages of the preparation of the land to the harvesting and processing of the crop. It provides some credit in cash to pay direct production costs, such as payment to farm hands and other employees and living expenses of the farmer's family during the growing season. It provides the rest of the credit in kind—in the form of chemicals and seeds, rented machinery, and services, such as technical assistance and ginning—which it then deducts from the value of the crop which it sells on the world market, along with cotton from other producing areas, as the agent of the producers. The growers thus reap profits from the production

---

[1] Many of its loans supported a political decision to help the collective ejidos of Lombardía and Nueva Italia at any cost. These experiments in communal farming were showcase examples of what could be done through the land reform. This support has become more selective in the past eight years. The Bank also withdrew from other ejidos where politics originally influenced lending policies. Its present management seems intent on keeping the Bank on a money-making basis.

[2] Banco Nacional de Crédito Ejidal, S.A. de C.V., *Boletín de Estudios Especiales* (México) VIII: 88 (15 May 1957).   [3] *Ibid.*, IX: 130 (10 July 1958).

and processing of the products and do not have to pay a middle-man for its disposal since the bank only charges the actual costs of administering its services plus a monthly interest charge of 1 per cent.

Table 27. *Agricultural credit in the Tierra Caliente*

Source and product	Area covered (hectares)	% Crop financed by loan	Credit granted '000s pesos
Banco Nacional de Crédito Ejidal			
1964–5	15,052		56,054
Corn	1,843	9·5	1,584
Cotton	11,667	27·8	52,195
Rice	960	8·0	1,325
Sesame	1,582	13·2	485
Cattle and bee-keeping			257
Others[a]			208
Banco Regional de Michoacán			
1965–6	6,409		14,472
Corn	2,277	11·7	926
Cotton	2,777	6·9	12,030
Sesame	752	5·4	338
Sorghum	595	n.a.	178
Cattle			1,000
Private banks, January 1965			13,881
Agriculture			10,593
Livestock			3,288
Ginning plants 1964–5			
Cotton	27,500	65·5	110,000
Melon packers 1965			
Melons	11,000	100·0	33,000

n.a. Not available.

[a] Includes beans, sugar mill, and pumping equipment.

Sources:

Banco Nacional de Crédito Ejidal, Apatzingán Office, Accounting Dept.
Banco Regional de Michoacán, Apatzingán Office, Accounting Dept.
Private Banks, Banco de México, SA.
Ginning Plants and Melon Packers, estimates made by the writer; accurate within a probable range of 25%.

The bank's importance in the financing of the cotton crop lies not so much in the size of its operations, which account for more than one-quarter of the crop, but in the example it provided of the profitability of such an undertaking. Private interests observed the results of the government bank with interest and responded to the favourable results with additional investments in plants for the initial processing of raw cotton and credit for cotton production. Although the bank provided a large part of the credit for the crop in the early stages of cotton growing in the region, the example it set by lending financial support to this very costly product and by processing the cotton in the region in its own gins was of paramount importance in inducing private enterprise to come into the region. The Banco Ejidal itself was not able to finance the further expansion of the crop because of the lack of financial resources which perennially plagues the institution.

In recent years the bank's financial resources have increased and its credit operations in cotton have expanded. The private sector has been retrenching slightly as the costs of producing cotton have risen and their profit margins declined. Therefore, even after the bank succeeded in stimulating private interests to undertake responsibility for a large part of the cotton production, it has continued to maintain its position as an important source of finance for the crop and has stepped in when private ginning plants were reluctant to continue to finance the crop. The bank's cotton operation may be considered a co-operative effort involving both the bank and the ejidatarios eligible for credit. The problem with the present arrangement is that the increase in land brought under cultivation has come from the more prosperous parts of the zone. As a result, there are constant complaints of discrimination against the less fortunate sections of the region.

More recently (1965–6), the bank has begun to exert an important influence in rehabilitating the lemon orchards in the Tierra Caliente. The Nacional Financiera, the publicly-owned Mexican development bank, transferred a large processing plant to the bank for operation. It has been operating at considerably less than full capacity for many years because of insufficient demand in export markets, but it has recently signed a contract for the export of lemon juice concentrates and oil derivatives. In an effort to encourage ejidatarios to improve their groves, it has been providing credit to produce the fruit and promising to buy it as it matures. The lemon plant is the most important producer of lemon products in the region and can transform the fruit into juice, citric acid, and oils, in addition to preparing wastes for forage and packing fruit for domestic and export markets.

The innovative activities of the Banco Nacional de Crédito Ejidal were not limited to cotton and lemons. In the early 1950s the bank joined other, already established, interests to finance the production of canteloupe melons for export to the lucrative North American market.[1] This financing was meant to complement the credit provided by the American melon interest which has been in the region for many years so that the total area planted with the melons might increase. This programme was rapidly terminated as Mexican capital moved in to finance this profitable crop and expand it to the limit of the demand for the product. The fact that the bank was unable to make satisfactory marketing arrangements for the melons in the eastern United States market reduced the advantage that the bank could provide to the ejidatarios over private sources of credit, and the bank withdrew in 1957.

The bank recently began construction of a sugar mill in Gabriel Zamora (Lombardía) to complement plans for the planting of sugar cane in various parts of the zone. Experiments at the agricultural station, which the bank helps to finance, indicate that yields will be almost four times as high as those realized in 1950 when sugar was in decline in the region. No new plantings have yet been made, and it is too early to judge the results of this experiment. It is indicative, however, of the bank's encouragement of further diversification of the region's agricultural economy.

The bank also constructed a rice mill to process the rice crop which it was financing in Lombardía and Nueva Italia. This crop has become less important in recent years because of the upsurge of cotton, but the bank continues to finance some ejidal production, which it then processes in its mill. Some maize and sesame growers also receive credit from the bank for their production

---

[1] Banco Nacional de Crédito Ejidal, S.A. de C.V., *Boletín de Estudios Especiales* (México) IX: 130 (10 July 1958).

costs, but these loans are insignificant when compared to cotton (Table 27 shows that in 1964-5 the bank financed about 1,500 hectares of sesame, 1,800 of corn, and less than 1,000 of rice).

The most striking thing about the bank's history in the Tierra Caliente has been its role as an innovator and entrepreneur in encouraging the region to diversify its agricultural economy and convincing private interests of the attractiveness of new lines of investment. This picture is in contrast to the usual conception of the bank as an inefficient instrument of the Mexican Government to subsidize the backward farmers in the collective agricultural sector. In the Tierra Caliente it has tried to pare its losses and has actively encouraged the expansion of commercialized agriculture in co-operation with private interests.[1]

The second public credit bank, the Banco Regional de Michoacán, is a branch of the Banco Nacional de Crédito Agrícola which provides credit for small private landowners throughout the nation. In the Tierra Caliente, the bank acquired the assets of a large landlord, William Jenkins, when he died in 1963; these facilities are now being used for the benefit of the bank's borrowers. Although its operations are much smaller than those of the Banco Ejidal, they have grown substantially in recent years and with this growth has come an effort to become more innovative. In 1960 it provided less than 2 million pesos of credit for about 4,500 hectares of unirrigated maize land, while in the 1965-6 agricultural cycle it lent more than 14 million pesos to the owners of 6,400 hectares for maize, cotton, sesame, sorghum, and cattle raising (Table 27).[2] Most of this credit was for 2,777 hectares of cotton, but the bank also lent 1 million pesos for 1,250 head of cattle in an experiment to determine how attractive livestock enterprises can be. In all, it financed crops on about one-fifth of the private land in the Tierra Caliente.

[1] In doing this the bank was strongly influenced by the personal intervention of important people in the region. Political arrangements and friendships established in the 1950s were important in the bank's consolidation moves and were the cause of the complaint that the bank was the tool of those who were naturally better off. A large part of the losses of former years is probably due to these arrangements and some of the ejidatarios who no longer have access to credit from the bank were probably victims of the campaign to eliminate these deleterious influences.

[2] Banco Regional de Michoacán, Apatzingán Office, Accounting Department.

The bank also operates an ice plant, and finances the operations of a ginning plant owned by some of its borrowers. All of these operations, however, are on a much smaller scale than those of the Banco Ejidal. Its recent entry into cattle-raising indicates that the bank is anxious to follow the tradition of the other national bank in the region by encouraging a diversification of the region's economy. Accordingly, the director of the bank was enthusiastic about the possible role his bank could play in avoiding stagnation because of limited demand for the products now produced in the region.[1] Both institutions, therefore, are combining their normal functions—the provision of inexpensive agricultural credit and technical assistance—with an entrepreneurial effort to ensure the future prosperity of the region by diversifying production.

In the private sector, the most notable example of such entrepreneurial activity with significant benefits for the region is the growth of melon and watermelon production. These crops are presently financed almost exclusively by the five to ten packers who have an interest in maintaining production so that they can fulfill their contracts to supply the fruit in the United States. They were first planted in the region more than two decades ago in response to the possibilities offered by the North American market and were financed by American interests. In the 1950s the Americans encouraged their Mexican workers to take over the financing, production, and embarking of the fruit, and remained in the region to assure sufficient fruit supplies for the four winter months during which the Tierra Caliente supplies the market. At the same time, the Americans are moving to other parts of Mexico in search of additional sources of supply of melons and other fruits.

In 1965, about 33 million pesos were loaned to farmers to finance melon production during the three month growing period. The farmers themselves supplied another 25 million pesos to pay the costs that the lenders would not cover.[2] No interest is charged for the loans, but the grower must sell his harvest to the

---

[1] Interview with Benito Casares, Director, Banco Regional de Michoacán, April 1966.
[2] These estimates of the amount of credit provided by the packers and the supplementary costs paid by the farmers are subject to a wide margin of error, perhaps as much as twenty-five per cent on either side of the cited figure.

packer providing the credit. Most of the credit was provided from Mexican funds accumulated from past profits from melon harvests in the Tierra Caliente; some growers were financed by American capital, but this source of credit has been declining in importance with the passage of time.

The entrepreneurial activity of the Americans in establishing melon growing in the Tierra Caliente was not unique; it also occurred in northern Mexico in connection with truck farming products and other fruits. It is now being expanded to other parts of Mexico and existing capital is being shifted into new areas as Mexican interests move into the established areas. This shift from foreign to domestic capital is encouraged by many of the Americans because it means that they can continue to expand their sources of supply for established products and experiment with new products without increasing their investment. The Americans are also providing the opportunity to diversify the agriculture of old and new regions alike. For instance, in the Tierra Caliente, cucumbers and other valuable vegetables for which there is a large potential market in the United States are being planted on an experimental basis.

The potential supply of this type of foreign investment in Mexico is probably increasing and could play a growing role in exploring the productive potential of new regions and the possibilities for diversification in other areas. As labour and land become more expensive in the United States, the development of new lower cost sources of supply in Mexico is being encouraged. The Americans have been willing to provide the working capital and technical assistance for such ventures which are usually undertaken in co-operation with ambitious Mexicans. In view of the limited resources for the expansion of the agriculture extension service and the small number of agronomists willing to work in the field, this additional source of help for improving the productivity of agriculture should be encouraged by the government.

The private cotton-ginning interests also provide credit to ensure a steady source of raw cotton for their mills and delivery contracts. Unlike the melon marketers, these companies did not pioneer the development of the crop; quite the contrary, their late entrance is rather surprising.

The cotton-ginning plants provided almost all the credit for production which was not supplied by the two government banks. They granted credit for more than 27,000 hectares of cotton production in 1964, of about 110 million pesos, more than double the credit appropriated by the Banco Ejidal for the purpose (Table 27).[1] The ginning plants were forced to extend credit to ensure a minimum supply of raw cotton and an adequate return on their fixed investment in ginning equipment. The ginning plants have agreements similar to those of the Banco Ejidal with the local agricultural input suppliers so that the planters received most of their credit in kind. They also supervise the planter and provide technical assistance to ensure that the supplies and money are properly used; the borrower is charged for these services, although it is really the lender's way of protecting his investment. Unlike those borrowing from the government banks, most planters who received credit from the processors must sell their raw cotton to the ginning plants and cannot reap the profits from ginning; the difference can be as much as 1,000 pesos per hectare, an important consideration in view of the rising costs of production of cotton. The borrower is charged $1\frac{1}{2}$ per cent monthly for the money he borrows from the ginning plants.

A third group of lenders is the merchants who sell agricultural inputs and other goods to local farmers. The input suppliers give credit in the form of deferred payments for goods purchased prior to the harvest and charge $1\frac{1}{2}$ per cent a month as interest. It is rare that they provide actual cash for living expenses or the payment of day-labourers. Since these firms are selling fertilizers, improved seeds, and insecticides, their clientele are members of the technically more advanced part of the population. These lenders are usually dealing with people who understand how to combine fertilizers, better seeds, and water to obtain satisfactory yields. Some farmers, however, cannot obtain credit from local banks and must resort to this higher priced credit; others may be reluctant to mortgage their lands as bank borrowing requires, as they may lose them in the event of crop failure. Suppliers

[1] This is a rough estimate which is probably within fifteen per cent of the amount lent by the ginning plants in 1964–5. Most of this capital comes from national organizations which finance production in several growing areas.

of agricultural inputs who benefit from increased sales will be more lenient with defaulters than will banks.

Other local merchants provide financial assistance for some of the farmers who plant traditional crops—maize, rice, and sesame. These are planted without fertilizers and no improved seeds are used; the maize and sesame are usually not irrigated during the rainy season. The credit is needed for the living expenses of the farmer and his family during the agricultural cycle. This is the most risky type of loan for the lender because the farmers are the least advanced and use primitive techniques whose success depends on the weather. If the crop fails, as it often does, the lender must write off the loan. It is also the most disadvantageous from the point of view of the borrower because of the unfavourable terms on which these loans are granted (often $1\frac{1}{2}$ per cent monthly interest plus a discount on the prevailing market price). The amount of credit available from the Banco Ejidal for these products (Table 27) is limited and so most people who cannot finance their own production out of the family's resources or day-labour during the agricultural cycle must sell their crop 'a tiempo', i.e. before it is harvested.

This credit permits the intermediaries to have a significant influence on the prices of crops in the region, in spite of the efforts of the government to provide a minimum price support programme for subsistence farmers. Although the official price of maize was 94 centavos a kilogram in 1965, the farmer rarely received more than 80 or 85 centavos for his product at harvest time in spite of the standing offer of the government price support agency to buy unlimited quantities of maize from the producers. Those people required to sell to merchants who lent them money for the crop often receive as little as 70 or 75 centavos per kilogram. The buyers of rice and sesame have an even tighter control over the market because there are fewer of them and the crops have to be processed before they can be used.

These sources of credit have played an important role in filling the gap left by other lending institutions. In the absence of credit facilities provided by merchants and supply houses, many farmers would not have been able to plant their land. These lenders are able to judge the performance of their customers and allocate the scarce supply of working capital among the most productive. In doing this, they are assuming a large risk because many borrowers are unable to provide any security for the loans. The higher cost of capital to the farmers that have to appeal to these sources of credit is a reflection of the lower productive potential and higher risk of the more primitive cultivation techniques. Nevertheless, the merchants undoubtedly do reap monopoly profits from their financial activities.

Finally the private banking system also provides a small amount of credit for agriculture in the Tierra Caliente. The total portfolio of the private banks in the region for agricultural loans was about 6 million pesos in 1961 and it grew to almost 11 million in 1965 (compared with more than 50 million pesos for cotton loans by the Banco Ejidal for the previous harvest). Livestock interests borrowed 1·8 million pesos in 1961 and increased their obligations to 3,330,000 pesos by the beginning of 1965. The rapid increase in loans (starting from a very small base) was partly the result of funds from the Alliance for Progress which were re-lent by the private banking system to small farmers at low interest rates (6 per cent annually). These banks cannot lend to ejidatarios because the farmers have nothing to pledge as security for the loans; they cannot mortgage their lands and many do not have agricultural machinery or other capital equipment to secure the loans. As a result, the banks limit their operations to the larger and more successful commercial farmers who pledge their land and equipment for the loans which carry a $1\frac{1}{2}$ per cent monthly interest charge.

We have seen that agricultural credit in the Tierra Caliente has been very influential in determining the amount of land planted in each of the commercial crops which are relatively expensive to cultivate, and has been important in determining which of the farmers have been able to take advantage of the land's economic potential. The decision to supply credit for certain crops is the main determinant of the resulting pattern of crops in the region. The Banco Nacional de Crédito Ejidal's role as an innovator in channelling resources towards the more valuable export crops and providing an instructive example has been decisive in the past development of the region. Private credit sources stepped in to supply working capital to other parts of the agricultural economy that the government banks were unable or unwilling to accommodate. The availability of private or public credit for cotton, melons, and watermelons, was of paramount importance in determining which of the farmers have prospered from the public investment programme. Credit for the other crops often gave the lender a great deal of control over the markets and planters he lent to.

Land tenure

These changes in the region's agriculture have not come about solely in response to the investment programme of the Tepalcatepec Commission. In addition to the important influence of agricultural credit on production in the Tierra Caliente, adjustments in land tenure patterns were a prerequisite for the success of the irrigation project. As we have seen, the expropriation of the Cussi holdings represented a significant change in the structure of land holdings and at the present time well over one-half of the land is nominally in the hands of ejidatarios whose rights are guaranteed under the constitution.

Ironically, some of the land distributed under the land reform programme has passed into the control of private moneyed interests who rent land from ejidatarios for commercial exploitation because the latter lack the working capital for adequate utilization of the irrigated lands. Such renting arrangements began shortly before 1960 when there was a need for large investments in land improvements so that farm machinery could be used. The land in the Tierra Caliente is very rocky and the cost of clearing the plots was beyond the means of most ejidatarios. Legal arrangements were worked out with people who wanted to farm the land. The usual terms were that they would clear the land in lieu of paying a rent and would have the right to farm the land for two years, usually a sufficient time to realize an adequate return on the land-clearing operation. After this operation, which cleared about 40,000 hectares, some continued to rent their land to the 'investors' and worked as day-labourers on their own land or on other plots.

As we discussed in Chapter 3, this development is illegal but is winked at by officials in the region. Much of the cotton, melon, and watermelon crops are planted on rented ejidal land under illegal or semi-legal arrangements.[1] This practice attracts much criticism of the way in which the Mexican land reform has been diverted from its goal of improving the lot of the peasant. According to this argument, influential and/or aggressive people are taking advantage of their position by working large tracts of land rented from ejidatarios. An examination of this point of view indicates that there might be less injustice in, and more economic benefits from, this practice than the critics would like one to believe. In usual circumstances it would be unwise for a person to rent his land to others if he thought that he could obtain a larger yield by working it himself. Field investigation in the Tierra Caliente did not indicate that there is any reason to doubt that this principle applies there. Explanations for possible differences in potential yields on the same plot were sought. We found that many ejidatarios did not have access to sufficient credit to use their land for the most valuable commercial crops. In some communities no credit was available, while in others it was not sufficient to permit every farmer to plant the more expensive commercial crops. This limited the range of crops which the peasants could consider to the traditional products of maize, sesame, and, in some cases, rice.

Credit availability, in turn, is a function of the technical capacity of the individual and his past experience with commercial crops. Thus, a person who has never cultivated cotton and did not have experience with fertilizers and chemical pest controls was not likely to be granted credit for its cultivation. The Banco Ejidal provides some technical assistance as does the local extension agent, but their resources are limited and most of their attention is devoted to the more successful communities. Private sources have expanded the technical base, but here again success breeds success and the poorer villages have not been able to obtain the initial assistance which would permit them to change their production methods.

[1] The local office of the Ministry of Agriculture estimated, on the basis of a survey, that about 68 per cent of the ejidal land planted in cotton was being rented and that this was as high as 89 per cent in the Cupatitzio-Cajones District in 1963. In 1965 the office estimated that about 65 per cent of the ejidal cotton crop was on lands rented to private interests.

Finally, many had never worked on irrigated lands before the advent of the Commission, and there is a widespread misunderstanding of the influence of water from a dependable source on crops. Even after more than five or ten years of regular irrigation, many seriously damage their crops by applying too much or too little water. Thus, the yields are lower even on subsistence crops than might be expected from a farmer with some familiarity with the new technology.

Insufficient credit and lack of technical knowledge combine to make it more attractive for some farmers to rent out their land, or arrange some variant on this form which is more legal, to others who can make better use of it. The farmers seem to consider their usufruct rights as capital grants which they have the right to dispose of in a way which maximizes their expected returns. Thus, the alteration of the ideal ejidal structure is beneficial from the point of view of increasing the productivity of the limited land available for cultivation. In addition, the ejidatario often works his own land and acquires technical knowledge about the cultivation of more valuable crops which he can and often does apply to his own production in future years. In this way, renting may be considered an improvement in individual welfare because the peasant becomes a free agent, to the extent that he is willing to bend the law to dispose of his resources in the most productive way possible given his own preference and production-possibility functions.

A second distortion of the Mexican land reform legislation which was also discussed earlier is the holding by single landowners of more than the legal maximum amounts of land in the Tierra Caliente, usually through family relations or nominees. Part of the reason why the land reform limited the size of the individual plots was the inefficiency of the *latifundistas* (large landholders) in pre-revolutionary Mexico. In modern Mexico, land no longer plays as important a role as it once did in terms of social prestige and the existence of large expanses of uncultivated lands invites expropriation. Thus, the efficient utilization of large private holdings is encouraged by the new institutional framework, although there must be a disincentive to make large investments of fixed capital which could not be recovered if the land were expropriated. Several well-known large landholders in the Tierra Caliente make good use of their lands by using modern technology and planting commercial crops. It is often argued that the transfer of their land to the peasants now working the land would reduce the high yields currently obtained because the workers would lack credit and technical expertise. There are no figures to let us compare yields of large and small farms in the Tierra Caliente. Ordinarily, however, we should expect small farms to have at least as high per acre yields as large farms, unless they were poorly managed or seriously handicapped by a lack of credit, since more labour is applied per acre. In addition, the current arrangement is contrary to the ideal of more equal income distribution. Nevertheless, it is impossible to deny that the present pattern of thriving commercial agriculture, privately owned and financed, is impressive and is contributing substantially to goals of national and regional development.

THE INDUSTRIALIZATION OF THE TIERRA CALIENTE

The Tierra Caliente's economy has not diversified greatly in response to the stimuli provided by the Comisión del Tepalcatepec's investment programme. During the past two decades the infrastructure has expanded so that low-cost transport and power are readily available. Economic activity has been stimulated by the increase in arable land and the rise in the value of agricultural production. In spite of these changes, there have been few additions to the number of industrial enterprises and most of them are satellites of the region's new agricultural products.

This is the sort of results that would have been predicted from Hirschman's analysis of linkage effects which we discussed in the first chapter. Primary products do not provide a broad-based stimulus for the industrialization of a region. According to Hirschman, even with the most modernized production techniques requiring the heavy use of capital equipment, the linkage effects would be very weak.[1]

Verification of this hypothesis is found in the experience of the

[1] Albert Hirschman, *The Strategy of Economic Development* (New Haven: Yale University Press 1958), p. 109.

Tierra Caliente. Most of the diversification that has occurred in the Tierra Caliente has been a response to the consumer needs of a rapidly expanding population rather than a response to induced forward linkages which might stimulate economic development. Chemical and farm machinery companies established local agencies to sell their products. Several groups opened servicing centres for agricultural machinery and aerial fumigation to satisfy the requirements of an increasingly complex agricultural technology. Nevertheless, the activities which stem from backward linkages employ very few people; all of the manufacturing and commercial activities employ only one-tenth of the labour force in the region (Table 13).

From the national point of view the significant growth in the use of agricultural machinery in the region may have contributed to backward linkages in the production of equipment, but the regional linkages were slight. The Ministry of Water Resources reported that there were 900 tractors in use in 1963. An estimate for 1966 places the figure at 2,000.[1] There were also 300 seeders and 371 work vehicles of all types working on irrigated lands in the Tierra Caliente during 1963[2]; the number has grown markedly since that time. Finally, several airfields serve the many small planes engaged in aerial spraying during the cotton and melon seasons. The income from sales and servicing is minimal in comparison with agricultural incomes; all of the farm machinery used in the region is probably worth less than one-half of the value of the 1965 cotton crop.[3]

The fabrication and mixing of chemical fertilizers was the second largest industry, after ice making, in the region in 1960 according to the Industrial Census.[4] It accounted for one-fifth of

---

[1] México, Secretaría de Recursos Hidráulicos, Dirección General de Distritos de Riego, Departamento de Estadística, *Informe Estadístico No. 27: La Mecanización Agrícola en los Distritos de Riego, Ciclo 1962–63* (Mexico, 1964). We made the 1966 estimate in collaboration with the agricultural extension agent in the region. [2] *Ibid.*

[3] This comparison was based on estimates of the average value of various types of equipment made by the salesmen. There is sufficient margin of error allowed for the statement to be accepted as an indication of the order of magnitude.

[4] The Census indicated that there was a sizable installation for the production of medicinal pharmaceutical products in Apatzingán which, according to interviews in the region, never existed. It is probable that an error in coding was made and that the data refer to the fabrication and mixing of chemical fertilizers.

the value-added in the basin, but employed less than 5 per cent of the industrial labour force. Most of the products mixed and packaged in the region are used locally and do not enter into the national distribution channels of the companies operating in the Tierra Caliente.

Other new elements have sprung up as part of the region's industrial sector. Forward linkages have created 'satellite industries' —those closely related to another activity and whose value-added is small in comparison with the value of the agricultural product itself. The newest and most important of these industries is the ginning plant. There are presently ten ginning plants which can process raw cotton before it is shipped to market. They represent the largest private investment of any kind in the region.[1] Two of the plants are owned and operated by the Banco Nacional de Crédito Ejidal and serve only those farmers working on land expropriated under the land reform programme. The first to operate in the zone was constructed in 1956. One of the private processing installations is co-operatively owned, and several others are wholly or partly owned by large national organizations with extensive cotton operations.

This processing increases the value of cotton by about 20 per cent. For example, in 1964, the rural price of a metric ton of cotton rose from 2,000 to 2,400 pesos once the crop had been ginned; for the harvest as a whole, this represented about 40 million pesos. The total fixed investment in this industry probably does not exceed 50 million pesos, which is only slightly more than the value-added by processing in one year. These establishments play an important role in financing the costs of the cotton crop. Their working capital greatly exceeds the fixed investments in the cotton gins.

There is, in addition, one unit for the extraction of cotton-seed oils. At present, most of the seed is sent to other areas for processing. The Banco Ejidal is planning to construct its own processing plant in the Tierra Caliente to avoid the costs of transporting the seed, thereby increasing the profits of the ejidatarios.

[1] Since seven of the largest ginning plants were constructed after the 1961 Industrial Census, no reliable quantitative data are available to support this observation.

There are other satellite industries in the Tierra Caliente. The Banco Ejidal has a rice mill and a large lemon processing plant. In addition, there are eleven smaller rice mills, seven lemon plants, and a number of melon and watermelon packing houses. The total investment in these establishments probably does not exceed 15 million pesos. As in the case of cotton, the fixed investment is less important than the working capital used to finance the production costs of the crop. The credit helps to ensure adequate rates of utilization of the processing capacity and to fulfill marketing contracts.

The area's lack of diversification is highlighted by the fact that ice-making was the largest industry in the region in 1960. It accounted for two-fifths of the industrial product and employed more than 70 per cent of the industrial labour force. Ice production is geared to normal commercial needs, but during the melon and watermelon harvest, all the ice is used to refrigerate the freight cars in which the crop is shipped to export markets. At the peak of the harvest, ice is brought in from distant cities to satisfy the demands of the melon packers.

There is very little other industrial development except that which has come about in response to the daily demands of a growing urban population. The making of *tortillas*, bread and other food products accounts for an important part of the increasing number of establishments in the region. One large plant went into operation in 1962 to process barium and calcium, which are mined in the nearby municipio of Tepalcatepec. Its production has probably increased the value of industrial production in the region by one-fifth, but it employs less than twenty-five people; generally an equal number of people are employed in the mine.

It does not appear that there will be further development of new industries in the region in the near future. Other industries which might be established because of forward linkages are limited and tend to be set up in other areas where there is an obvious labour surplus and a more temperate climate. Since the reduction in transportation costs by road and rail, there is less incentive to move into the area to process anything other than the most bulky of raw material such as cotton and barium.

Additional processing (e.g. cotton spinning or the purification of barium) is usually located nearer to the larger markets.

Unless other natural resources are found which require the construction of additional processing plants in the Tierra Caliente, it is hard to conceive of any attraction for industrial location in the region. Mexico has embarked on a policy of equalizing electricity tariffs throughout the nation, and therefore has vitiated the advantage of having abundant supplies of inexpensive hydro-electric power nearby. Transportation facilities are a two-way blessing from the point of view of regional development—they provide easy access to markets, but they also provide easy access for manufactured goods from other regions. The region has not been able to attract an adequate permanent labour force for its agricultural needs, and its remoteness from other population centres would make it difficult to draw skilled people for industrial occupations, even if they were available.

The Commission's investment programme has had limited success in sparking the industrial development of the region. Only a few satellite industries were established and the prospect for additional industrialization is dim. These results were to be expected given the type of programme that the government has undertaken in the basin and the lack of specific incentives to locate in a region which, in itself, cannot offer any comparative advantages to the investor.

THE EFFECTS OF THE COMMISSION'S SOCIAL INVESTMENTS

The Tepalcatepec Commission's social investments deserve special attention because of the effect they had on the area's living conditions and for the attention drawn to them as a justification for a public investment programme in the region. These programmes were directed towards reducing health hazards, upgrading educational levels, and improving urban facilities.

As noted in Chapter 5, the social investment programme accounted for less than 10 per cent of the Commission's investment expenditures through 1965. It is evident that the Commission's main responsibility was the exploitation of the region's natural resources for economic development rather than the provision of facilities to improve health and educational facilities. The Commission's relatively small expenditures in these fields, however, were not the only public investments in the basin for such purposes; the Ministries of Education, Health and Welfare, and Water Resources provided most of the operating funds for the projects built by the Commission and built others with funds from their budgets. Unfortunately, data were not available on the size of the expenditures by other governmental dependencies.

With such limited expenditures, the impact of the Tepalcatepec Commission's social investment programme was predictably limited. The most striking improvement in living conditions was the reduction of the basin's mortality rate by about one-third during the 1950s, from 14·1 deaths per 1,000 population in 1950 to 9·6 in 1960; the decline in the Tierra Caliente was even sharper, from 16·5 to 10·6 deaths per 1,000 population (Table 12).[1] This decline was slightly greater than that for the nation which was from 16·2 to 11·5 during the same period. Part of this change was due to the virtual eradication of malaria from the region. In 1947, eighty-eight people died from malaria in the six municipios which then composed the Tierra Caliente; by 1955 the number had been reduced to twenty-five registered deaths. It continued falling until in 1960 there were only two deaths, and in 1964 no deaths from malaria were reported.[2] The Commission made only a small contribution to the malaria campaign which is still supported by contributions from the Mexican government and UNICEF.

The Commission's major contribution to the reduction of the mortality rate was the construction of drinking water and sewage systems which checked the rise of intestinal and gastric disorders. In 1947, these maladies claimed more lives than malaria. According to the Oficina de Difunciones, 141 people died of various intestinal diseases in 1947. Since that time, the proportion of people dying from this cause has fallen, although the absolute number of people who died in 1964 increased to 172. Intestinal

[1] The reduction in mortality rate is a reflection of improvements in health conditions. This improvement, however, is not fully reflected in these statistics because it also resulted in higher productivity for members of the labour force and improved living conditions in general.

[2] México, Secretaría de Industria y Comercio, Dirección General de Estadística, Departamento de Difunciones. These figures are not based on medically certified reports and, therefore, should be considered approximate.

problems caused about 17 per cent of all deaths in 1947 and 11 per cent in 1964.

Another characteristic of the region when the Commission was formed was its high rate of homicides. It was common knowledge that the lack of communications and poor health conditions created an ideal hide-out for fugitives from the law. Their presence was the cause of a great deal of lawless behaviour. According to official statistics, there were seventy-seven homicides in 1947 which accounted for about 9 per cent of the total deaths.[1] In 1964 there were 115 homicides reported—almost 8 per cent of the total deaths. Even allowing for substantial under-reporting in 1947, it appears that the recent prosperity has not reduced the homicide rate, although it is probable that the causes for this violence are now different. No longer a good hide-out for criminals, the region does have a large migrant population, especially during the cotton-picking season, which causes tensions and conflicts which are often resolved by force. It would be hard to determine the proportion of deaths caused by this new factor, but many residents blame the temporary agricultural labour force for the disruptions.

On the other hand, the region's recent prosperity has probably also contributed to the reduction in the mortality rate from other causes. The rise in regional incomes enabled the population to be better fed and obtain more adequate medical treatment. As a result, productivity probably rose as did life expectancy. These potentially quantifiable benefits from the improvement in economic conditions in the region were not measured in this study but should not be ignored in the final evaluation. In addition, there are doubtless benefits from a healthier environment which are not subject to quantification but will also be added to the Commission's credit.

Educational improvement was another important part of the Commission's social investment programme in the basin. Numerous schools were built in co-operation with state and local governments and some financial assistance was provided to pay

[1] México, Secretaría de Industria y Comercio, Dirección General de Estadística, Departmento de Difunciones. There is probably a significant bias in these figures due to under-reporting, especially in 1947. Unfortunately, there are no other sources which might aid in correcting the data.

extra teachers in the basin. In spite of this attention, the proportion of literate people in the basin rose slower than in the nation
as a whole (excluding the capital city) and by 1960 this proportion
had fallen below the national average.[1]

The government's impact on educational and health conditions
is certainly understated by the figures cited. The quality of education was undoubtedly improving as were the facilities and the
opportunities available to each successive generation. Falling death
rates do not reflect the improvement in health for those who
continue to live and, therefore, can be more productive and lead
more satisfactory lives. On the other hand, the Commission was
not the only official organization working to improve conditions
and therefore the assignment of even these benefits is difficult.

The Commission encouraged the colonization of uncultivated
lands to achieve a more rational utilization of the region's economic potential. Several ejidos were formed for those having rights
to land grants under the land reform, but for whom there had not
been sufficient land in other parts of the Tierra Caliente and in
neighbouring zones. In 1958, 200 families were organized into a
community in the Tierra Caliente. The migrants came from the
Tierra Fría and each family was given a 10 hectare ejidal plot to
farm. There were no other organized attempts to colonize parts
of the region. Nevertheless, the population swelled as farmers
from other parts of Mexico came to the region in search of land
and work. Merchants and shopkeepers looking for business
opportunities in the prospering region joined them. Some of
these people settled down in the region and took advantage of
the availability of land and irrigation to plant commercial crops.
New ejidal communities were formed by some while others purchased formerly barren land for cultivation and transformed pasture into cropland. Still others established themselves in the commercial life of the community.

Temporary farm workers flocked into the region to pick the
cotton and melon crops. During the 1964–5 cotton harvest, the
largest in the history of the Tierra Caliente, approximately 15,000

---

[1] The reduction in illiteracy is also only a rough measure of educational improvement. It seems likely that one of the effects of the Commission's intervention
was an improvement in the quality and length of schooling available to school
age children. There is, as yet, no satisfactory way of measuring this.

men were needed to supplement the local labour force. These workers came from other cotton areas, mostly in northern Mexico, as well as from nearby rural areas where there is a great deal of disguised unemployment. The cotton picking season lasts almost 100 days and is followed by the melon and watermelon harvests, so that the labour force absorbs a large number of temporary workers for more than one-third of the year.

Skilled workers were attracted to the region by the high wages offered by planters and investors who needed foremen and machinery operators as well as agronomists, trained salesmen, and myriad other skilled workers essential for the development of an agricultural economy. Many of these people did not establish homes in the region, but merely stayed there during the agricultural cycle and returned to their homes and families for the rest of the year.

As a result of the immigration of these various groups of people, the towns in the region grew rapidly. Apatzingán more than doubled its population during the fifties, from 8,300 in 1950 to 19,500 in 1960, while Zaragoza (Nueva Italia) spurted from 4,750 to 8,900 during the same period.[1] The region as a whole experienced a doubling of its population during the decade and was still growing fast during the first half of the 1960s. Almost 23,000 people were estimated to have migrated into the region up to 1960 (Table 12).

The permanent immigrants into the Tierra Caliente were less numerous, however, than the emigrants from other parts of the basin. More than 17,000 people were estimated to have left the highland regions during the ten-year period. Even the development of labour-intensive crops in a prosperous agricultural economy was insufficient to absorb the population growth and idle labour force in the neighbouring regions where agriculture was stagnant. The other social investments, like educational facilities, probably increased emigration from the highland areas as knowledge of alternative ways of life and employment opportunities become more widespread.[2]

---

[1] *Population Census, 1960.* Michoacán, p. 4.

[2] Since 1960 immigration into the Tierra Caliente probably increased because of the prosperity occasioned by the large increases in commercial production. This may have reversed the net outflow observed during the 1950s.

The better road system played its role in increasing the outward flow of people from the less attractive parts of the basin like the Tierra Fría and increasing the population pressure in other cities where unemployment among unskilled workers was already a problem. Undoubtedly, the roads also facilitated the importation of new goods and ideas into the zone, thereby stimulating demand for products through the demonstration effect. Because of the comparative economic unimportance of much of the mountain region, most of the justification for these roads rests on the general objective of bringing some of the benefits of Mexican development to remote Indian areas. The roads improved labour mobility, a mixed blessing, and widened the market for certain consumer goods while accomplishing an important political function—improvement in the integration and unification of the nation.[1] The roads make it easier for the population to make its wishes known and for the government to implement its decisions.

On the whole the Commission's small expenditures were most valuable in endowing the region with more and better facilities to promote social welfare. Education and health were the principal targets of this effort, but improved mobility and better public services in urban communities were added to the package of social investments. Even recreational needs were considered when the Cupatitzio National Park was conceived. This particular project now attracts many tourists to the whole basin—another benefit which should not be overlooked. Illiteracy and intestinal illness, however, are still major problems in the region and could absorb large amounts of additional social overhead capital.[2]

[1] Steiner, *Criteria for Planning Rural Roads in a Developing Country*, pp. 108–11.
[2] Charles Myers suggested that there is considerable under-investment in education throughout rural Mexico: *Education & National Development in Mexico* (Princeton: Princeton University, Industrial Relations Section, 1965), Chapter 4.

7

AN ASSESSMENT OF THE
COMMISSION'S ACTIVITIES

In the first part of this book we presented a discussion of the objectives of the river basin programme and have now illustrated it with a case study of the Tepalcatepec Commission's activities. We now want to use this case study to assess the performance of the Tepalcatepec Commission, which we shall do in this chapter, and the strategy as a whole, which we shall consider in the next and final chapter. Here we shall suggest that the Tepalcatepec project was overall an attractive one, whose productivity justified the decision to undertake it. It will be necessary, however, to make some qualifications of this judgment, since by no means all the scheme's objectives were satisfactorily fulfilled, and the pace of agricultural development was fairly slow to gain momentum.

We shall begin the analysis by investigating those changes which contributed to national development without regard to their effects on the regional economy. These changes were basically due to the agricultural potential unleashed by the availability of irrigation water and the hydroelectric potential of this water before it was distributed in the irrigation canals. However, the project has made a substantial contribution to national income and earnings of foreign exchange and has also affected the supply of some scarce and superabundant factors of production.

We then examine these same developments, and others, strictly from the point of view of the region's own development. In this part of the analysis our concern is limited to those changes in production and living standards which had a direct or indirect impact on the inhabitants of the Tierra Caliente, regardless of their influence on the rest of the nation.

The investments by the Tepalcatepec River Basin Commission amounted to more than 500 million pesos (in 1960 prices) during the first eighteen years of the Commission's existence. In that time a substantial network of irrigation canals and a complementary road system were constructed to facilitate agricultural development in the Tierra Caliente. The increase in agricultural output, measured in value terms, is the principal benefit produced by the investment programme and the only one which was subjected to measurement.

We shall treat hydroelectric power generation, in which the Commission co-operated with Federal Electricity Commission in the construction of certain joint works, separately. Joint costs were allocated according to the main use to be made of the part of the project in question. The arbitrariness inherent in any allocation of joint costs could not, of course, be avoided altogether.

Agricultural development

It is not necessary to review the process by which we arrived at the estimate of net agricultural product in Chapter 6; instead we shall use this as the basis of measurement of net agricultural benefits to irrigation. The step is not a difficult one but it involves asking a hypothetical question: what would have happened in the Tierra Caliente had the Tepalcatepec Commission not been created? This question is important because even without the investment there probably would have been some increase in the value of agricultural production although it would have been smaller than that actually observed. In 1947 there were already irrigation facilities in the Tierra Caliente; these might have been extended privately. A change in crop composition would probably have taken place—the first melon production had already been started, for example, and would have grown in the absence of the Commission's investment.

One indication of the likely magnitude of such hypothetical change can be obtained from examining agricultural performance in a region with similar physical endowments which did not have the benefit of large-scale government investment programmes until recently. Such a region, called Ciudad Altamirano, is in the neighbouring state of Guerrero.[1] Information of the changes in the region during the 1950s can be obtained from agricultural census data.

The history of the Ciudad Altamirano district does not permit an exact comparison with the Tierra Caliente of the Tepalcatepec basin. In 1950 there were only small-scale private irrigation facilities in the region. In 1953 the Ciudad Altamirano Irrigation District was created. Several pumps, a dam to store irrigation water, and complementary canals were installed for irrigation, which began in 1954. In some ways, this increases the attractiveness of the Ciudad Altamirano zone as a 'control' region because the Michoacán area had irrigation canals at the beginning of the period under observation. However, since these public irrigation works in Guerrero were not yet constructed in 1950, the figures for the region alone would overstate the progress that might have been expected in Michoacán. To compensate for this, two other municipios were included in the control region. These municipios will soon enjoy the fruits of irrigation as a result of the construction of storage dams for irrigation by the Balsas Commission. Their inclusion diminished the effect of the introduction of irrigation in Ciudad Altamirano during the middle of the period but did not completely eliminate it. A comparison of the changes in the Tierra Caliente and in the control region is presented in Table 28.

In the control zone, cultivated land increased by 29 per cent and yields rose by 54 per cent, from 536 to 635 pesos per hectare, during the 1950s (Table 28). This increase in the productivity of the land (a result of improved technology and a changing composition of crops) and in the area under cultivation formed the basis for the adjustment in the value of the agricultural production in the Tierra Caliente. The rate of growth of the value of agricultural production in the control region, approximately 7 per cent per year, was applied to the increased production observed in the Tepalcatepec basin and the net agricultural output reduced accordingly, before the increase in net agricultural output over the

[1] We are grateful to Ing. César Buenrostro of the Balsas Commission for his suggestion for using this region as a control area.

Table 28. *The agricultural sector in the Tierra Caliente and in the 'control' region*

	Tierra Caliente[a]	Control region[b]
Population		
1950	55,191	76,238
1960	111,585	91,525
% Change	102·2	20·1
Work force		
1950	17,969	24,396
1960	32,739	30,656
% Change	82·2	25·7
Agricultural labour force		
1950	13,753	20,451
1960	25,617	25,582
% Change	86·3	25·1
Cultivated area (hectares)		
1950	42,317	44,374
1960	105,664	57,355
% Change	149·7	29·3
Value of production ('ooos 1960 pesos)		
1950	34,479	23,786
1960	181,067	47,297
% Change	425·2	98·8
Monetary yields per hectare ('ooos 1960 pesos)		
1950	815	536
1960	1,714	825
% Change	110·3	53·9

[a] Tierra Caliente comprises the municipios of: Apatzingán, Buenavista, Gabriel Zamora, La Huacana, Parácuaro, Tepalcatepec, and Zaragoza, Michoacán.
[b] The control region in Ciudad Altamirano comprises the municipios of: Arcelia, Coyuca, Pungarabato, and Zirándaro, Guerrero, and San Lucas, Michoacán.

Sources: Lines 1–9: *Population Censuses, 1950 and 1960, Michoacán and Guerrero;* lines 10–18: Appendix A for the Tierra Caliente. *Agricultural Censuses, 1950 and 1960, Michoacán and Guerrero* for control region.

base year was determined (Table 29, Column 4).[1] The growth in agricultural output, net of costs and without allowance for expected productivity increases, is the estimate of the benefits which were attributed to the investment in irrigation by the Tepalcatepec Commission during the 1950 to 1970 period.[2]

In estimating costs and benefits we have accepted straightforwardly prices in peso values (converted to constant prices) at which market transactions took place. As we argued in Chapter 1, this is unlikely to be the ideal way to make an evaluation of investment projects in underdeveloped countries, since market prices of project outputs and inputs are usually far from representing relative social scarcities of products and factors. Unfortunately the use of a more sophisticated set of prices would have involved a great deal more information (and time) than was available and would also have required value judgments which are very difficult to make—for example, did Mexico achieve an ideal balance between investment and consumption during the period 1947–65, or should less have been consumed and more invested?

Although we have not made any price adjustments, it is worthwhile indicating in which direction adjustments might need to be made. We need to consider whether there is any distortion of market values from more appropriate social values that could affect benefits or costs systematically and so bias any assessment. Considering first the cost side, our data do not permit us to

[1] This rate of increase of the net value of agricultural production, in constant prices, is very high—almost twice as great as the national average—and could not be expected to continue over the 50 year life of the project. Consequently the benefits measured in this study are probably a conservative estimate of the actual situation. This effect is offset by the introduction of a discount rate (see below) which renders future income much less important than present production.

[2] The net benefits reported in Table 29, Column 4, are calculated from the data in Tables 22 to 25 inclusive. The sharp decline in net benefits projected after 1966 was, in large part, due to the declining prospects for cotton production in the region. Even if these projections are off by a wide margin they will affect the internal rate of return very little because of the effect of discounting on benefits and costs as far from the start of construction as this.

This method for measuring the benefits from irrigation attributes all of the increase in the productivity to a single factor of production—water. In effect, it is an estimate of the Ricardian rent attributed to this one factor after all other inputs into the production process have been paid their competitive price. It is a 'hypothetical computation of the maximum amounts which farmers would be willing to pay if they were perfectly rational entrepreneurs' (Otto Eckstein, *Water Resource Development* (Cambridge: Harvard University Press), p. 19). The rationale for this was discussed in Chapter 1.

Table 29. *Costs and benefits of the Comisión del Tepalcatepec's investment programme*
('000s 1960 pesos)

		Economic investments		Agricultural benefits from the Tierra Caliente	
	All costs (1)	Total (2)	Tierra Caliente (3)	Actual (4)	Alternate (5)
1947	5,691	5,415	4,364		
1948	25,722	23,447	18,049		
1949	29,284	27,600	18,615		
1950	31,765	30,414	28,037		5,908
1951	32,493	30,672	28,721	−10	11,034
1952	40,916	37,558	35,221	1,070	27,598
1953	42,039	40,132	36,734	2,796	29,128
1954	35,487	34,390	32,252	3,715	34,206
1955	39,643	38,303	32,256	5,908	33,522
1956	35,462	30,725	23,803	11,034	46,506
1957	42,503	35,189	21,686	27,598	67,638
1958	35,500	28,195	17,229	29,128	78,329
1959	20,875	17,672	12,164	34,206	81,539
1960	26,560	24,245	19,310	33,522	109,699
1961	10,800	9,938	8,864	46,506	106,830
1962	12,687	8,670	4,737	67,638	97,417
1963	13,188	9,005	6,499	78,329	98,955
1964	13,230	10,691	3,462	81,539	83,486
1965	9,838	7,398	3,319	109,699	72,566
1966[a]	7,000	7,000	3,500	106,830	75,000
1967	7,000	7,000	3,500	97,417	75,000
1968	7,000	7,000	3,500	98,955	75,000
1969	7,000	7,000	3,500	83,486	75,000
1970	7,000	7,000	3,500	72,566	75,000
1971–99	7,000	7,000	3,500	75,000	75,000
Total	741,638	687,659	474,322	3,166,932	3,534,361

[a] Projections are based on Comisión del Río Balsas estimates.

Sources:

Column 1: Table 11.

2: Table 11. } Only those costs attributable to economic investments
3: Table 18. } and current operating expenses are included in these
columns.

4: Table 26.

5: Column 4, moved five years ahead.

separate expenditures on direct labour inputs and other inputs, let alone to value intermediate inputs and capital goods at world prices. Although there is, as we have discussed, a great deal of unemployment in Mexico and although the provision of employment is a major national objective of the Mexican government, the use of actual money wages in place of estimated shadow wages may not be very misleading. In the basin itself, there is plenty of evidence of near-full employment of labour at least at peak seasons, with a tendency for any sharp increase in the level of economic activity to lead to increased wages. In other words, money wages may not seriously underestimate the opportunity cost of labour inside the basin.

It may here be objected that the short-term opportunity cost of expanding employment in the basin overestimates the social opportunity cost for the nation as a whole. The expansion of employment opportunities in the basin creates an opportunity for unemployed labour to move to the basin and be productively employed. But the costs in terms of additional consumption involved in this process are likely to be considerable, and, as argued in the first chapter, the appropriate shadow wage for otherwise unemployed unskilled labour is not likely to be very far from the the money wage paid. Where labour employment expansion involves the use of trained and skilled people, who are in no sense unemployed in Mexico, then there is no case for valuing their services at less than the market wage.

Inputs of goods and services bought by the Commission itself and by farmers producing project outputs came from both domestic and foreign producers. As we described in Chapter 2, Mexico's policy has been one of import substitution behind heavy protective tariff barriers. The average price differential between domestic and foreign manufactured goods was recently estimated to be of the order of 25 per cent (with a wide dispersion).[1] If, as we suggested in Chapter 1, expenditures on domestically produced inputs were valued at world prices they would probably be lower. Most important inputs were of producer's goods which enter the country under low tariffs, and there the use of world

[1] For a further discussion of this see Timothy King, *Mexico: Industrialisation and Trade Policies Since 1940.*

prices would make relatively little difference. But on balance, project expenditures expressed in terms of Mexican prices are greater than if world prices had been used.

In contrast, the agricultural output of the project was sold mostly at world prices or below. Domestic prices for maize and bean output, it is true, are higher than world levels, but these products are relatively unimportant in the total. Exported output, which includes the very important cotton and melon crops, usually receive lower than world prices since exports have been taxed throughout the period. In recent years, taxes on agricultural exports have diminished in importance. Where world prices have fallen, a reduction or complete exemption of export taxes and the adoption of a sliding scale that depends on price has frequently followed.

It therefore seems that the effect of our method of estimating benefits and costs is to tend to underestimate social benefits and overestimate social costs. As we shall see, in spite of this, the return on project expenditures was high by the standards normally applied to such projects, though low enough to leave open the question of whether a higher return might not have been obtained by investing the funds elsewhere in the economy.

In Table 29, costs are analysed in several different ways in order to examine the sensitivity of the results to changes in assumptions as well as to look into possible alternative ways of using public investment resources. The first column of Table 29 itemizes all of the costs incurred by the Commission since its formation in 1947. No attempt is made to separate out those expenditures which were made to improve the standard of living of people in the region but which might not have increased the region's measurable economic product. This is done in Columns 2 and 3 where only those investments which were categorized as economic in Chapter 5 are included along with some part of the current expenditures which are attributable to the operation of the irrigation system and the administration of the economic investment projects. In the third column only those costs attributable to the Commission's economic investment in the Tierra Caliente are presented; this is done in order to compare them directly with the measure of benefits used in this book: the increased agricultural production in the Tierra Caliente arising from the activities of the Tepalcatepec Commission.[1]

In Chapter 1 we discussed the rationale for our calculations of the internal rate of return. The results for a series of different alternatives are given in Table 30. Under the most severe analysis, i.e. when the benefits from the Tierra Caliente were compared to the total costs of the project, the scheme showed an internal rate of return of about 10.2 per cent. When only the economic investments in the Tierra Caliente were used as the cost base, the internal rate of return rose to 12.8 per cent.[2]

Given the caveats in determining the social values of output and the resulting biases in our data, these rates of return might be considered respectable. They are, however, perhaps rather low in terms of the marginal rates of return available in the private sector, although it is impossible to get good data to determine what this level might be. Conversations with businessmen, and various bits of evidence such as the fact that small entrepreneurs are observed to borrow from private investment banks at very high rates indeed (reportedly these are sometimes in excess of 20 per cent[3]), suggest that the expected rate of return on new investment is substantially higher than the average 13 to 14 per cent earned in the United States.[4] Rates of return of less than 15 to 20 per cent invite the conclusion that a higher rate of return

---

[1] The time streams in Table 29 were projected to 1999 to provide data for the estimated fifty year life span of the project. These projections were made with the help of technicians in the Balsas Commission. Because of the effect of a discount rate on returns which are in the distant future, adjustments of as much as ten per cent in the size of the various streams only marginally affects the results of the internal rate of return analysis.

[2] It should be remembered that at several points in our analysis, the data produced conservative estimates of the agricultural benefits from the Comisión del Tepalcatepec's investment programme. One of the most important of the factors biasing the results downward is the estimate of the expected progress in the region had the project not been undertaken. If we had not adjusted benefits to take account of the expected growth in the absence of the project, the latter internal rate of return would have been 13.4 per cent.

[3] W. Paul Strassman, *Technological Change and Economic Development* (Ithaca, New York: Cornell University Press, 1968), pp. 124–5.

[4] Tobin reported that 'Phelps . . . has estimated the annual rate of return on tangible [private] investment in the US to be about 14 per cent in 1954'. 'Economic Growth as an objective of Economic Policy', *American Economic Review*, LIV (May 1964), p. 15. Stigler estimated the average rate of return in manufacturing industries to be 6.26 per cent in 1954 but this rate should almost be

could have been achieved by using the resources in the private manufacturing sector.[1] The Mexican Ministry of Water Resources uses a discount rate of 8 per cent in its economic analysis and this is clearly achieved in this case, and the Ministry of Public Works' criterion—12 per cent—was also met.

Many of those involved in making policy decisions about the Tepalcatepec Commission would be astonished to learn that the project could be considered in any way only marginally successful in its economic returns. It is usually regarded as being a really out-standing success. This reflects a failure to appreciate the rationale of discount rates, either for measuring returns from alternative

Table 30. *Measures of the programme's profitability*

	Benefits / Total costs	Benefits / Economic investment costs	Benefits / Economic investment costs: Tierra Caliente
A. Actual and projected benefits			
Internal rate of return (%)	10·2	11·0	12·8
B/C ratio			
0% discount	4·3	4·6	6·7
10% discount	1·0	1·1	1·4
20% discount	0·4	0·4	0·5
B. Alternative benefits			
Internal rate of return (%)	17·3	18·7	22·4
0%	4·8	5·1	7·5
10%	1·6	1·8	2·2
20%	0·9	0·9	1·1

Source: Table 29.

doubled to take account of the effect of corporate taxes on the profit rate. *Capital and Rates of Return in Manufacturing Industries* (Princeton: Princeton University Press for the National Bureau of Economic Research), p. 35.
[1] It should, however, be noted that high private returns owe a great deal to the protection mentioned above; if evaluated at world prices the social rate of return in manufacturing might be very much lower in most industries.

investments, or for conveying notions of social time preference. If a discount rate is not used, the project is indeed attractive. Without a discount factor (i.e. the opportunity cost of capital is zero), the project shows a benefit–cost ratio of 4·3 when the benefits in the Tierra Caliente are compared with the total costs of the project (Table 30); this ratio was as high as 6·7 if only the Tierra Caliente cost base is used.

The difference between the two analyses is a result of the long time-lag between the completion of the irrigation facilities and the impressive growth in agricultural output of recent years. The policy-makers' unwillingness or inability to incorporate discount rates into their evaluations of the project has meant that they do not understand how very costly was this delay. In Chapter 6 we described the slow response of farmers and their creditors to the new opportunities created by the Commission's investments in the Tierra Caliente. Additional expenditures for agricultural experimentation and extension and new injections of credit might have speeded the transition to the new commercialized modern agriculture now characteristic of the zone. This might also have helped to reduce some of the other problems of income inequality and land tenure that have arisen in the region.

Such complementary investment in agricultural development, if effective, might have increased the stream of benefits sooner than it actually did increase. To determine the effect such a change might have had on the investment, the stream of benefits was moved forward five years and the benefits compared to the costs. The alternative stream of benefits (Table 29, Column 5) yielded markedly high internal rates of return (17·3 per cent when all the costs were included and 22·4 per cent with only the Tierra Caliente's investment) and favourable benefit–cost ratios with the use of discount rates greater than zero (Table 30). This finding confirms that a quicker adaptation to the new environment by all parties would have made the project a much more profitable one.[1] The change in the benefit–cost ratio at a zero discount rate

[1] This lag in response to the opportunity to produce cotton cannot be satisfactorily explained by market forces alone. During the period 1950–5 total Mexican cotton output approximately doubled but cotton output in the Tierra Caliente was nonexistent, while the irrigated area under maize rose by about four times.

was not as marked as it was when the rate was higher. Using the Tierra Caliente cost base, the new ratio was 12 per cent higher than the original estimate without a discount rate, and it was 64 per cent higher with a 10 per cent discount rate (Table 30).

In conclusion, the project could have been substantially improved if additional resources had been invested in the diffusion of the appropriate technology and the establishment of sufficient credit facilities to speed the response to the new environment. An important lesson to be learned from this study, therefore, is that further emphasis should be placed on the problems of adjusting the productive structure of the region to the new investments with sufficient speed to take full advantage of a largely indivisible addition to a region's social overhead capital. If private initiative is not prepared to step in to provide these facilities, then the government must organize the effort to ensure that its investment is fully used as rapidly as possible.

Hydroelectricity

Although the Commission did not play an important role in the development of the hydroelectric potential of the region, it did co-operate with the Federal Electricity Commission (CFE) in the construction of the two dams. These projects have not been discussed up to this point because they are completely separable parts of the development programme, but this hydroelectric potential was probably an important factor in the selection of the basin for development.

When the Commission started work in the basin the small quantity of hydroelectric power generated in the basin was entirely for local markets. Electricity generation jumped markedly during the 1950–65 period as two large power plants were constructed along the Cupatitzio river. The two plants, the Cobano and the Salto Escondido, are located on the river just above the Tierra Caliente where the water is used to irrigate the cotton and rice fields (Fig. 4). In the preliminary evaluation of the area's economic potential, the team of engineers noted that the Cupatitzio,

because of the outflow from its springs—15–17 m³/s in the dry season...,
as well as the steep slope of its bed...which in 30 kilometers drops 1200

meters..., offers some of the most important hydroelectric potential in the Republic, not only because of the total potential generating power, but also for the low unit cost of the works, which will also be used for directing the water to the irrigable lands on the plains of Antunez.[1]

Experience bore out these remarks, as can be seen in Table 31. Not only were 125,000 additional kilowatts of installed power added to the system but costs of production fell dramatically. One of the most important reasons for this drop in costs was the low initial construction costs and attractive operating characteristics afforded by the river; because of the almost constant flow throughout the year from the springs which feed the Cupatitzio, it was not necessary to build large reservoirs to store water.

No further increase in the installed generating capacity within the Tepalcatepec river basin is anticipated during the next decade. Regional consumption is not growing fast enough to warrant further investments, as we shall shortly see, and there are several other hydroelectric projects nearby which have greater priority in the allocation of investment funds. In the state of Michoacán, about 336,000 kilowatts of additional capacity will be available in 1971 when La Villita is completed on the Balsas river near the Pacific coast. This project, part of the regional development scheme for the coastal area, will provide energy for a vertically integrated steel mill as well as for the future growth needs of the area for many years to come. Another Balsas river project, El Infiernillo, became operational in 1964 and currently has an installed capacity of 672,000 kilowatts with which to supply the growing Mexico City market. Neither of these projects are directly linked to the plants on the Cupatitzio river, which form the Lázaro Cárdenas system.

Electricity consumption in the basin has not increased as fast as production, in spite of the fact that growth in consumption has been much faster than the national average. In 1964 total electricity available for sale in Mexico was almost 256 per cent greater than that available in 1950 but in 1964 regional sales were

---

[1] Comisión del Tepalcatepec, *Características de la Cuenca del Tepalcatepec*, 1950, p. 9.

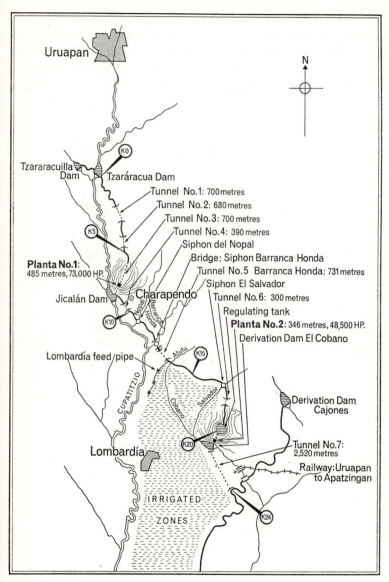

FIG. 4   Hydroelectric works on the Cupatitzio river.

Source: Ministry of Water Resources, Tepalcatepec Commission. *Memoria de los Trabajos Realizados, 1947–52* (Uruapan, México, 1952).

533 per cent higher than in 1950.[1] As a result of the rapid increase in production, large surpluses have been available for export to the neighbouring regions where industrial demands are large and constantly growing (Table 31). Since there is no difference in electricity tariffs by region there is no locational advantage to placing a plant near a source of power and thus the availability of power has not provided an impetus for the industrialization of the region.

Table 31. *Electricity production in the Lázaro Cárdenas system, 1950–65*

| Year | Installed Capacity (kW) | Generating costs per kWh[a,b] (1960 pesos) | Electricity Sales ('000s kWh)[a,b] | | |
			Total within region	Sales outside region	Total sales
1950	8,010	13,183	12,397	2,984	15,381
1951	8,090	10,771	12,985	5,079	18,064
1952	8,090	12,177	19,379	6,207	25,586
1953	8,090	11,318	20,269	13,275	33,544
1954	8,090	7,651	9,069	5,359	14,428
1955	34,100	4,418	14,500	74,685	89,186
1956	60,110	2,850	17,926	144,990	162,917
1957	60,110	3,659	20,785	185,025	205,810
1958	60,110	5,521	26,910	143,596	170,506
1959	60,110	8,303	32,556	105,324	137,881
1960	60,110	6,815	37,278	151,614	188,892
1961	60,110	5,249	50,811	218,254	269,064
1962	132,560	4,304	51,804	268,417	302,221
1963	132,560	3,051	69,045	471,345	540,390
1964	132,560	3,922	78,470	534,944	613,415
1965	132,560		93,950	546,744	640,694

[a] Includes electricity purchased from other systems for distribution by Lázaro Cárdenas System.
[b] 1950–3 data not comparable with 1954–65 data.

Source: Comisión Federal de Electricidad; information prepared at request of the authors, and financial reports.

[1] Data on consumption of electrical energy was collected for an operating area of the CFE which is larger than the hydrological basin defined by the SRH. Approximately two-thirds of the energy sold in the CFE district was sold to the districts of Apatzingán, Zaragoza, and Uruapan in 1965. The basin accounts for about eighty per cent of all the energy reported sold in the region in Table 31.

According to its projections, the CFE does not anticipate any dramatic increase in regional electricity consumption during the coming decade. Their construction programme is based on the assumption of a continuation of the steady rate of growth in demand of somewhat less than 10 per cent resulting from higher incomes, the normal growth of new commerce, and the programme of rural electrification. Most of this increasing demand will be supplied by existing generating capacity while new plants are constructed in other parts of the Republic to satisfy the demands of the regions outside of the basin currently being supplied by the Lázaro Cárdenas System. It is likely, however, that a third generator will be added to the Salto Escondido plant sometime during the 1970s, although no plans have been elaborated for this project. This will add almost 25 per cent to the installed capacity of the region.

Attempts to quantify the rate of return on the investments in hydroelectricity production were frustrated by the lack of sufficient data and pricing policies which are designed to encourage the use of electricity by industry. Data supplied by the CFE show that the investments along the River Cupatitzio had a negative return. It is probable, however, that the social rate of return to investment in power facilities was high, since the unit costs of construction were low and the plants enjoyed a high rate of utilization. Part of the explanation for this negative return is the relatively lower rates charged to industrial users of electricity production, which accounted for the bulk of the consumption of the energy produced in the region. Another factor may be the book-keeping practices of divisions within the Electricity Commission; it is possible that the energy is sold to the distributing divisions at a low price and that they are the ones that actually reap the profits. A fuller examination of the subject would be required to ascertain which of these explanations is most important or if there were other factors which produced the unexpected results.

At the time the plants were initially constructed there were severe shortages of electricity in the neighbouring industrial states and the power from the Cobano plant was needed for the continued growth of the region. Since that time, this power has been integrated into the national power grid and represents only a very small proportion of national production. This production, however, is about twenty-five times greater than consumption in the basin, even after the recent upsurge in economic activity. Thus, the electricity did represent an important contribution to the economic development of neighbouring states at a time when electricity was scarce and since that time the inexpensive power from this region has been used as base power in the national electricity network.

The foreign sector

In Chapter 1 we discussed the view that a shortage of foreign resources might impose a separate constraint on development from a shortage of domestic resources. The distinction appeared more valid in planning for a short period than for the length of time over which we are considering the performance of the Tepalcatepec Commission. Over a longer period there are a great many things that almost all countries can do to equate the relative scarcities of home and foreign resources. Over the life of the Tepalcatepec Commission Mexico has devalued twice, substituted domestic production for imports on a considerable scale, and maintained exchange convertibility, and it is difficult to see foreign exchange as the one binding constraint on her development.

Nevertheless, the need for new exports has been a constant anxiety among Mexican policy-makers. Undoubtedly they value projects like the Tepalcatepec Project, which makes a substantial net addition to foreign exchange earnings, much more highly than a project of equal domestic profitability but which made no net contribution to improving the balance of payments. The Papaloapan Commission estimated that the import content of their total investment from 1947 to 1956 was 31.7 per cent.[1] Using a roughly similar percentage here (which is probably an overstatement for the Tepalcatepec Commission's projects since they are on a smaller scale) would give us total imports of about 160 million pesos (1960 prices) between 1947 and 1965. In addition, other investments, particularly agricultural machinery, will also

[1] Comisión del Papaloapan, *Economía del Papaloapan*, Vol. 1, p. 202.

have absorbed much foreign exchange. But the Commission estimated the value of cotton output, in the 1962–3 cycle, at 209 million pesos.

Since cotton is Mexico's most important export crop, this can be considered as 209 million pesos of foreign exchange. This would cover the use of foreign exchange by the Commission, and probably most of that required to buy tractors, cotton gins, aeroplanes, etc. In addition, there have already been several other agricultural cycles of cotton, each as large as the 1962–3 harvest, and of canteloupes, melons and watermelons as well as other crops. The scheme is therefore quite clearly a net earner of foreign exchange.

As pointed out above, the region has also seen the withdrawal of much foreign capital from the financing of the crops and its replacement by local capital accumulated from agricultural profits. This foreign capital has, in many cases, continued to be used in other parts of Mexico to spur the search for new regions where crops in high demand in the United States may be profitably grown. In this sense the Tepalcatepec basin not only has been a net earner of foreign exchange but it also has freed the resources it originally required for use in other parts of Mexico.

The supply of domestic factors of production

There has been considerable controversy over the relative importance of shortages of particular factors of production in restricting the rate of economic development. As we pointed out in Chapter 1, this is very much an empirical matter, and any light that studies such as this one can throw on it the better. The tapping of otherwise unutilized sources of capital and entrepreneurship is potentially a valuable contribution of a public investment project to national development.

It appears that a lack of entrepreneurship did reduce the return from investment in the early years of the project, but that later the project may have been useful in increasing the supply of commercially-oriented enterprising farmers. In Chapter 6, we saw that one of the most serious limitations of the Tepalcatepec development programme was the slow start it made in utilizing the new resources which the irrigation works provided. Only after substantial stimulation by the Banco Nacional de Crédito Ejidal did the region begin to use the potential that had been developed. In the process farmers were trained and the market mechanism began to function so that those residents willing to take risks began to avail themselves of the opportunities to bring additional land under the plough for their own profit. This initial stimulation was provided, perhaps a little late, by a forward looking public institution which rarely has been given credit for such actions in the past. It may be an overstatement to say that the resources it stimulated are really entrepreneurial—they may only be managerial—but they did play an important role in developing the region and shaping its present economic structure. There is no evidence of any unutilized sources of capital in the region before the project that started could be tapped by the project. Undoubtedly for most of the period the Tierra Caliente was an importer of capital to finance both public and private investments. It would be extremely difficult to estimate at what time the region began to reverse this flow of capital—if indeed it has already done so (which is probable but not certain). Although agricultural profits increased rapidly throughout the decade 1955–65, this was also a period of rising investment in agricultural credit, processing plants, and in agricultural machinery and other inputs. If, as seems probable, the growth of output is coming to an end it is likely that future profits will not be matched by new investment. The American capital which initiated the planting of canteloupes and watermelons has already been able to move on to other regions, being replaced by local capital accumulated from past profits. According to well-informed local sources, the investment in the physical equipment of the cotton gins was recovered after two cycles in every case and the sizable working capital needs were supplied by accumulated profits after about five cycles of large-scale planting (in other words, by 1966–7).

It may be worth noting that the private banking system has probably been able, on balance, to channel funds out of the region in recent years. Its portfolio of loans amounted in 1965 to less than 20 million pesos while there were almost 30 million pesos in demand deposits in the region in that year; savings accounts represented almost 12 million pesos.

Finally, the region has been able to attract substantial immigration into the region which might have otherwise moved to traditional population centres where unskilled labour is already unemployed. The Tepalcatepec Commission openly encouraged this influx of new people. A colonization programme was implemented under the leadership of Lázaro Cárdenas but the majority of the newcomers needed no special incentives and came in response to the plethora of new opportunities.

Since 1960 immigration has continued, perhaps at a faster pace. It is possible that the immigration into the Tierra Caliente has become so large that it offsets the outflow from other parts of the zone. Whether this is or is not the case, by 1960 the project had been able to retain (on balance) about 40,000 more people in the region than might otherwise have been expected to be there.[1]

THE REGIONAL VIEWPOINT

Regional economic development

The contribution of the project to national development has also been its contribution to regional development. But there were specifically regional economic and social objectives in undertaking the project. In spite of the generally favourable outcome of the analysis of the preceding section of this chapter, it is clear that these developments did not have the desired impact on the region itself: the benefits accrued to the nation as a whole, and to certain individuals, but the regional impact was limited.

This is most clearly presented in the description of the industrial development in the region. The induced investment in related industries was severely limited, and only those industries whose

---

[1] Data from the control region indicate that there would have been an emigration from the Tierra Caliente of 22.8 per cent of the 1950 population, or 14,310 people, during the decade had conditions not improved. Thus, the investment programme in the Tierra Caliente attracted 37,465 more people to the region than might have been expected had the Commission not existed: this number is slightly less than the number who emigrated from other regions in the basin.

cost structure made location near the source of raw-material supply determinant are found in the zone today. Without a favourable electricity pricing policy the abundant power resources of the region did not contribute to the other features of the region to attract a more diversified industrial base.

Agricultural development did raise incomes of people in the region. Not only were new lands opened for cultivation but old lands became more productive. The impact of this development was shifted, to a great extent, to other regions because of the limited industrialization of the Tepalcatepec river basin. There are two components of economic growth in the region—growth as a result of larger numbers of people, and as a result of higher incomes for these people. The first type of growth increases the demand for food products and basic services which are often supplied locally while the second depends much more heavily on manufactured and processed goods and services which are supplied from outside the region because of the lack of a local industrial base.

The regional impact was further limited by the way in which the agriculture of the Tierra Caliente evolved. With the signing of rental agreements and the limited availability of credit, only a small proportion of the people in the area were able to participate in the prosperity brought by the irrigation project. Most of the ejidatarios on whose land cotton and melons were grown, were forced to rent their plots to those private and ejidal planters who had access to credit from the Banco Ejidal or the ginneries. They worked as day-labourers, often on their own lands, and received a wage for this labour in addition to the rent for their lands. This income is an improvement over the returns that might be expected from continuing to plant traditional crops on the land. Those that received credit enjoyed substantial improvements in their income and although much of this was reinvested, there was some improvement in the living standards of these planters. Even in this area, therefore, income was quickly concentrated in the hands of a relatively few farmers.[1]

[1] For a further analysis of this process of income concentration as well as some suggestions for redistributing income see David Barkin, 'Income Distribution during Agricultural Development' *Social Research*, 1970 (forthcoming).

An assessment of social investments

The increase in population in the Tierra Caliente during the first decade of operation of the project was accompanied by significant improvements in health and sanitary conditions. Malaria has been almost completely eliminated as a health hazard while other maladies, including intestinal disorders, have been significantly reduced by the construction of sewage systems and other facilities. Illiteracy has also been reduced markedly through intensive campaigns and the expansion of the school system. The problem of evaluating the social investments which had an important impact on living conditions in both Tierra Caliente and in the rest of the basin, is very difficult. For example, various measures of educational advance are possible—the percentage of any particular age group enrolled, the numbers of teachers per head of population, the literacy level, etc.

Even if it were possible to measure unambiguously educational output it would be a mistake to see expenditures for education solely as an investment to increase productivity. In large part, education is a durable consumer good that can enrich the lives of the people who receive it. The social aspect of the Commission's work throughout the basin is an attempt to bring the benefits of progress made by the Mexican nation to rural areas. This is both a straightforward attempt to redistribute income in order to assure a minimum standard of life for all citizens and, particularly in the Tierra Fría, a reflection of the belief that Mexico cannot be a truly unified nation while pockets of her citizens remain scarcely touched by any progress made since the sixteenth century.

These statements are equally appropriate for the health measures and for many of the expenditures on secondary roads in the highland areas where communities have been linked to public transportation routes for the first time. The urban facilities, described above, also served this function and are a source of pride for all residents of the region, both urban and rural. They are a symbol of the fact that the Mexican Revolution has truly been able to reach the more distant parts of the nation and weld it into one people.

In spite of these contributions, perhaps the most important

effect the Commission had on regional development was the attention it drew to the area as a focus for government investment. The social investment programme was miniscule in relation to the needs, but the induced expenditures by other agencies and by the communities themselves were of greater importance in improving the well-being of the inhabitants.

THE VIEW FROM 1947

In Chapter 1 we suggested that any *post hoc* project assessment should examine the predictability of a project's outcome. To what extent would it have been possible to anticipate a programme's future development and thereby justify its profitability before the construction was undertaken? With the wisdom gained from the passage of time, we are now able to say that the project was probably a worthwhile one but the question of whether an economist would have made a similar judgment in 1947 remains.

The major aspect of this problem would be the ability of experts in 1947 to predict the course of events in the region's agricultural development. On its formation one of the first acts of the Commission was the establishment of an experiment station in cooperation with the Ministry of Agriculture, and this focused its attention on cotton. Although there were only 12 hectares of planting in 1950, it seems clear that the agronomists were convinced of the potential value of this product early in the life of the Commission. The analyst in 1947 might not have foreseen the long hiatus between the development of the technology for cotton planting and its adaptation, as we have pointed out elsewhere, and might therefore have predicted a pattern of benefits from the project closer to the alternative presented early in this chapter.

The contribution of hydroelectricity production was of paramount importance to the nation in the early 1950s when there were occasional blackouts throughout the central part of the country because of a shortage of generating capacity. The several power plants which were constructed were readily foreseen and eagerly anticipated by government planners and industrialists.

On the other hand, the claims that the Tepalcatepec Commission's presence diversified economic growth in the basin or even in the Tierra Caliente beyond growth of the agricultural output appears to have been unduly optimistic, even for 1947. It is hard to know what lay behind such forecasts of extensive industrialization but it certainly would be hard to substantiate anything more grandiose than the processing plants and servicing centres which sprang up during the first two decades of growth. The Tierra Caliente is still far removed from the principal markets on the Mesa Central in spite of the construction of good roads and the inauguration of regular rail services. The climate requires air conditioning in most offices and in plants which cannot be left open for ventilation. Finally, there is a shortage of labour which certainly affects locational decisions. Manufacturing production and transport costs would therefore be relatively high. In the light of these considerations, the view of the Tierra Caliente as a new growth pole, which seems to have been conjured up by those pressing for the investments, should not be viewed as more than rhetoric in assessing the project, for no steps were taken to encourage industrial development in the region.

In the social sphere, the plans to change the environment and make the Tierra Caliente a healthy place to live, and one well integrated into the national network of transport and communications, were accomplished early in the Commission's life. In the higher reaches of the basin, communities and people had been isolated for decades and the Commission's programme of road and school building, and electrification played an important role in integrating the region into the nation. It may also have accelerated the pace of outmigration to other, more prosperous parts of the country.

Finally, it may be asked whether the 'hiding hand' observed by Hirschman had any impact on progress in the Tepalcatepec basin.[1] It may be a tribute to the project's engineers and planners or to the generosity of the region's physical endowment that no large unforeseen obstacles seem to have arisen which required large changes in plans or which, if anticipated, would have threatened the incorporation of the project into the Mexican

[1] See Chapter 1.

public investment programme. One possible positive development was the discovery of sizable deposits of high grade iron ore in a nearby zone which is presently being developed by the steel industry in co-operation with the government.

Thus, the analyst making an evaluation similar to the present one but twenty years earlier might have finished his report with an enthusiastic recommendation for the immediate implementation of the investment programme. His findings might have been that the rate of return exceeded 20 per cent and that the other benefits from changes in living conditions and the possible attraction of people away from Mesa Central were more than sufficient to justify the project even if it did not promise the spontaneous growth of the region, beyond the increase in agricultural output.

THE HUMAN RESPONSE

The large changes in the Tierra Caliente's economic and social structure have been accompanied by adjustments in farmers' attitudes. Differences in technical ability and wealth currently observed in the region are the result of different responses by the farmers to government intervention.

Perhaps the greatest differences in wealth and income are the result of the limited availability of credit due to the narrowing of the market for the new commercial products. The less risk-averse took advantage of the offers for assistance at the beginning and have continued to receive credit if their crops have been profitable, while those who hesitated have not been able to do so.

One of the important ways to speed up the adaptation to the new agricultural potential of a region is to reduce the apparent risk to the farmer from experimentation. This could be done by guaranteeing the farmer his opportunity cost in subsistence crops for the land he places under commercial products.[1] In this way, an inexpensive system for reducing risks can be used to speed the transition from traditional to modern farming and thus improve the returns to public investments made in agriculture.

---

[1] The guarantee would have to be conditional on the actual cultivation of new crops on land now used for subsistence crops to avoid a situation in which land remains fallow in expectation of a guaranteed minimum income from the government.

Finally, those farmers with access to credit and knowledge of new cultivation techniques are proving themselves responsive to price changes and switch from one crop to another as the economic situation advises. Sesame production is expected to increase as people find ways to improve the yields of the crop and control of the market is wrested from the few merchants in Apatzingán who now dominate it. There is no reason to doubt that this group of farmers will continue to show this responsiveness and perhaps provide some of the financial resources that the other farmers need for their conversion to more valuable crops.

This analysis adds further evidence to the growing literature on the rationality of peasant farmers. There is nothing to indicate that the farmers in the Tierra Caliente did not act in their own best interests by either accepting or rejecting the offers of assistance in clearing their lands. It does suggest that by reducing the risks to be faced by farmers, agricultural development can be speeded up.

This assertion of the rationality of the peasant does not mean, however, that he can be left alone to fend for himself. The differences in the region's economic levels are mostly the result of unequal access to credit and technical assistance. The farmer without these resources needs protection against those seeking to gain control of his rented land; the injunction against disposing of land granted under the land reform provision of the Constitution serves this function. Under this arrangement, the farmer always has the option of terminating the contract and returning the land once he obtains the necessary resources, either on his own or from government sources. Economic rationality, therefore, should not imply, as is sometimes argued, that the peasant can be abandoned by the government and left to react to the freely working forces of the market.

8

RIVER BASIN PROJECTS
AND REGIONAL DEVELOPMENT

The strategy of promoting regional development through river basin schemes has, as we have already shown, both a political and an economic side. From a national economic point of view this strategy involves heavy agricultural and hydroelectric investments. We have already discussed the contribution that such investments have made to national economic growth. In the case of a successful scheme like the Tepalcatepec project this contribution has been impressive. It is likely that the Fuerte project would also prove to have made a high return on investment, but we did not measure this in any detail. On the other hand the Papaloapan project appears to have been relatively unsuccessful. There is little more that we can usefully say about this here, though we shall have something to say about effects of the projects on factor supplies which contribute both to national and regional development objectives.

In this chapter we discuss first the rationale for using integrated river basin schemes to carry out public investment in irrigation, hydroelectric schemes and other social overhead capital, rather than entrusting each item of investment to other agencies which in Mexico normally carry on such investments. We approach this question from both political and economic angles. We then conclude by summarizing the economic contributions that the projects have been able to make to Mexican regional economic development objectives, drawing both on the detailed analysis of the Tepalcatepec project presented in Chapters 5, 6 and 7 and the earlier descriptions of river basin projects in Chapter 4, and by considering the implications for regional development policies generally.

THE USE OF INTEGRATED RIVER BASIN PROJECTS

Economic rationale

As we suggested earlier, especially in Chapter 3, it is unlikely that the Mexican government would have created new agencies to administer the regional development programmes if these had not promised to make a substantial contribution to the national development effort in addition to their impact on the regions in which the projects were located. The distinction between the effects of the programmes on the growth of national income and its regional distribution is an important one, however, in considering regional economic development policies.

In most of the cases discussed, the focus of the investments has been on the fuller utilization of existing natural resources as a part of the national development effort. The government has never provided special incentives so that new enterprises would locate in these river basins rather than somewhere else. Rather, the river basin programmes have focused on providing basic social overhead capital and developing the agricultural and hydroelectric potential of a region. With an emphasis on primary industries and the absence of any specific inducements to change their traditional locational patterns, new firms rarely found any advantage in locating in regions far removed from large population centres and from the centre of power.

This type of regional development will depend, in the absence of positive inducements, on establishing an export-base. The comparative advantage of any newly developed area, if it has one, is likely to be in primary production which determines the character of the initial export-base. The fact that river basin schemes will, if successful at all, emphasize agriculture as the export-base (except where the availability of minerals and inexpensive electric power foster metal industries) is a point in their favour. As we have seen with the Tepalcatepec and Fuerte projects, irrigation development can have an impressive effect on local agricultural output and incomes. The results of the Papaloapan project are a reminder, however, that this is not an inevitable result of river basin development. Irrigation here has proved particularly disappointing—the works have been expensive and their utilization low. Although irrigation in the Gulf region does have an effect on productivity, those critics who argue that irrigation in the areas where it is truly indispensable should have taken priority are probably right.[1] The chief work of the Ministry of Water Resources, however, has always been irrigation, so that a bias in its favour in the Papaloapan and Grijalva projects seems almost inevitable. In an arid, tropical country like Mexico, irrigation is in most regions a necessary condition for high agricultural productivity. The agricultural development that Mexico has experienced in recent decades is usually attributed principally to the growth in area irrigated.[2] But a spread of the irrigable area is not a sufficient condition for agricultural progress. Communications, credit, technical assistance, and perhaps also other social overhead investment, are necessary. So whether co-ordinated within one agency or not, the basic elements of the strategy appear well chosen to promote agricultural development, and it is difficult to think of any alternative strategy that could have had similarly successful results in this respect.

But for sustained development, agriculture may be far from ideal as an export-base. In the first place, its products are those for which, beyond a certain point at least, income elasticities of demand are likely to be low, and the terms of trade between the region and the rest of the country may deteriorate. Secondly, its 'linkage' effects on other producers may be small. Even though an advanced agriculture buys a high proportion of its inputs from non-farm sources, spatially such a market is very diffuse and does not appear to have much effect on the location of major industries. An example of this might be the lack of industry in vast areas of the United States Midwest, particularly in the Plains states. For agriculture in an underdeveloped economy, which will be less mechanized and will therefore buy less of its inputs from non-farm sources, this will be even more true. The same is true with respect to the location of manufactured consumer goods industries. Backward 'linkage' effects are therefore small. In addition, value-added in processing most agricultural

---

[1] Moisés T. de La Peña, *El Pueblo y su Tierra: Mito y Realidad de la Reforma Agraria en México* (México, D. F.: Cuadernos Americanos, 1964), pp. 455–6.
[2] For example, *ibid.*, p. 206.

products is a fairly small proportion of the gross value of output. The experience of both the Tepalcatepec and Fuerte projects supports this argument. Other primary production and local processing, such as those of forest products, may take advantage of the social overhead facilities now provided in the basin. Examples are the Tuxtepec paper factory in the Papaloapan basin, one planned (but never built) in the Tepalcatepec basin, and the barium operation with its plant in Apatzingán. But nothing in Mexican experience suggests that such production is likely to have more than a minor impact on gross regional income.

The absence of any self-sustained regional economic development is specially important in view of our discussion of the problems confronting the capital city of Mexico. In Chapter 2 we pointed out that congestion costs arising from the rapid development of industry in the Valley of Mexico and the growth of its population have greatly increased and are a cause of great concern to some policy makers. It also seems likely that the benefits from economies of agglomeration are no longer increasing and may even be declining with the growth of the Federal District; in view of this it does not seem surprising that other industrial centres are developing in the neighbouring states just outside the Valley of Mexico where they remain within easy travelling distance of the capital.

The river basin development programmes did, however, facilitate the process of incorporating technical externalities within each basin directly into the planning process. In the Tepalcatepec river basin, the simultaneous execution of both irrigation and hydroelectric segments of the development plans was probably the most efficient way of using the government funds. Similarly, the construction of roads for communication purposes also requires some co-ordination with the future commercial and passenger demands for surface transport. Co-ordination by the Commissions, however, does not imply that the appropriate amount of investment will be allocated to the project. There is no technically determined amount of road investment, for example, which must be combined with a given irrigation project. Presumably there is an absolutely rock-bottom minimum of indispensable roads before an irrigation scheme can become at all productive. Beyond this point, which may represent quite a large investment, additional 'road inputs' will continue to increase the productivity of the irrigation scheme, but eventually at a diminishing rate which may even fall to zero. Most of the interesting questions of transport policy are likely to fall in the stage where marginal productivity is diminishing but positive. This is where the decision whether to pave a road is likely to fall, or, in an advanced economy, whether to build a motorway. In Chapter 1 we encountered the Hirschman argument that it may be better to let the government be induced to expand the road network by the prior growth of the private sector rather than expand the network and hope that it will induce private activity to use it. This argument is at its most plausible during this stage.

There is a danger, as Hirschman points out, that government agencies may push road building too far; a bottleneck may be considered politically much more undesirable than the much less obvious underutilization. Road building may even be pushed beyond the point where an increase in investment would have no effect on productivity at all. Such has perhaps been the case with some of the roads in the Papaloapan basin. Giving one agency the power to co-ordinate investments evidently does not eliminate this danger. In fairness, it should be stressed that underutilization may result only from indivisibilities, and economies of scale may justify building ahead of demand.

Although the productivity of all activities in the basin depends to some extent on the existence of a road network, there will be obvious variations in this. The stage at which improved roads have no effect on productivity may be reached for some activities long before it is reached for others. If all activities were simultaneously and centrally planned, then conceptually one activity or group of activities would determine where the margin of road building was to lie. This is particularly clear when we are considering expansion in terms of a denser network of roads, rather than an increase in the volume of traffic that a particular road can handle in a given period (because in the latter case total demand would inevitably be part of the calculation). Making the road network denser is the type of expansion most relevant to the development of river basins in Mexico, but on the Mesa Central, expanding the carrying capacity of roads is perhaps equally important. Decisions on paving a road have something of both aspects, since not only the carrying capacity of a road is affected but also the quality of service that it can give.

Very often in a newly opened agricultural region, irrigation may be one of the group of activities that determines the extent of the network. But it is also possible that it may be more necessary to co-ordinate the bulk of road investment with the expansion of activities in a neighbouring region, or with mining, or with tourism. In the case of the Fuerte basin, for example, the highway that forms the principal tourist and commercial route between Central Mexico, Baja California, and the Pacific Coast of the United States crosses the lower basin. The fact that the Fuerte Commission has only been slightly concerned to use its road building powers reflects the fact that the area it serves has been well supplied with roads for other purposes, and that further road investment on its part—other than some local farm roads—would have little effect on the productivity of its other invest-ments.

Probably one may argue analogously for other social overhead investments, such as health and education expenditures, although two things should be mentioned here. The first is that the con-sumption component of such investment is likely to be more important here than in the case of transport investment, so that the effects of productivity may be unimportant in deciding at the margin how much should be spent on each. The second is that little work has been done on the technical relationship between such investment and the productivity of other investments, and it is much harder to generalize about the effects of different amounts on productivity.

Political rationale

While the economic case for making a river basin the focus for the co-ordination of regional public investment does not seem in general to be particularly strong, in Mexico the strategy makes a great deal more sense if political as well as economic factors are considered. It has, as we discussed, often proved extremely difficult for the Mexican government to achieve any co-ordinated planning of public investment and a large number of decentralized spending agencies exist. The River Basin Commissions represent an attempt to co-ordinate government expenditure under a semi-independent agency on a regional basis.

Difficulties in the co-ordination of public investment have often in the past reflected the strong personalistic pattern of Mexican politics where national leaders have become identified with definite ideas or policies. Although Scott reports that this trait of *personalismo* has been on the decline,[1] the Papaloapan project is a good example of a scheme whose founder is identified with its development. A symptom of this decline is the disappearance of the old *caudillos*—leaders whose power derived not from constitutional authority but from their personal and military following. This decline may be making co-ordination easier to achieve, which may be why there has been the trend from the River Basin Commission as an agency which simply spends money, towards one which plans and co-ordinates non-water resource investment as well, even that which will be undertaken by some other government agency. It is interesting that both ministries with a special responsibility for co-ordinating public investments—the Ministry of the Presidency and the Ministry of National Properties (Patrimonio Nacional) were fairly recently established (during the administration of López Mateos). Nevertheless, it is apparently true that political jealousies and rivalries and personal followings remain and continue to make co-ordination difficult. According to Scott, *personalismo* has been replaced by a more formal policy-making process giving a greater role to a professional bureaucracy and functional interest groups.[2] Neither of these is particularly likely to foster easy co-ordination—administrative agencies may be every bit as anxious not to share their functions with other agencies, as politicians are to avoid dividing power with other politicians.

One reason for using a River Basin Commission to achieve co-ordination of public investment within a region is that this appears to be a widely acceptable way for a President to try to do this. He can argue, based on TVA's successes, that there is some special need to integrate activities within a river basin. Some other

[1] Scott, *Mexican Government in Transition*, p. 13.　　　　[2] *Ibid.*, p. 9.

spatial unit might seem to be more sensible, but this might arouse strong opposition. River basins cross state boundaries, and this strategy may be the only practicable way of co-ordinating investments in different states. It may appear the only legitimate way of avoiding channelling funds through a corrupt state government. Having established a Commission, the President can then use it flexibly for a wide variety of activities; the Tepalcatepec Commission was used to study the potential development of iron ore deposits that were not even within the basin over which it had jurisdiction.

On the other hand, as we saw in Chapter 4, there are many situations where using a river basin as the planning unit seems inappropriate. If basin-wide planning is useful, it is because the interdependencies between different investment projects within the basin are substantially greater than those between investments inside the basin and those outside it. If the basin is too diverse, like the Balsas basin, then this is true only for a very narrow range of investments; and if, like the Lerma basin, the boundaries of the basin are quite unimportant from an economic standpoint, then this condition also will not hold. Although the flexibility of the Commissions has sometimes taken them out of their basins for odd jobs, so far they have not been empowered to carry out extensive planning outside the watershed. We can put this in terms of our earlier analysis. In Chapter 1 we discussed the concept of incomplete synoptic analyses at different levels of policy-making. The River Basin Commissions represent an example of this, particularly in their planning rather than in their investing function. They do not consider all national objectives in their work; they are concerned only with small areas of the country, and they ignore side effects (usually called 'external effects' or 'spillovers' in public investment discussion) on other objectives such as price stability, and ignore effects outside the basin. They can themselves be considered the result of higher-level incomplete synoptic policy decisions.

The success of such a strategy depends on two things. First, it depends on the extent to which there are problems that can be solved within the basin, with insignificant side effects on policy decisions with respect to matters outside the basin or to other objectives, so that these can be reasonably ignored by the Commissions. Second, it depends on the extent to which solutions reached in policy decisions will be unaffected by the side effects of other policy decisions.

Centralized co-ordination of decision-making imposes a cost in information handling and flexibility. In addition, there may be other costs in terms of individual freedom of decision, opportunity for initiative, Hirschman-type stimuli, and so on. Decentralization of decision imposes a cost where, by neglecting the interdependence of decisions, the total productivity of the system is less than it would have been under ideal, centralized co-ordination. The choice of a planning unit involves balancing these two. It may be hypothesized that were the Lerma-Chapala-Santiago basin to become a true planning unit it would be a poor one. With a large and complex economy, many of the costs incurred by centralized co-ordination would be incurred here. But because the basin is bound up so closely with the development of the whole Mesa Central, including the Valley of Mexico, there are likely to be a large number of interdependencies between investment decisions inside the basin and out, and ignoring those taken outside will be costly.

Other river basins may make better planning units, because they have some common problems whose solution does not depend too largely on investments made outside the basin. Even here, the major common problems of the upper basin are not likely to be those of the lower basin, causing the dichotomy of functions of the Papaloapan and Tepalcatepec Commissions, or leading the Fuerte Commission to ignore the upper basin.

MEXICAN REGIONAL ECONOMIC GROWTH

A satisfactory return on the investment in a river basin project, such as we found for the Tepalcatepec project, implies that the project made a satisfactory contribution to increasing aggregate national income. This is probably a sufficient justification of Mexican policies, at least in the Tepalcatepec and Fuerte basins. The projects, however, need to be considered in the light of other objectives. In the first place, the effect of the projects on the supply of factors of production must, as we discussed in Chapter 1, be assessed. Secondly, although the return on a project may be satisfactory in national terms, the results may disappoint those who hoped that it would lead to greater regional development.

The effect of a project on the supply of factors of production can be considered by separating out its effects on the absorption of otherwise unemployed labour, and its effects on tapping unutilized supplies of other human and natural resources and capital inputs. Both are of course beneficial to the economy, but the first is likely to be a more direct government objective because it would clearly improve the distribution of income and remove a source of political disaffection. The importance of the second depends on the empirical question of whether the unutilized resources exist; if they do, and can be tapped, they may have a cumulative effect leading to the exploitation of other unutilized resources.

In Mexico, the numbers of people benefiting directly from the projects has been very small indeed in relation to the agricultural population as a whole or even compared with new entrants to the labour force. As a strategy either for decentralizing the location of economic activity or for stemming the flow of migrants to urban areas, the schemes achieved very little. In Chapter 4 we gave some very rough indication of the marginal cost of employment of men in colonization schemes exclusive of the costs of some major items of capital expenditure, such as multiple purpose dams or major roads whose costs cannot be allocated to separable parts of a project. These figures suggest that the expense of sufficient projects to have a serious impact on the location of the agricultural population would be enormous. On the other hand, it is probably true that the cost of equipping an additional man with modern industrial techniques would be much greater, and in this respect the employment effects of these schemes must be regarded as satisfactory.

The achievements of the projects in tapping other unutilized resources depends on two things. First, such resources must actually be present, and second, a successful strategy to utilize these resources which do exist must be formulated. The Mexican experience we have examined does not suggest that there are any large quantities of potential entrepreneurs or frustrated savings in the outlying regions just waiting to be used. But the more successful projects did succeed in encouraging even small-scale farmers to move to more rewarding, if riskier, and more exacting, crops and induce local saving and investment. Hitherto unutilized natural resources were of course extensively employed—the effects of this are for the most part calculated in any cost-benefit calculation of the return on agricultural and hydroelectric investment.

But in realizing the potential here the Tepalcatepec project, at least, stimulated only a slow response from the private sector, even in primary industries where government investment reduced costs and increased potential profits for a whole range of possible business ventures. Public investment projects are generally designed on the assumption that further government intervention to supply fixed or working capital will not be necessary. If the private response is slow, then the return on public investment is greatly reduced. It may also be politically or administratively impossible for the government to find financial resources or personnel to provide all needed complementary resources.

With the various qualifications we have discussed, it is clear that the more successful projects have made a valuable contribution to Mexican development. Where they have been most disappointing is in the cumulative effects on regional growth, for the reasons given in the first part of this chapter. The Mexican government did not attempt a strategy which was capable of leading to regional industrialization at least in any forseeable period of time. Whatever lip service it may have paid to the idea, it is likely that it was perfectly aware that regional industrialization would have required a quite different approach. In most regions industrialization is probably attainable only at the cost of continuing subsidy from other regions, except in regions which are endowed with raw materials whose processing usually takes place near their location rather than near the market, such as steel in the Balsas river basin and petrochemicals on the Gulf Coast. The Mexican government has quite clearly been unwilling to promote regional development at the expense of national economic growth.

REGIONAL DEVELOPMENT POLICIES RECONSIDERED

In the first and third chapters we suggested that the concern for regional development arose from two different types of problems: regional inequalities and the costs of urban congestion. The first problem leads to dissatisfaction with the existing regional distribution of income and often to sharp political pressures seeking change.

Economies of agglomeration, which make it attractive for people and firms to settle in close proximity to each other, are often overshadowed by the costs of congestion imposed on people and public services in a large urban area. Here too there is pressure for the creation of special policies to encourage the decentralization of future growth if not the actual dispersion of existing economic activity and population.

The Mexican experience suggests that the combination of these pressures, discussed in much greater detail in Chapters 2 and 3 of this book, was insufficient to warrant costly policies of decentralization which would weaken the national development effort. The regional development programmes pursued by the Mexican government appear to have been undertaken primarily in the hope that they would make significant contributions to national development goals rather than redistribute income to the unfortunate people who had remained in the backwash of Mexican economic progress. When analysing this experience, it seems clear that policy-makers have been willing to sacrifice very little in response to demands for a more equitable regional distribution of national income.

Furthermore, the Mexican experience suggests that the creation of an export-base is not a sufficient condition for the cumulative economic growth of a region. The experience gained during the past decades about the importance of linkage effects is confirmed by our analysis. Without compelling technical or financial incentives for the location of new investment in an area, other considerations like proximity to the market and economies of agglomeration are likely to play a dominant role in locational decisions.

It therefore seems clear that a more positive strategy than river basin schemes is needed to achieve the development of lagging regions. Social overhead capital is only a permissive policy which will not necessarily bring development in its wake. Furthermore, it is extremely easy to provide too much investment and difficult for the policy-maker to decide the appropriate level to induce necessary private investment without waste. A more effective regional policy must also include some restraints on investment elsewhere or positive inducements to invest in the developing regions. Such a policy would probably require some sacrifice of economic growth in favour of achieving the objective of regional balance.

Appendices

A

CHANGES IN THE STATISTICAL BASE FOR THE ANALYSIS OF AGRICULTURAL PROGRESS IN THE TIERRA CALIENTE[1]

During the course of the field investigation in the Tierra Caliente, it became very apparent that the 1960 Agricultural Census was wholly inadequate for the purposes of this study. In order to quantify the benefits arising from the construction of the irrigation system discussed in this book, it was necessary to obtain as realistic a picture as possible of the situation so as to be able to analyse the changes from the base year to the present. This appendix presents the official data which suggested the need for the revisions which were taken for this evaluation.

In order to adjust the census data, two sources of agricultural statistics were used and related to other information available in the field to obtain a complete picture of the agricultural situation during the 1950–60 period. The census is based on an enumerative procedure with the information supplied by the farmers or their representatives in the field. The data are supposed to include all the agricultural establishments in the country, grouped by type and size of land tenure: private property greater than 5 hectares, private property of 5 hectares or less, and land distributed under the land reform regardless of the size of the individual holding. In addition, a special questionnaire is distributed with the population census to obtain information about livestock in towns and villages. These data, according to the Law of Statistics of Mexico, are confidential and cannot be used for any fiscal purposes. In spite of this provision and the efforts of the directors of the census to explain its safeguards, many people believe that their confidences will not be kept and give imprecise and sometimes false information. It is also often the case that many cannot remember the information asked in the census because it has no importance for the management

[1] This Appendix is taken from a monograph by Barkin: *Cambios en la Agricultura de la Zona de Tierra Caliente, Michoacán, 1950–1960* (Chapingo, México: Escuela Nacional de Agricultura, 1965).

of their farms. There is also an unknown coefficient of censal evasion—that is, farms that escape enumeration. With these considerations in mind, we thought it necessary to revise the data to obtain a better idea of the magnitude of the deviations of the census data from the actual situation.

A second source of agricultural statistics is the Department of Agricultural Economics (DEA) of the Ministry of Agriculture and Livestock (SAG). The DEA publish information on the area, yields, and production of each product. Using the information on rural prices, one can compute the value of the harvest. These figures are estimates of the annual municipio production by municipio presidents and careful counts are unlikely to be made. Adjustments are made to aggregate these data on the state and national levels. The DEA's statistics can only give an approximate indication of the situation in any one year because of the way in which they are collected.

The last source of information on agricultural production is the administration of the irrigation districts for those areas under the control of the Ministry of Water Resources (SRH). The information is supplied by those in charge of the operation of the irrigation canals and verified by the permits which each farmer is supposed to obtain before each agriculture cycle. Unfortunately, only since 1958 has collection of this information been mandatory and districts under the control of de-centralized organizations, like the Comisión del Tepalcatepec, were the last to comply with the regulations. This information only refers to the irrigated land and thus does not include production data on dry-farming. The data on production are estimates based on theoretical yields and fixed rural prices. They are often unreal estimates, and as a result only the area figures are reliable, and even these have their flaws.

Each source collects a different type of information. The census provides the best idea of subsistence production, which does not reach the market and predominates in the smaller units, because it alone makes direct enquiry to small farmers. On the other hand, the census appears to be less adequate in obtaining data on commercialized production. In these cases, there is the possibility that the information estimated by the municipio presidents or by the canal workers in the irrigation districts are closer to reality. The information from the SRH is useful as a check to analyse the other sources when they refer to production on irrigated lands.

Tables 32 to 34 present the actual data from the three sources mentioned above. By comparing them with the revised figures used for

Table 32. *Data for the 1949–1950 agricultural cycle in the Tierra Caliente,* Michoacán[a] (principal crops)

Crop	Source	Harvested area (hectares)	Volume (tons)	Value ('000 pesos)	Yield (kg./ hectare)	Rural price (pesos/ton)
Totals	1	36,068		17,338		
	2	20,687		12,240		
Beans	1[b]	587	196	143	334	729
	2[b]	168	155	113	323	730
Corn	1[c]	20,208	17,503	5,612	865	321
	2	6,950	5,710	1,759	822	308
Cotton	1	12	25	38	2,070	1,520
	2					
Lemons	1[+]	2,580	11,167	3,881	4,328	348
	2[+]	1,513	9,385	3,285	6,200	340
Melons	1	1	3	1	3,150	369
	2[d]	79	359	144	4,544	400
Rice	1[+]	4,813	11,254	3,901	2,338	347
	2[+]	7,468	13,749	4,381	1,841	319
Sesame	1[+]	7,539	3,555	3,219	472	905
	2[+]	3,765	1,652	1,487	439	900
Sugar cane	1	289	15,601	468	53,983	30
	2	665	32,060	862	48,211	27
Watermelons	1	39	215	75	5,506	351
	2[d]	79	522	209	6,608	400

[a] The Tierra Caliente includes the municipio of the Apatzingán, Buenavista, La Huacana, Parácuaro, Tepalcatepec, and Zaragoza. In addition, the municipio of Uruapan is included when it was evident that the data refer to Lombardía; this is indicated by +.
[b] Includes the volume and value of beans planted with corn but not its yield.
[c] Includes the area, volume, and value of corn planted with beans but not its yield.
[d] The data are for 1950 since the harvest takes place in the first quarter of the year.

Sources: 1. México, Secretaría de Industria y Comercio, Dirección General de Estadística, *III Censo Agrícola, Ganadero y Ejidal, 1950, Michoacán* (México, D.F., 1957).
2. México, Secretaría de Agricultura y Ganadería, Dirección de Economía Agrícola. Data from 1949.

the evaluation of actual progress in the Tierra Caliente (Tables 22 and 24) it is possible to appreciate the order of magnitude of the errors contained in the official publications. The adjustment process is described in greater detail in the monograph cited at the beginning of this Appendix and in Barkin's doctoral dissertation.

Table 33. *Data for the 1946–1947 agricultural cycle on irrigated land in the Tierra Caliente, Michoacán*

Crop	Harvested area (hectares)	Volume (tons)	Value ('ooos pesos)	Yield (kg./hectare)	Rural price (pesos/ton)
Total	9,701		9,885		
Camote	33	99	20	3,000	200
Corn[a]	2,931	2,216	1,158	756	522
Fruits	1,198		2,480		
Lemons	970	8,725	1,745	8,995	200
Pasture	313	10,955	66	35,000	6
Rice	3,164	6,961	2,784	2,200	400
Sugar cane	1,035	51,750	1,552	50,000	30
Vegetables	57		80		

[a] Of these 2,391 hectares, 53 were planted with chile and corn, with a value of 119,280 pesos, and 300 hectares were planted with corn and beans with a value of 371,250 pesos.

Sources: México, Secretaría de Agricultura y Ganadería, Dirección General de Distritos de Riego, División de Planeación, Sección de Estadística Agrícola, *Informe Estadística No. 2* (México, 1948).

Table 34. *Data for the 1959–1960 agricultural cycle in the Tierra Caliente, Michoacán[a] (principal crops)*

Crop	Source	Harvested area		Volume (tons)	Value ('ooos pesos)	Yield (kg./hectare)	Rural price (pesos/ton)
		Total (hectares)	Irrigated (hectares)				
Total	1	51,775	17,245		59,723		
	2	40,171	24,798		83,215		
	3	70,859	70,859		206,520		
Beans	1[b]	692	474	583	728	565	1,250
	2[b]	515	n.a.	471	617	360	1,310
	3	728	728	1,092	2,184	1,500	2,000

Table 34 (*contd.*)

Corn	1[c]	26,600	5,620	25,553	18,973	986	743
	2	12,910	4,510	10,740	7,196	832	670
	3	33,974	33,974	76,922	61,538	2,264	800
Cotton	1	1,599	1,134	2,749	6,203	1,719	2,256
	2	4,045	4,045	9,854	24,524	2,436	2,489
	3	4,100	4,100	12,300	28,900	3,000	2,350
Lemons	1	3,554	n.a.	9,282	7,240	2,612	863
	2			not available			
	3	4,614	4,614	28,656	7,997	6,211	279
Melons	1	1,280	1,251	5,611	2,691	4,384	480
	2[d]	5,180	5,180	32,742	16,041	6,321	490
	3	4,362	4,362	32,534	32,534	7,459	1,000
Rice	1	6,166	4,766	9,218	7,946	1,495	862
	2	7,745	6,545	11,617	10,025	1,500	863
	3	12,090	12,090	40,860	35,220	3,380	862
Sesame	1	10,136	2,379	5,723	10,928	565	1,909
	2	5,988	730	3,907	7,384	652	1,890
	3	7,098	7,098	4,478	10,757	631	2,402
Sugar cane	1	24	17	1,098	51	45,730	42
	2	337	337	16,988	819	50,410	48
	3	269	269	1,614	97	6,000	60
Watermelons	1	1,724	1,604	10,897	4,963	6,321	455
	2[d]	3,451	3,451	26,364	16,609	7,631	630
	3	3,624	3,624	68,232	27,293	18,828	400

[a] The Tierra Caliente includes the municipios of Apatzingán, Buenavista, Gabriel Zamora (Lombardía), La Huacana, Tepalcatepec, Zaragoza, and Parácuaro.
[b] Includes volume and value of beans planted with corn but not its yield.
[c] Includes area, volume, and value of corn planted with beans but not its yield.
[d] The data are for 1960 since the harvest takes place in the first quarter of the year.

Sources: 1. México, Secretaría de Industria y Comercio, Dirección General de Estadística, *IV Censo Agrícola-Ganadero y Ejidal, 1960, Michoacán* (preliminary data).
2. México, Secretaría de Agricultura y Ganadería, Dirección de Economía Agrícola; data from 1959.
3. México, Secretaría de Recursos Hidráulicos, *Informe de Labores, 1959-60* (México, D.F., 1961), pp. 594-6.

B

DEVELOPMENT OF NET AGRICULTURAL BENEFIT FIGURES IN THE TIERRA CALIENTE, MICHOACAN

The net agricultural benefits from irrigation (Table 26) were based on the information on gross production presented in Tables 22 and 24 and the cost data summarized in Tables 23 and 25. This Appendix describes the basis for the elaboration of the net benefit figures and the statistical basis for Table 26.

The first step in estimating the benefits was the determination of the profits from agricultural production in the Tierra Caliente during the 1950–65 period and estimates for profits for the period 1966–70. This was done by determining the distribution of land in each year by type of crop (Table 35) and then obtaining the amount of profit that might be expected from each crop in each year. The yearly profit level for each crop was obtained by determining the trend of profits from 1950 to 1960. In practice, a weighted average of the profits in 1950 and 1960 was taken with the weights changed for each year. With the exception of rice, which was adjusted for the period 1965–70 to take account of the important change in technology discussed in Chapter 6, 1960 profits were applied to the period 1960–70.

This method of determining the profits from agricultural production is based on the supposition that production in the Tierra Caliente did not influence prices for the products it was supplying and that the agricultural prices used in calculating returns were based on the agricultural situation in an average year. In the case of cotton, the price was determined on the world market. In the case of melons and water-melons, the price was determined on the United States market.[1] Fortunately, both 1950 and 1960 were considered 'average' years by the region's farmers.

[1] Although the Tierra Caliente is an important supplier of melons and water-melons to the American market during the short period in which domestic suppliers do not have any harvests to market, the buyers base their purchase plans on demand conditions in the market, which they can gauge quite well. The harvest programme is adjusted to this schedule to limit the supply of fruit to the market and thus maintain some price stability. The prices used for these crops in the estimation of agricultural profits were averages which took this factor into consideration. This is discussed at greater length in Chapter 6.

Table 35. *Area planted by crops in the Tierra Caliente, Michoacán, 1950–1970*

	Total (hectares)	Beans Wet	Beans Dry	Corn Wet	Corn Dry	Corn and beans	Cotton	Lemons Wet	Lemons Dry	Melon	Rice	Sesame Wet	Sesame Dry	Sugar cane	Water-melon	Other
1950	42,317		587	2,600	19,510	200	12	3,146		256	6,852	1,500	6,387	658	79	530
1951	42,842		700	2,500	19,300	200	12	3,200		250	7,000	1,500	6,500	600	80	1,000
1952	45,350		800	3,000	19,250	250	150	3,500		300	8,000	1,500	6,500	500	100	1,500
1953	51,625		900	5,000	20,100	400	200	4,000		400	10,000	1,500	6,500	500	125	2,000
1954	55,625		1,000	7,000	21,000	500	300	4,000		1,000	10,000	1,500	6,500	200	125	2,500
1955	63,314		1,100	10,200	22,200	600	500	4,458		1,335	11,661	1,464	6,536	129	131	3,000
1956	67,300		1,000	10,500	21,500	1,000	1,500	4,500		4,000	12,000	1,500	6,500	150	150	3,000
1957	76,150		1,000	12,000	20,800	1,200	5,000	5,500		4,000	12,000	1,500	7,000	150	3,000	3,000
1958	82,600		1,000	15,000	20,600	1,400	4,000	5,500		3,900	13,000	1,500	7,000	300	3,400	3,000
1959	92,450		500	22,000	19,500	1,500	8,450	4,500	2,000	4,200	13,000	2,500	7,000	300	3,000	2,500
1960	105,664	1,000	501	33,537	20,152	1,603	4,099	5,674	2,500	4,552	13,828	3,331	7,359	553	3,964	2,698
1961	106,600	1,107	500	29,000	16,500	1,500	12,000	6,000	2,706	5,100	14,000	3,500	8,000	500	4,500	2,500
1962	107,400	1,000	500	22,000	11,000	1,000	25,000	6,000	2,000	6,200	13,500	3,500	8,000	200	5,000	3,000
1963	106,500	500	500	16,600	9,200	800	34,000	6,000	2,000	5,800	12,000	4,000	8,000	100	4,600	3,500
1964	107,700		500	14,000	9,500	500	36,000	6,000	2,000	6,200	12,500	4,000	8,000		5,000	3,500
1965	109,500		500	12,500	7,000	500	42,000	6,000	2,000	6,000	12,000	4,000	8,000		5,000	4,000
1966	109,000			12,500	7,000	500	40,000	8,000		6,000	12,000	6,000	8,000		5,000	4,000
1967	103,000			14,000	4,500	500	35,000	9,000		6,000	12,000	7,000	5,000		5,000	5,000
1968	108,000			14,000	4,500	500	35,000	10,000		6,000	12,000	10,000	5,000		5,000	5,000
1969	114,000			15,000	4,500	500	35,000	10,000		6,000	12,000	15,000	5,000		5,000	6,000
1970	109,000			15,000	4,500	500	30,000	10,000		6,000	12,000	15,000	5,000		5,000	6,000

Source: See text.

The estimate of net agricultural profits (Table 26, Column 2) had to be further adjusted to take account of changes in productivity which might have occurred had the Commission not intervened in the region. These changes, as explained in the body of Chapter 7, might have taken place because of an increase in cultivated area as a result of privately financed irrigation projects, an expansion of non-irrigated farming, or increases in productivity as a result of technological improvements.

These combined factors resulted in a doubling of agricultural output during the decade of the fifties in the Ciudad Altamirano control region. This doubling implies a compound rate of growth in agricultural production in the region of slightly more than 7 per cent annually, the rate that was used in trying to eliminate the 'independent' influence of 'normal' progress over time from the estimates of net benefits. The last column of Table 29 presents the results of these calculations.

INDEX

257

Index

204, 290, 231, 239–41, Uruapan–Apatzingán, 134; telegraph, 150; telephone, 150
Comparative advantage, 237
Confederación de Trabajadores de México, 79
Confederación Nacional Campesina, 79
Congestion, 3–4, 65–70, 89, 239, 247
Constitution (Mexican), of 1814, 125; of 1857, 51; of 1917, 53
Control zone, see Ciudad Altamirano
Corn, see Maize
Cortés, Hernán, 43
Costa Sierra (Sierra Madre del Sur), 48, 108, 120–1, 124, 126, 130, 138–41, 144, 146–51
Costs, 215, 217–18
Cotija-Quitupan, 133
Cotton, 44, 46, 111–12, 145, 148, 155, 158–64, 167–71, 179–81, 197, 198n, 225, 230, 232, 253; costs, 164, 173–6; financing, 187–91; introduction of, 168–70; processing, 193–4, 202, 225; prospects for, 180–1; slow response to opportunities in, 168–9
Credit, see Tierra Caliente, agriculture, credit
Cupatitzio (River of the Singing Waters), 123, 137, 209, 221–2, 225
Cupatitzio-Cahones, 133, 198n
Cussi, Dante, 128–9, 186

Decision-making, 72–85, 242–4; decentralization, 244; synoptic vs. incremental approach, 25–8, 243
de la Peña, Moisés T., 54n, 160n, 165n, 238n
Demand factor, 238
Department of Agricultural Economics, 250
Díaz, Porfirio, 51–2, 128
Díaz del Castillo, Bernal, 43n
Díaz Ordaz, Gustavo, 82, 106
Directly productive activities, 15–17, 29
Discount rate, 38–40, 218–21; Tepalcatepec Commission, 218–20
Drinking water, see Social overhead capital
Durango, 58, 63, 110, 113

Eckstein, Otto, 23n, 24, 214n
Eckstein, Salomón, 129n
Economies, of agglomeration, 3, 18, 64–7, 239, 247; of scale, 3–4

Education, 65, 131–2, 150–2, 156–7, 209, 231, 241; improvements in, 206–7; school construction, 136–7
Ejidos, 53, 75–9, 112, 196–8, 207
Electricity, 55–6, 65, 83, 87, 102–4, 106, 114, 204, 211, 221–6, 232, 237; consumption of, 222
El Infiernillo Dam, 108, 222
Entrepreneurship, 9–10, 16, 19, 30–1, 168, 185–97, 227; American, 193; see also Banco Nacional de Crédito Ejidal
Exchange rate, 10, 33–4, 226
Experiment station, 135, 175
Exports, 6–7, 86, 226–7, 237–8, 247
External effects, pecuniary, 29n

Federación de Sindicatos de Trabajadores en el Servicio del Estado, 79
Federal District, see Mexico City
Federal Electricity Commission, 104, 112, 115, 221–5
Fernández Bravo, Vincente, 107n
Fertilizers, 163, 177, 201
Fish breeding, 136
Flood control, 86–103, 115
Foreign sector, 226–7
Forest products, 125, 147, 149
Fruit production: bananas, 47, 49, 97, 163; canteloupes, 227; coconuts, 163; lemons, 129, 155, 158–62, 164, 170–1, 175–6, 183, 187, 189–90, 251–3, 255, processing plants, 203; mangoes, 163; melons, 148, 158–62, 164, 167–71, 173, 175–6, 178–83, 188, 192–3, 197, 227, 230, 251, 253, 255, American interests, 181–2, 190, packing houses, 203; pineapples, 97; strawberries, 114; watermelons, 148, 155, 158–62, 164, 167, 169–71, 173, 175–6, 180–3, 192, 197–8, 227, 251, 253, 255, packing houses, 203
Fuerte Commission, 45, 94, 109–13, 236–7, 239, 241, 244
Fuerte River Basin, 241

Gabriel Zamora (Lombardía), 126, 190
Garnsey, Morris E., 57n
Gill, Mario, 110n, 111n
Grijalva Commission, 47, 94, 102–7, 238
Gross Domestic Product, see National income

Index